MW01504889

A Blessing, Not a Burden

My Parents' Remarkable Holocaust Story
and My Fight to Keep Their Legacy Alive

11/10/24

Steve:
Never Give up!

Alex Kor

Graham Honaker

Dr. Alex Kor with Graham Honaker

Pediment Publishing, a division of The Pediment Group, Inc., Vancouver, Washington 98682

www.pediment.com

© 2024 by Dr. Alex Kor and Graham Honaker

All Rights Reserved. First Edition Published May 2024.

Second Edition Published August 2024.

Printed in the United States of America.

Library of Congress Control Number: 2024904495

ISBN: 978-1-63846-092-3

Dust jacket photos:

Front cover, left: Camp director's office of Stutthof concentration camp. Courtesy Muzeum Stutthof

Front cover, center: Kor family. Courtesy Alex Kor

Front cover, right: Main gate and railroad to concentration camp of Auschwitz Birkenau

Inside back flap: Alex with his parents. Courtesy Butler University

I dedicate this book to my late parents, Eva Mozes and Mickey Kor. These words from Bette Midler seem very appropriate:

Did you ever know that you're my hero
And everything I would like to be?
I can fly higher than an eagle
For you are the wind beneath my wings
It might have appeared to go unnoticed
But I've got it all here in my heart
I want you to know I know the truth, of course I know it
I would be nothing without you

A.K.

To Dr. John Abrams
One of my all-time heroes—your tireless effort to better
the lives of others is a shining example to us all.

G.H.

Advance Praise for
A Blessing, Not a Burden

This book by Dr. Kor, along with Graham Honaker, chronicling the incredible lives of his parents Eva and Mickey Kor as they managed to survive the unimaginable horrors of life in a concentration camp during the Holocaust is a must read. As discrimination of all kinds continues to rise across this country and the world, Dr Kor's story of perseverance, love and forgiveness is more poignant than any time since the Holocaust. With antisemitism skyrocketing, this book spotlights the atrocities of the past while lighting a path forward to a better and more tolerant future. Thank you, Alex, for providing us with the gift of your parents and your amazing story!

—*Josh Schertz*
Head Men's Basketball Coach, Saint Louis University

Mickey Kor was one of Purdue University's most fervent fans. From his college days, where he spent hours in Lambert Gymnasium to the hundreds of games he attended at Mackey Arena and Ross Aide Stadium, few cared more about their alma mater than Mickey. He and his wife Eva embodied the principles that we seek to instill in our players here, including toughness, resilience, and passion. Featuring fascinating stories from Mickey's Purdue past, including his introductory encounter with John Wooden, *A Blessing, Not a Burden* is a must-read for Purdue fans, and all readers in need of inspiration.

—*Matt Painter*
Head Men's Basketball Coach, Purdue University

In July 2018, the Davidson College Men's Basketball team journeyed to the Auschwitz death camp and had their eyes opened to a life changing experience. Guided by Eva Mozes Kor, a Holocaust survivor and a Mengele twin, and accompanied by her son, Alex, the Davidson players and coaches were presented with a powerful and incredibly personal view of the horrors of the Holocaust. Stunned, shocked, and moved to tears, they left Auschwitz determined to share this experience with their families, friends, and classmates. Eva became a hero to all of us.

Now, Alex Kor together with Graham Honaker has written a book that shares the heartbreaking and heartwarming stories of Eva and her husband Mickey Kor, a Holocaust survivor of Buchenwald. It's a story about overcoming overwhelming adversity and consistently finding the courage to fight and the determination to survive.

Eva and Mickey created their own hope when no one gave them any reason to live another day. Remarkably, as insurmountable obstacles greeted them each day, they turned every dead end into a pathway to another destination. Their extraordinary perseverance is a model for all of us.

How fitting that Eva's favorite song became "The Impossible Dream." Eva's life and Mickey's life are compelling statements about fighting the unbeatable foe and bearing with unbearable sorrow. They won the battle of life, refusing to surrender, and turning every negative into a positive.

Twenty-four hours each day they were greeted with the challenge to give up and surrender or fight and survive. The Nazis stole the lives of Eva and Mickey. Eva and Mickey took their lives back. This book is a must-read for every one of us as we face the daily challenges of contemporary culture and strive to cross the finish line.

—*Bob McKillop*
Retired Davidson College Men's Basketball Coach

A Blessing, Not a Burden is the story of so much suffering yet at the same time, so much spirit. It is a spirit I got to see firsthand when I interviewed Eva Kor at Auschwitz in 1985, on the 40th anniversary of its liberation. She spoke of her horrors but also of her forgiveness. As if it's not enough that against all odds, she survived the Nazi death camp, she also survived something even worse: Dr. Josef Mengele, the so-called "Angel of Death." As one of the hundreds of sets of identical twins who became experimental fodder in Mengele's degenerate lab at Auschwitz, she survived his persistent and perverted procedures while he murdered other twins just to have corpses for his experiments. Her spirit is something to emulate. Her life is something to honor. This book does just that.

—*Greg Dobbs*
Emmy Award–winning former ABC News *correspondent*

Though not Indiana natives by birth, Eva and Mickey Kor were the consummate Hoosiers. From their against-all-odds survival to their peace-spreading message based on forgiveness and their home in Terre Haute, Indiana, their relentless and optimistic example inspired not just Hoosiers, but the world over. Their creation of the CANDLES Holocaust Museum and Education Center has educated thousands of young people and attracted visitors from across the globe. In 2020, we established "Eva Education Day" to further spread her message of resiliency, perseverance, and forgiveness. In *A Blessing, Not a Burden*, readers will learn more about Eva's teachings and find inspiration in Mickey's own example of courage and fortitude. I highly recommend reading the story of Eva and Mickey Kor and learning how the human spirit can powerfully persevere, restore, and become a beacon of light for others to follow.

—*Eric Holcomb*
Governor of Indiana

I met Eva at the Indy 500 during her reign as Grand Marshal and was instantly enamored with her and her remarkable tale of perseverance. Having invented "Pictionary," I have a great admiration for people who focus on the task at hand. Eva's focus was on bettering the world and she worked tirelessly to do so. In *A Blessing, Not a Burden*, readers will gain an appreciation for Eva and Mickey's decades-long efforts to make a difference. You'll also get a glimpse into their sense of humor, an attribute instrumental in helping them overcome the most trying of circumstances.

—Rob Angel
Entrepreneur, Explorer, and Philanthropist

Eva and Mickey Kor were an inspiration to me and a beacon of light to thousands. In *A Blessing, Not a Burden*, Alex Kor portrays his parents' inspiring work and devotion to the freedom of the human spirit. It's an honor and a privilege to have known them.

—Elliott Gould
Award-Winning Actor

Eva and Mickey Kor's lives are remarkable tales of survival, strength, and determination. While managing USC Shoah Foundation's Dimensions in Testimony team, I had the privilege of meeting Eva as she recorded her interactive testimony. Her story is unforgettable; her resilience, her drive to teach others through her own experiences, and her capacity for forgiveness have left an indelible imprint on me.

As a second-generation German, not of Jewish descent, I have spent the last thirty years capturing and sharing the stories of Holocaust survivors to ensure that we remember, raise awareness, and combat contemporary antisemitism. With the passing of these survivors and witnesses, the responsibility falls to us—the next generations—to determine how best to carry their messages forward. Although I never met Mickey, through Alex and Graham's book, I have the opportunity to encounter both Eva and Mickey together. The book is, indeed, A Blessing!

—Karen Jungblut
Director Emerita of Global Initiatives, USC Shoah Foundation

My first exposure to Eva Kor came in the 1980s. A general indifference to Hebrew school vanished for a day when she ventured from her Indiana town (Terre Haute) to mine (Bloomington) and spoke with candor, passion, and relatability to our group of Jewish adolescents. We sat rapt and she spoke. Without sandpapering her experience, she told her story: her interrupted childhood; the horrors of the Holocaust and experiments imposed upon her by Dr. Mengele; persistent antisemitism in the Midwest. She gave us a glimpse of humans' most monstrous capabilities. And at the same time, she represented the opposite: that is, the very best in humanity. Bottomless grace, courage, pliability, and an extraordinary capacity for forgiveness. Eva Kor was born in Hungary, held captive in a Polish concentration camp, and lived in Israel. Still, she is an American original and American hero. Now more than ever, it's imperative her story—her blessing—is told, considered, and admired.

—*Jon Wertheim*
Correspondent
60 Minutes
CBS News

Bravery and fortitude always make for compelling reading, and modern times provide no greater exemplars than the incredible Kors. How one wishes that their story was of only historical interest, but the world keeps reminding us that their struggle must constantly be not just remembered but renewed. *A Blessing, Not a Burden* captures Eva and Mickey's extraordinary resilience and reminds us all of the power of the human spirit to overcome.

—*Mitch Daniels*
Former Governor, State of Indiana
Former President of Purdue University

Alex Kor has written an extraordinary autobiography, actually an autobiography and two biographies, one of his mother, famed Mengele twin survivor Eva Mozes Kor, and the other of his less well-known father Mickey Kor, he too a Holocaust survivor. The result is rare insight into two fascinating people and the opportunities and obligations of their son to continue and enhance their legacy. I have read his mother's many writings, seen her films, and shared many experiences with her including a trip to Auschwitz, which included a rare visit to Block 19 and lunch with her hours before she died, when she handed me a speech she wanted to give at the 75th anniversary commemoration of the liberation of Auschwitz, which I read at her memorial. And yet, there was much that I learned in this book about her achievements and her struggle. For many readers Mickey Kor's story will be less known but his support for CANDLES and for his indomitable wife so essential. Alex has done them and himself proud. Compellingly told, he has written a story well worth telling, well worth reading.

—*Michael Berenbaum*
Director Sigi Ziering Institute
Distinguished Professor of Jewish Studies, American Jewish University

In a time when there are fewer and fewer survivors to hear Holocaust testimony from, we must hear their stories through their children and through their friends. *A Blessing, Not a Burden* is a heroic story told by Alex Kor, and a lesson in inspiration, love, faith, and hope. It is a must-read for every sports fan and a must-read for every citizen of the world who believes in humanity.

—*Rabbi Erez Sherman*
Senior Rabbi, Sinai Temple

Over the duration of her eighty-five years on this planet, Eva Kor's voice impacted millions. Through the USC Shoah Foundation's Dimensions in Technology (DIT) initiative, we were able to preserve her voice for decades to come. I had the privilege of asking Eva more than 1,000 questions for the project and came to truly appreciate her philosophy on forgiveness. In *A Blessing, Not a Burden*, Alex Kor adds further context to his mother's stance while vividly recounting his parents' uplifting life journeys. Our goal for the DIT project was to permanently document the narratives of Holocaust survivors via enhanced technology. Alex has done this in the form of a written account, and reminds us of how imperative it is to safeguard these stories for future generations.

—*Stephen Smith*
Former Executive Director, USC Shoah Foundation

I've been privileged to have known Alex Kor for more than thirty years. During that span, I came to learn about the extraordinary story of his parents, Eva and Mickey. Eva wrote to me decades ago and shared words that still resonate with me. Her encouragement to never give up, to forgive your worst enemy, and to strive to eliminate prejudice made an indelible impact on me. I sought to instill those same lessons in my players over the years and was fortunate to have Eva speak to several of my teams. In *A Blessing, Not a Burden*, Alex introduces Eva's lessons to a wider audience and recounts Mickey's own extraordinary journey as well. Eva preached that we should always "do the next right thing." I hope readers will come away from this memoir inspired to make the world a better place and heed Eva's words of wisdom.

—*Jim Crews, Former Head Men's Basketball Coach at Army, St. Louis University, and the University of Evansville*

My brief encounter with Eva Kor at the Indianapolis 500 led to a meaningful friendship, and her example of forgiveness profoundly impacted me. In *A Blessing, Not a Burden*, her son Alex describes in vivid detail how both Eva, and her husband Mickey, became true "rock stars" and inspirations for us all.

—*Nikki Sixx*
Cofounder and Bassist of Mötley Crüe

TABLE OF CONTENTS

17   Author's Notes

23   Prologue

25   Timeline

31   Chapter 1: Independence Day

37   Chapter 2: The Taste of Freedom

57   Chapter 3: Hope Was in Short Supply

81   Chapter 4: Love Language

99   Chapter 5: The Unlikeliest of Destinations

117   Chapter 6: My Toughest Match

127   Chapter 7: For Herself

145   Chapter 8: It's Not the Critic Who Counts

157   Chapter 9: A Permanent Reminder

167   Chapter 10: You Can Go Home Again

191   Chapter 11: Burned Again

201   Chapter 12: A Different Platform

223   Chapter 13: Crossing the Goal Line

237   Chapter 14: Fortunate Son

255   Epilogue

259   Acknowledgments

264   Endnotes

Author's Notes

It began with a letter. In September 2014, I had plans to visit Baltimore, Maryland, for a fundraising trip. As Senior Development Director at Butler University, I was tasked with raising big dollars and Dr. Alex Kor, class of 1983, was a prime donor "target" (we use very crass jargon in our profession). The year before, I'd briefly bumped into Alex at a pregame reception for a Butler-Georgetown basketball game, but he blew me off. Alex denies this, but it's true! Given the previous year's stiff arm, I was less than optimistic that he'd respond to my letter. To my surprise he agreed to a meeting.

I've long prided myself on preparation prior to meeting with a donor, and this time would be no different. What was distinctive was the type of research employed. I had limited knowledge of the Kor Family but knew they were from nearby Terre Haute, Indiana, and that Alex's mother Eva was a Holocaust survivor. In addition to probing Alex's professional achievements and potential wealth, I spent weeks listening to Eva Kor's lectures and was mesmerized by her commanding presence. Her harrowing tale of surviving the horrors of the Auschwitz concentration camp and ghastly experiments of Dr. Josef Mengele was unfathomable. Even more remarkable was her forgiveness of the Nazis— how could she possibly make amends to these monsters?

Alex, of course, picked one of the more expensive restaurants in Baltimore for dinner. Dining over crab cakes on the Chesapeake Bay, we spent three hours conversing and immediately developed a strong rapport. Our conversation bounced back and forth, from his mother's stirring tale to college basketball—we both were massive hoops junkies. I learned that his father Mickey was also a Holocaust survivor, having endured the Buchenwald concentration camp in Germany, and was a die-hard Purdue Boilermaker fan. Alex shared that his mother (seventy-nine at the time) was lecturing more than 150 times annually and had no plans of stopping. She'd spoken all over the world on the topic of forgiveness, but incredulously never at his alma mater. I assured Alex that we'd change that and left dinner as a man on a mission. Upon arriving back at my hotel, I realized that I'd forgotten to solicit him for a donation.

Back on campus, I immediately contacted Butler President James Danko. Conveniently leaving out that I'd failed to secure a donation from Alex, I emphatically pitched the President on bringing Eva to Butler. He agreed and a few weeks later sent an email informing me that she'd be our 2015 commencement speaker and honorary degree recipient. I was over the moon and so was Alex.

Venerable Hinkle Fieldhouse is the site of Butler's commencement exercises and a packed house arrived for BU's graduation on May 9, 2015. Built in 1928, Hinkle is one of the most iconic sports venues in the country. In addition to serving as the home for the Butler Bulldog basketball teams, the final scenes for the movie *Hoosiers* were filmed there and it long played host to the Indiana high school basketball championships. Seven United States presidents have spoken at Hinkle and in the 1940s it housed Naval officers during World War II. More history was to come on this muggy, but ebullient day.

The backstage reception area was abuzz when Alex escorted his parents into the green room. The Kors received a warm welcome and Eva immediately bonded with soon-to-be graduates JoJo and Jill Gentry. The Gentrys, like Eva and her sister Miriam, were identical twins and received one final history lesson before graduating as Eva recounted her trials at Auschwitz. Joining President Danko and the trustees on stage once the ceremony began, Eva gazed out on a capacity crowd of 9,200 people. It hit me that over a seventy-year span, she'd gone from the selection platform at Auschwitz to the commencement platform at a leading University and was set to receive Butler's highest honor.

I'd heard many commencement addresses—some good, few great, and many that were sleep-inducing. Eva's was by far the most riveting speech I'd ever heard. She detailed her journey, from the wretched conditions at Auschwitz, to her liberation, and then finally to her courageous and controversial adoption of forgiveness. Generating thunderous applause, several standing ovations, and a torrent of tears, few cared that she went ten minutes over her allotted time. Her closing words hit me the hardest. Gazing into the eyes of the 1,000 plus graduates, Eva implored each of them to hug their parents following the ceremony.

Upon "graduating" from Auschwitz, she wasn't afforded the opportunity to hug her own parents, who'd been murdered in the camp's gas chambers. She then motioned to Alex to join her on stage where she locked him in a warm embrace. Goosebumps. And there wasn't a dry eye in the house. I'd witnessed some thrilling moments in my years of watching basketball in Hinkle, but never experienced the feeling of nirvana like I did that May morning.

James Marshall Crotty, a writer, was on hand for the address and felt so moved that he penned an essay in *Forbes* magazine on how Eva's speech touched him. "I couldn't help but tear up when Mrs. Kor explained how she came to write a widely criticized public letter forgiving her Nazi tormentors, and eventually to hug 'the accountant at Auschwitz' Oskar Groening. She did so, she said, not to absolve Nazi crimes, as widely believed, but to regain her serenity and agency," wrote Crotty.

Fundraisers never miss an opportunity to capitalize on big moments, and I decided this was the perfect time to endow a scholarship in Eva's honor. In a matter of weeks, we'd raised the minimum $50,000 needed to endow the scholarship, which is appropriately awarded to a student in Butler's Peace and Conflict Studies program. President Danko was so impressed with Eva that he invited her to return to speak that fall. I collaborated with our operations staff and was miffed upon their insistence that she speak at the Schrott Center, a smaller, 400-seat venue on campus. Knowing this wouldn't satisfy demand, I pressed hard that it be held at historic Clowes Memorial Hall. Built in 1963, Clowes had played host to stars like Bob Hope and David Letterman and could hold 2,100 people. With the President's assistance, we secured Clowes and her fall lecture easily sold out.

On the morning of her talk, I went to ensure the venue was ready and was greeted by bomb-sniffing police dogs, a painful reminder of the ever-present threat of antisemitism. Eva had been liberated for seventy years and still dealt with the "crime" of being Jewish. The majority of the 2,100, mostly non-Jewish attendees that night would have no clue of the bomb inspection, yet she'd faced this out-of-sight, out-of-mind discrimination for eight decades. Eva again brought the packed house to tears, and I felt that I'd finally fulfilled my promise to Alex.

As my friendship with Alex blossomed, our work to honor his parents' legacies took on more meaning. In 2017, we collaborated with our friend and filmmaker Ted Green who produced *Eva A-7063*, a documentary on her life that premiered across the country and ended up winning multiple awards. The film debuted at Clowes in the spring of 2018 to another large audience. An educational curriculum was developed from the film and used in public schools across Indiana–vital in a state where a state senator recently brought forth legislation mandating that teachers be impartial when discussing Nazism.

On July 4, 2019, I received an early morning text from Alex asking that I call him immediately. With a pit in my stomach, he confirmed my fears and shared the news of his mother's passing, noting the sad irony that she'd died during her annual pilgrimage back to Auschwitz. The first person I contacted was President Danko, who immediately offered Butler as a site for her funeral. On August 19, I had the honor to speak at her memorial service and barely kept it together. She'd made such an impact on me, even encouraging me to forgive a family member whom I hadn't spoken with in years. Though she wasn't physically present, Eva Kor inspired the crowd at Clowes Hall one final time.

After Eva's passing, I got to spend more time with Alex's dad Mickey. I loved needling him whenever Butler beat Purdue and drafted off his contagious optimism. He was hospitalized in 2021, and I'd periodically visit him in his hospital room in Lebanon, Indiana. He'd converted the room into his own Purdue man cave and always had a smile on his face. I so much admired how Alex cared for his father and was envious at how close a relationship they had. Mickey's passing in October 2021 brought much sadness, but I took solace in the optimistic outlook he held until the very end. It wasn't surprising; he'd done it for more than ninety years through some extraordinarily trying circumstances.

Over the course of our friendship, Alex and I spent a lot of time together. There were Butler games, NCAA tournaments, dinners, and counseling sessions on how he might find his own "Mrs. Kor." So far, I—along with Jdate, a Jewish matchmaking site—have failed miserably. Alex had long aspired to author a book on his life as the son of Holocaust survivors, and I'd grown tired of his talk without action. In the summer of 2023, I told him that we were either going to write it or drop the subject. I'd published two books in the last three years and was burned out, but the one project that could get my juices flowing again was this one.

I wanted to help Alex tell his story for several reasons. While many knew about his mother's narrative, his father's narrow escape at Buchenwald wasn't widely known. Nor was Alex's battle with cancer and how Eva and Mickey helped lift their son out of despair by reminding him of the hurdles they'd overcome. There was also an emotional pull for me given my fondness for Eva and Mickey. They were true heroes to me, and for years their picture sat atop my desk at Butler. In December 2022, a pipe burst above my office, destroying my files, books, and many of my pictures. Somehow my photo of Eva and Mickey made it. Even in death, they still survived. I hope this book honors their legacy and is yet one more way to keep their narrative alive.

The Kor Family's story is just as important now as it's ever been. In recent years, the Tree of Life Synagogue shooting in Pittsburgh, the disgusting display of white supremacy in Charlottesville, and closer to home, antisemitic graffiti spray-painted onto an Indianapolis synagogue had deeply impacted me. If I drove an hour and a half south, I could find the home of one of the country's prominent Holocaust deniers who'd helped lead the Charlottesville rally. Even two years after the January 6 attack on the Capitol, I couldn't erase the image of the rioter donning a "Camp Auschwitz" T-shirt.

In 2022, I co-authored my second book, *Unbracketed*, which highlighted the Davidson College basketball team's 2018 trip to Auschwitz led by Eva. Alex and I were later invited to speak at Davidson and at the Sinai Temple in Los Angeles on Davidson's experience. I also presented at a New Jersey synagogue along with Davidson College coach Bob McKillop and my co-author Jerry Logan. Our panel discussion came just a week after NBA star Kyrie Irving tweeted a link to *Hebrews to Negroes: Wake Up Black America*, a 2018 film driven by antisemitic tropes about Jewish people lying about their origins. Just days prior to our talk, multiple bomb threats were called in targeting synagogues in New Jersey. It was nearly eighty years after World War II ended and I had to ask: how much progress had we really made? A little more than two months after Alex and I started writing, Hamas terrorists launched a surprise attack on Israel and infiltrated the country by air, land, and sea. On October 7, 2023,

1,200 Israelis were killed by Hamas, marking the largest mass murder of Jewish people on a single day since the Holocaust.

Disturbing studies revealing how younger generations lacked even a basic knowledge of the Holocaust also motivated me. In 2020, the US Millennial Holocaust Knowledge and Awareness Survey showed a "worrying lack of basic Holocaust knowledge" among adults under forty, including over one in ten respondents who didn't recall ever having heard the word "Holocaust." I hope this book reaches young people to educate and remind us that we can never forget. I have two young daughters and dream that one day they will pass this work along to their children and grandchildren.

Recently, Alex and I were having lunch with a mutual friend who is also Jewish. He was perplexed as to my involvement in these projects given that I am not Jewish myself. I believe all of us have an obligation to fight discrimination, but my own family background has an interesting tie to this book. My father-in-law, Hans Morsbach, grew up in Nazi Germany and was a member of the Hitler Youth, a mandate for young boys in that era. His family escaped Germany after the war, and he went on to become a successful businessman in Chicago. He was a role model for me and fought tirelessly against discrimination up until his death in 2011. I hope that in a small way, this book honors him as well.

A few years ago, Alex admitted to me that he almost tore up the letter that I sent him in 2014. He knew I was coming to call on him for money and had been through this song and dance before. I'm so glad he kept the letter and our appointment. My journey with him and involvement with this project has been an honor. I also gained one of my very best friends along the way.

—*Graham Honaker*
Indianapolis, Indiana

Prologue

My family's story is not an easy one to tell—or to hear. History has documented many versions of the atrocities that occurred during World War II. And to have close, first-hand accounts of that history right in the immediate family is *not* something I take lightly.

My name is Alex Kor, and my mother and father each spent time in Nazi concentration camps during the terrible time that Adolph Hitler and the Nazis terrorized Europe.

Eva, my mother, was an incredible force of nature.

Mickey, my father, was a loving pure heart.

Despite the horror of their youths, they found a life together and built an incredible future.

After a time, they both miraculously learned to forgive.

There is a lot of life, death, pain, struggle, and love shared on these pages. I would like to share my family's journey, so you might join me in appreciation of their legacy.

Timeline: Eva Mozes Kor and Mickey Kor

1925

October 24: Rachmiel "Mickey" Kor born in Riga, Latvia

1934

January 31: Eva and twin sister Miriam born in Portz, Transylvania, Romania

1940

Nazis occupy Romania

June 17: Soviet forces begin occupation of Latvia

1941

July 1: Nazis invade and occupy Latvia

October 18: Mickey's father, Scholom, is murdered while walking to work

October 23: Mickey's mother, Mirka Kor, and brothers Leo and Shlomo are relocated to the Riga ghetto

December 8: Mirka Kor is murdered

December: Leo, Shlomo, and Mickey moved to the "small" ghetto

1943

June: Mickey becomes prisoner of Kaiserwald concentration camp

September: Eva and family under house arrest in their village

1944

March: Eva and family are sent to the Cehei ghetto

May 25: Eva and family arrive at Auschwitz-Birkenau camps as part of the Hungarian transport

May: Eva and Miriam held captive at Auschwitz concentration camp and used in human medical experiments by Nazi Dr. Josef Mengele

May: Mickey arrives in Stutthof concentration camp

November 3: Mickey gets relocated to Duderstadt (Polte-Werke), a subcamp of Buchenwald

November 19: Mickey is officially registered into the Buchenwald system

1945

January 27: Eva and Miriam liberated from Auschwitz

February: Eva and Miriam housed at Auschwitz I

March: Eva and Miriam taken to a convent in Katowice, Poland, facilitated by the Polish Red Cross and a Jewish relief organization.

April: Mickey taken on a death march

April 15: Mickey is liberated by the 250th Engineer Combat Battalion and meets Lt. Col. Andrew Nehf

March–May: Eva and Miriam stay in a DP camp in Katowice, Poland, with Mrs. Csengeri and her twins

May–July: Eva and Miriam stay in a DP camp near Czernowitz, Soviet Union, with Mrs. Csengeri and her twins

Summer: Mickey arrives in Frankfurt, Germany, with the 250th

July–October: Eva and Miriam stay in a DP Camp at the former Shultz Ghetto near Minsk, Belarus, Russia, with Mrs. Csengeri and her twins

October: Eva and Miriam return to Portz for a short time

October: Eva and Miriam travel to Cluj, Romania, where they live with their Aunt Irena until 1950.

1946

May 10: Mickey leaves Bremerhaven, Germany, for the United States

May 21: Mickey arrives in the Port of New York

August: Mickey enrolls in the State Lab High School, Terre Haute, Indiana

1948

Mickey becomes a naturalized citizen

1950

June 25: Eva leaves Communist Romania for Israel, arriving in the Port of Haifa.

Until 1952, Eva lives in the Youth Aliyah Villages

1952

Eva serves in the Israeli Military as a draftswoman until 1960, reaching the rank of Sergeant Major

1952

Mickey graduates from the Purdue University School of Pharmacy

1952–1954

Mickey serves with the US Army as a military pharmacist in Osaka, Japan

1960

April 27: Eva and Michael Kor get married

June 19: Eva joins Michael in the United States

1961	**April:** Son Alex is born
1963	**March:** Daughter Rina is born
1965	**September 22:** Eva becomes a naturalized citizen
1984	Founding of CANDLES organization
	Eva returns to Auschwitz-Birkenau for the first time since 1944
1985	**January:** 40th Anniversary of the Liberation of Auschwitz
	February: J'Accuse mock trial in Jerusalem at Yad Vashem
1986	Eva arrested at the Capitol Rotunda
1993	**June:** Miriam dies
1993	**October:** Eva travels to meet Dr. Hans Munch
1995	**January:** 50th Anniversary of the liberation of Auschwitz
	Dr. Munch documents the operation of the gas chambers
	Eva's declaration of forgiveness
	May: CANDLES Museum and Holocaust Education Center opens in Terre Haute, Indiana
1995	Mickey retires from working as a pharmacist and begins working as a CANDLES docent, twice weekly
1999	Eva sues the Bayer Corporation
2000	*Echoes from Auschwitz* is published

2003	**November:** CANDLES Museum destroyed by arson
2005	**April:** Museum rededicated
2006	*Forgiving Dr. Mengele* documentary released
2009	*Surviving the Angel of Death* is published
2010	Mickey issues a declaration of forgiveness to the German people
2014	Eva testifies at the trial of former Nazi Oskar Gröning trial
2015	Eva awarded honorary degree at Butler University
2016	Eva featured in "Dimensions in Testimony"
2017	Eva named Indy 500 Grand Marshal
	Eva receives Sachem Award
2018	*Eva: A-7063* documentary released
2019	**July 4:** Eva Kor passes away in Kraków, Poland
2019	Mickey issues a statement in the trial of former Stutthof guard Bruno Dey
	August 4: Celebration of Eva's Life at Indiana State University
	August 18: Celebration of Eva's Life at Clowes Hall–Butler University
2020	Mural of Eva created in downtown Indianapolis
2021	**October 19:** Mickey Kor passes away

CHAPTER

Independence Day

> "I have so much work to do here on Earth."
>
> —Eva

It was July 1, 2019, and my mother and I were in a familiar place, holed up in a stuffy hotel room in Eastern Europe. Even at nightfall, the outside temperature hovered around 90 degrees and it didn't feel much better inside.

Before nodding off to sleep, I turned to her and said, "Mom, you know… you aren't getting any younger. When are you going to start taking it easy? Maybe it's time to start cutting back on your hectic schedule."

She'd turned eighty-five in January and was still giving more than seventy-five lectures per year, a number of them outside our home in Indiana. When not on the speaking circuit, her days were filled with fielding interview requests, responding to letters and emails, tending to her museum, and tweeting on her newly beloved social media platform. Recently featured in an award-winning documentary, she was fresh off a year-long promotional tour for the film. I'd long admired the passion she held for her work but was concerned about the toll it was taking on her. In recent years, she'd experienced heart, knee, and shoulder issues and had both hips replaced. I wanted her to enjoy her final years. Following my plea, she stared at me as if I were from Mars.

"Alex, my dear son," she said, "I have so much work to do here on Earth. There is *no* way that I can cut back."

For more than a decade, my mother had led an annual expedition to the Auschwitz-Birkenau concentration camp near Kraków, Poland. The trip was marketed through the CANDLES Holocaust Museum and Education Center, which she founded in 1995 in our adopted hometown of Terre Haute, Indiana. The trips, often sold out months in advance, were populated by people of all ages from all over the United States and occasionally other countries. For their own personal reasons, they'd chosen perhaps the most horrific site in the history of mankind for their summer vacation. Over a five-year period from 1940–1945, more than 1 million people were murdered at Auschwitz, a pivotal locale in Adolf Hitler's Final Solution aimed at eradicating the Jewish people. This was the twenty-fifth time I'd accompanied her and the reason I found myself in Kraków on this scorching summer evening.

Each day, over a seven-day span, my mother would lead the tour group through Auschwitz. An expert guide, she knew every inch of the grounds, able to recount in vivid detail the concrete selection platform where deportees were dumped, many soon to be sent off to the gas chambers. She could evoke the rancid smell in the barracks and mimic the sound of rats scurrying around at night as desolate captives sought sleep. She was able to describe it all so precisely because Auschwitz had once been my mother's home.

My mother was Eva Mozes Kor and prisoner A-7063 at Auschwitz. In 1944, along with her parents and siblings, she was forcibly taken by cattle car from her tiny village in Romania to Auschwitz. As her family descended upon the selection platform, Nazi guards ripped my mother and her twin sister Miriam away from their parents and older sisters. It was the last time the family would ever be together. My mother and Miriam survived the barbaric medical experiments of Dr. Josef Mengele, aka the "Angel of Death," and they were liberated in 1945.

When my mother ventured overseas for these trips, my father Mickey was left to hold down the fort at the museum. A Holocaust survivor in his own right, my father had survived multiple concentration camps, including the notoriously brutal Buchenwald concentration camp near Weimar, Germany. His parents had also been murdered by the Nazis, and he'd narrowly escaped execution in the waning days of World War II. Though he supported my mother's annual expedition, he never joined us at Auschwitz. His own memories of the Holocaust were still too vivid and agonizing.

———————————————————

A couple of days after we arrived in Kraków for her latest sojourn to Auschwitz, my mother woke up with a mild cough, not uncommon as she occasionally suffered from upper respiratory infections. I was already with our group at Auschwitz, observing the sullen reactions from the attendees. Many wept as they reflected on the evil and sheer magnitude of death that had transpired nearly seventy-five years prior. My mother rested until 11:30 a.m. and then took a private car to the camp to reunite with us. As we awaited her arrival, to my surprise twenty-five students from the Young Men's Ensemble of the Los Angeles Chorus showed up to greet her. They were touring and performing in different locations across Europe and, while visiting Aushwitz that morning, had gotten word that my mother was due to arrive momentarily. While I was flattered, I informed their director that we had a tight schedule and needed to stick to it.

At that instant, my mother rolled up on her golf cart and barked out, "What's going on here? Who are these young men?"

Steven Kronauer, the director of the group, responded, "Eva, we are the Young Men's Ensemble from the L.A. Children's Chorus, and we would like to sing a few songs for you in Yiddish."

As they began singing, my mother (never shy) interrupted them and said, "Can you sing my favorite song, 'The Impossible Dream'?"

Kronauer replied that they weren't familiar with it.

"I know the song," my mother shot back. "You can follow me."

Outside the camp, with Auschwitz's foreboding tower looming in the background, my mother led the choir in a rousing rendition of her beloved tune.

To dream the impossible dream
To fight the unbeatable foe
To bear with unbearable sorrow
And to run where the brave dare not go

A crowd soon gathered and tears, including my own, began flowing. Of the many amazing moments in my mother's life, this was one of the most surreal. In a seventy-year span at Auschwitz, she'd evolved from captive to band leader.

After the impromptu concert, my mother conducted her afternoon tour before departing for the hotel, worn out, but in good spirits. She later held court during our group dinner and then headed upstairs. While she and I reflected on the day's happenings, one of the attendees snapped a picture of us. Little did I know that the photo would be the very last taken of my mother and me.

At 3:00 a.m. that morning, I was awakened by coughing and rushed to her side. "Are you okay, Mom?" I shouted. She replied that she was and settled into bed, sleeping peacefully without a sound. She awoke at 5:45 a.m. and hollered, "Alex, you need to wake up! We have a long day ahead of us at Auschwitz! Help with my blouse, and I will fix my coffee and take my medicine."

I began to get dressed and said something to her. When she failed to respond, I pivoted to see her slumped over and foaming at the mouth. She was unresponsive and I screamed, "*Mom! Not here! Please do not die here, not now!*"

Our nurse and another staffer rushed in from the adjoining room, and we laid my mother on the floor and began CPR. I hurtled to the lobby to inform the hotel staff that we needed the paramedics immediately. Six minutes later, EMTs were in the room. They worked on her for the next hour. In tears, I pleaded to her that she couldn't die, not here and not on this day.

At 7:11 a.m., the paramedic turned to me and said, "There is nothing we can do. She's gone."

In shock, I was unsure of how to inform my father and sister, who were both back home in Indiana where it was the middle of the night. I thanked the paramedics as they departed and, at their request, handed both a copy of my mother's book, *Surviving the Angel of Death*. About twenty minutes later, another man entered the room.

"Hi, my name is Yossi and I'm the hotel manager. I'm Israeli and greatly admire your mother. Can I say a prayer with your mother and ask that you kiss her?" In my stupor I consented, and Yossi said the Kaddish, an ancient Jewish prayer recited in memory of the dead. I kissed my mother and can still recall how frigid she felt.

They say that when you die, your life flashes before your eyes. As my mother lay lifeless, her life flashed in front of mine. Memories raced through my head—my childhood, my mother's arduous journey to find forgiveness, and all the past visits with her to Auschwitz. One of her mantras was, "I want my life on this earth to count for something." Inconsolable and alone in the hotel room, I took solace that her life had counted for something and that she'd impacted tens of thousands of people in her eighty-five years. Three days earlier, she'd reiterated how much work she still had to do. That morning, I was acutely aware of how much work she'd done.

Eighty-five years is a long life, but the end had transpired so quickly. Less than twenty-four hours ago, we were singing joyfully with a group of young men from California, celebrating how my mother had realized the impossible dream. It was here at Auschwitz on January 27, 1945, that against all odds she was liberated. The cruel reality that she'd died near the same place as her greatest triumph brought me to my knees. And then it hit me. The day of her death was just as significant as the place. It was July 4, 2019. She had passed not only in the shadow of Auschwitz, but in the dawning hours of Independence Day, a holiday that held immense significance to her.

CHAPTER

The Taste of Freedom

> "It was a time to be or not to be."
>
> —Mickey

There were few things that a kid growing up in the 1960s cherished more than a bottle of Coca-Cola. My friends and I loved going to the local drugstore and (for a dime!) buying a cold bottle of Coke. It was a ritual for us after playing hoops or baseball, but truth be told, we never needed an excuse to down a cold one. Yet my excitement always seemed to pale in comparison to my father's. Coca-Cola was a staple at our family meals. Sporting a grin a mile wide, my father gripped a Coke bottle as if it were a trophy. I couldn't understand his unbridled enthusiasm for something so simple as a bottle of soda until he first shared the extraordinary story of his liberation with me. I was twelve years old.

The Kor Family (from left) Mirka, Shlomo, Zorri, Leib, Rachmiel, and Scholom Kor.
COURTESY ALEX KOR

My father was born Rachmiel Kor in Riga, Latvia, on October 24, 1925. The youngest of four boys, his father Scholom was a shoemaker and his mother Mirka, a homemaker. An excellent cook, Mirka was renowned for her latkes (potato pancakes). My father's grandfather was a rabbi in Lithuania and according to some family members, his last name was not Kor, but Kalt. In German, *Kalt* means cold and since Rabbi Kalt was a devout Jew, he changed the name to Kor—the Hebrew word for cold. The product of deeply religious parents, my father, along with his brothers Leib, Zorri, and Shlomo, was educated at a Jewish school.

As a child, my father was a voracious reader and kept up with world events from an early age. Every morning, he'd pore through the newspapers and to the surprise of his teachers, could rattle off the names of British and French cabinet members. Sports (especially soccer) and music were his great passions, but his family's financial circumstances limited his participation in both. Mirka did her best to make do and constructed a ping pong table using a board and a newspaper for a net. The boys played for hours on end, marking the beginning of my father's lifelong love affair with the game. One of his favorite childhood memories was attending a performance by the American opera singer Marian Anderson at the Latvian National Opera in Riga. He also loved venturing to the Riga harbor, where he marveled at the international ships even if he couldn't understand the languages being spoken aboard them. My father grew up poor but embraced the simple pleasures of his youth. Years later, he lamented that those in power couldn't appreciate the same tranquility in his writings:

My father Rachmiel "Mickey" Kor as a young boy. COURTESY ALEX KOR

This peaceful period didn't last too long. Somebody sitting in the high government office could not see that people live in peace in this world. A group of people was not satisfied with what they had. They wanted more. Their own country was too small for them, and they made plans for aggression. The group I am talking about was established in Germany.

I was young when all this took place, sometimes age doesn't mean anything. It is hard to describe my feelings at that time when everything was moving toward a war. I could not realize why do people have to build guns to destroy other people. Why do people claim other territories that belong to others? I asked myself. Why? There was no answer. [1]

As ominous rumors swirled around Germany and its powerful new leader, my father and his family grew anxious.

"I felt terrible at that time and kept asking myself questions," he remembered. "Why don't they do something? Why don't they take some actions against Hitler? But there was no answer." [2]

His anxiety heightened following the signing of the Munich Agreement on September 30, 1938. Germany, Britain, France, and Italy had reached

a settlement permitting German annexation of the Sudetenland in western Czechoslovakia. My father later shared that he knew, at that point,

My father (second row, far left) with his sixth-grade class.
COURTESY ALEX KOR

that war was inevitable and called the following weeks, "the calm before the storm."[3] He long held that war could have been avoided if Neville Chamberlain, Britain's Prime Minister at the time, had rebuffed Hitler's efforts at annexation.

Gone were the sweet sounds of the opera; in their place, other voices evoked terror. My father and his family often huddled around their radio and listened to Hitler's bravado-filled speeches. Hitler "drove me crazy," recalled my father. "If somebody had given me a gun, I would have gone to Germany and killed that man. It was rather impossible, but a lot of impossible ideas come into a young person's mind."[4] He was thirteen years old at the time and while every teenager wrestles with uncertainties, the happenings in Germany caused him much angst because they seemed so far out of anyone's control. "I was very restless at this time," he remembered. "I asked questions at school, home, every place, and nobody knew the answer. There was no answer."[5]

On June 17, 1940, Soviet troops began their occupation of Latvia under the provisions of the 1939 Molotov–Ribbentrop Pact with Nazi Germany and its Secret Additional Protocol. The Soviet Union annexed Latvia and over the next year, 35,000 Latvians were deported to eastern regions, many of them to Siberian camps. My father grew extremely frustrated with Soviet rule. He abhorred communism, a voting system he deemed corrupt, and the oppression of free speech that prohibited any criticism of Stalin. The ensuing year would be coined the "year of terror" and my father's sentiments aptly reflected the period:

Rumors were going around about the concentration of German troops along the border with Russia, but nobody would believe it.... I still remember my feelings at

The Kor Brothers (from left) Shlomo, Leib, Rachmiel, and Zorri. COURTESY ALEX KOR

that time and stopped to think about those rumors, "They are true, they are false, they are true, they are false." This is the way my mind worked then; I was restless. I didn't tell anybody about my feelings because I didn't want to make people panic, but I knew things looked bad. I also knew that there could be no understanding between two such opposite ideas: Nazism and Communism. I also knew that the two dictators, led by such strong hands as Hitler on one side and Stalin on the other, will not agree and will not change their attitudes. I was frightened, and the most unusual dreams came through my mind. I saw in dreams fire, airplanes, guns, soldiers, tanks, attacks, people running, and so on. [6]

At 5:00 a.m. on June 22, 1941, Hitler launched Operation Barbarossa, ordering his troops across the Soviet frontier, through Lithuania and into strategic Latvian localities.

My father vividly recalled Hitler announcing over the radio, "I gave my army the order to cross the Soviet border in order to fight Bolshevism." [7]

My father tried in vain to volunteer for the Russian army but was refused due to his age. "Not that I liked the Russians," he wrote, "but anybody that fought the Germans was my friend and ally." Since he couldn't fight, he invoked a higher power, praying that "God would make them (the Russians) successful." [8]

The following day, the Germans began bombing Riga:

A hail of bombs came over the city and we all ran to get shelter. Some made it and some didn't. My hate against the Germans grew. I was reading the newspapers before about the bombings at Rotterdam, Warsaw, and London but now I happen to see it with my own eyes. I thought I just could not realize why human beings drop bombs from the sky to destroy other human beings. The crime was big. Someday, I thought, they will get repaid for it. But when, when, when, when?

The Germans went ahead. Nothing could stop their blitzkrieg. Thousands and thousands of Russian soldiers fell into German prisons. The Germans used their propaganda. Broadcasts in the Russian language called the Russians to give up. Entire Russian units went over. Treason began in the Russian Army. The situation was critical. My feeling was then desolate. It made me that sore, I almost cried. I just couldn't forgive the world why they didn't make Hitler stop. I just couldn't understand it. [9]

The Germans followed the bombardment by invading Riga on July 1, 1941, a day forever etched in my father's memory.

This is a day which I'll never forget. For the first time I saw German soldiers. Their tyrannic faces seared me. They were occupying the whole city. Pride, glory, and happiness was expressed in their faces, which meant melancholy and madness to me. This day means very much to me. It was the day I lost my freedom and the beginning of a period which the history of mankind has never seen before. I'll never forget July 1, 1941. [10]

The Germans corralled Riga's Jewish residents, including my father, his brothers Leib and Shlomo (Zorri had been drafted by the Latvian Navy), and his mother, into a ghetto that was sealed off in October 1941, just one day shy of my father's sixteenth birthday. Upon his arrival, my father was reunited with his brother Leib, who had already been forced into the ghetto along with his wife Basseva and their two-year-old daughter Slata. When he pressed his mother on what offense they had committed, she simply responded, "the crime of being Jewish." His father never made it to the ghetto. On October 18, 1941, Scholom Kor was murdered by Nazi

The Riga ghetto. COURTESY YAD VASHEM

sympathizers on his way to work, having committed the "crime" of walking on the wrong side of the street.

Constructed primarily in run-down sections of Eastern and Central Europe, ghettos were used as points of delineation: captives were selected either for slave labor or for death. The Riga ghettos allowed for only 3-4 square meters per person and housed nearly 30,000 people, including approximately 5,000 children and 8,000 disabled and elderly people. The ghetto was secured by the Latvian police force and surrounded by a barbed-wire fence and wooden barriers. Those who got too close to the barbed wire were sometimes shot and killed by the ghetto guards. Ghetto houses had no electricity, plumbing, gas, or central heating and one hospital served the entire population. Food ration cards, distributed solely to slave laborers, allowed for small servings of turnips, cabbage, potatoes, and rotten fish. Those who tried to smuggle food in were beaten. Sexual relations were forbidden and women who got pregnant were forced to have an abortion. Children born alive were killed by poisoning. Such were the living conditions for the Kor family in late 1941.

By early December, rumors swirled in the ghetto that something drastic was about to happen. My father later composed an essay entitled "The Great Massacre" that captured an ominous turn of events in the ghetto that month:

The air was cold, frosty, and rough; the mood was bad and the morale low. How can you even think of a good mood when you are enclosed in a ghetto surrounded with barbed wire and armed guards. I could notice something unusual that day—hundreds and hundreds of drunk German guards. German troopers kept gathering around the ghetto and the feelings were indescribable. It meant danger and rumors came around that the Germans were planning to evacuate (as the Germans described it) all women and children and physically unfit men.... This was a terrible day and a most terrible night. I really don't know what words to use to describe those twenty-four hours. [11]

Forbidding anyone to leave the ghetto, Nazi troops demanded that women and young children gather their belongings for an "evacuation" set for the following morning. Young adult and able-bodied men like Shlomo and Leib were to remain in the ghetto to be used as laborers.

My father, whose fate was less certain, recognized this "evacuation" was a ruse: "We knew this meant death," he later recalled. One of the few possessions Mirka packed was a flower-patterned tablecloth. When the family would gather for meals, Mirka would throw the cloth over whatever makeshift table they could find or even simply place it on the ground. She hoped it would serve as a reminder of the serene moments they'd once enjoyed. Years later, my father came to realize that Mirka's use of the tablecloth was also her way of keeping the family "human."

My father, Mirka, Shlomo, and Leib waited for hours, resigned to their fate:

We all knew what this meant and there was no time to raise the feelings of each other. This was our destiny and there was nothing we could do about it, so we decided just to let it go. The time went very slow, every minute was like an hour and every hour like a day. We didn't even think of taking luggage because we knew there was no reason to. We just waited to get "picked up." [12]

My grandmother was an incredibly courageous woman. She comforted her three sons and insisted that my father not accompany her the following morning:

My mother said, "Rachmiel, you're young, your whole life is ahead of you, I'm not going to let you come." She started to cry and said, "I don't want you to come, I don't want you...to die." She said the last word softly so I couldn't hear her. This was a mother's love to her son, a mother's devotion to her son. [13]

My father was deeply conflicted. At the age of sixteen, he faced either imminent death or the overwhelming guilt of leaving his mother to perish alone. Protesting vehemently, he recalled thinking, "No, I'm not going to let her go by herself. My life wouldn't mean anything, anyway without my mother."[14]

Mirka ultimately won out. "I am not going to let you come," she instructed my father. "I am going, but I don't want you to die."

The following day, Nazi soldiers pounded on the door while my father hid in a back room. Guards asked Shlomo if anyone else was present in the house to which he responded there was not. With a rifle in her back, Nazi guards forced his mother out of the house as my father, rife with shame and despair, looked on through a back window:

I rushed to the window and saw them leading her down the street. She didn't see me, and this was the last time I saw her. What a way to separate a child from his mother. I didn't even get to say goodbye, she was gone. [15]

The Germans, drunk on both alcohol and power, progressed from room to room in the ghetto, rounding up thousands of terrified women and children. The captives were moved to the Rumbula Forest and lined up before German firing squads. In a two-day event on November 30 and December 8, German Schutzstaffel and Latvian auxiliary forces executed between 26,000 and 29,000 Latvian Jews, including fifty-two-year-old Mirka Kor as well as Leib's wife Basseva and daughter Slata. The mass execution was the second largest massacre (only surpassed by the Babi Yar slaughter in Ukraine) of the Holocaust until the implementation of the concentration camps.

A month later, my father visited the site of the Rumbula massacre and recalled the scene:

I happened to be at the place where the shooting took place. I saw nothing. They were all buried right after the massacre in order not to make it known to the public. All kinds of items that these unfortunate people had thrown away were still scattered all over the area. I even found a little doll that some little girl had thrown away.

There was no sign of the flower-patterned tablecloth that Mirka had carried with her when she left. All was gone.

This is the way I lost my mother; this is what Germany has done to me—murdered my mother. I couldn't even find her grave. [16]

One of the motivations for the massacre was to make room for a transport of German Jews coming into Latvia. The surviving Jews were held in an area known as the "small" or "Latvian" ghetto. Twenty thousand Jews soon arrived from Germany, Austria, and the Protectorate of Bohemia and Moravia to Riga and were incarcerated in the "big" or "German" ghetto, a separate establishment from the Latvian ghetto. Approximately 1,000 of the German Jews were executed upon their arrival and the majority of the remaining population killed in the Rumbula Forest. My father, Shlomo, and Leib remained in the Latvian ghetto from October 1941 to June 1943.

The Kor brothers were three of approximately 5,000 men spared and exiled to the Kaiserwald concentration camp where they were used as slave labor for German companies.

While on work detail, Shlomo killed the Nazi guard on watch, managed to escape to Germany, and eventually fled to the future state of Israel.

Zorri, who had become an officer in the Latvian Navy, hadn't been so lucky. Upon discovering his Jewish heritage, Zorri's comrades killed him and threw his body overboard into the Baltic Sea.

Both Leib and my father have almost identical imprisonment journeys. They were taken by the Gestapo Riga on September 4, 1943, to the Kaiserwald camp, which lay just a few miles outside of Riga. Constructed by Jews from the Riga Ghetto in March 1943, the camp's first occupants were German convicts. Jewish captives (approximately 15,000) in the Baltic region were sent through Kaiserwald before being transferred to other labor camps. Though not an extermination camp, evil pervaded at Kaiserwald nonetheless. Dr. Edward Kresbach, the camp's chief physician, was known as "The Needle" for his eagerness to murder patients. Forcing inmates to perform physical exercises, Kresbach would evaluate their strength and then identify the 2,000 weakest to be executed.

Inmates were put to work by large German companies in the production of electrical goods. Other prisoners were slave laborers in factories and mines, on farms, and inside the camp. My father and Leib worked in the SS construction yard from April 2, 1944, to July 31, 1944.

"Waking up in the morning still alive was an occasion of silent jubilation,"

The KL Stutthof Concentration Camp.
COURTESY DANUTA DRYWA, STUTTHOF MUSEUM ARCHIVE

my father remembered about this period. Kaiserwald was vacated in August 1944, and only those aged eighteen to thirty survived the selections. My father, now nineteen, and Leib, several years his senior, evaded death once again, this time being saved only by virtue of their ages.

Months later, in late October 1944, the two brothers boarded a German ocean liner docked at the Baltic Sea. Armed Nazi guards ushered the captives onboard and kept keen watch for potential escapees. Perplexed, my father wondered where the ship was headed:

I went to the rail where I could be a minute by myself and looked toward the sea. The view was beautiful at dusk as the sun slowly set. I tried to think about what was going on—we were sailing, but where to? I asked myself but there was no answer and I just stood there looking toward the sea.... I almost started to dream, but someone "woke me up." A German guard was walking up on deck and knocked on my shoulder. In a brutal voice, he said, "Hey, don't you know that you don't belong here? Your place is down below. The deck is for people, for humans only." I walked down below and kept thinking of that last sentence, "The deck is meant for human beings!!" As if I am just an animal. Someday, someday, I thought. [17]

Forced down to the ship's hull, my father joined hundreds of captives

My father's Personal Identification Card at Buchenwald.

huddled together in suffocating heat. Storms rocked the ship the first few days and my father imagined, "If some Allied ship had come and captured that convoy, we would be free. But this was only a dream." Instead, the journey only worsened:

The third day of the "beautiful voyage," the supply of drinking water was about to run out. People almost fought each other to get a drink of water. Just plain, simple water became the most serious problem of life. People would have given the best valuables they own (if they had any) to get a drink of water. This was the first time in my life that I found out that not always are diamonds, gold, and jewelry the dearest things. Here I was sailing on a boat where water, just plain water, was more valuable than gold and jewelry. It was awfully hot below and some people started to cry, begging for water, but the Germans didn't care. They had enough water upstairs and that's all they cared for. The cries of the people increased, and I just watched them.

Eventually, the Germans ran a fire hose from the sea down into the hull and barked, "Drink you thirsty creatures." Dirty salt water came through that hose, but people were glad to drink it. They had little cups, little glasses. Some, not having cups, opened their mouths so the stream running from the hose with "drinking water" could land in their mouths. What a picture that was! I wondered if this was the twentieth century! [18]

The following day, my father learned that they were destined for Danzig, Germany, where the ship docked on the fifth day of the voyage. He was

The Buchenwald Concentration Camp. COURTESY BUCHENWALD MEMORIAL ARCHIVE

astounded to be on German soil, but he quickly understood why they'd been brought to Danzig:

Was there anything behind this? What was the reason for the departure? I kept on asking these questions but no answer. A whistle blew and they put us in little boats and down a little river to our "new home"—to another concentration camp, this time on German soil. [19]

Their new home was Stutthof, a camp situated in a wooded marsh 20 miles east of Danzig. Initially constructed as a civilian internment camp, Stutthof transitioned into a labor "education camp" in November 1941. Most of the prisoners perished in the brutal conditions. Typhus epidemics wiped out thousands and those too feeble to work were killed by gassing or lethal injection. More than 60,000 of the 110,000 laborers ultimately died. My father became prisoner number 95 997. He and his brother were two of the 50,000 survivors of Stutthof.

My father and Leib's confinement at Stutthof didn't last long. On November 3, 1944, along with 500 men and 300 women, they were transferred to a sub-camp of Buchenwald near Magdeburg. On the brothers' registration cards, guards scribbled "none" under the question of "crimes committed?" It was another piercing reminder that the only offense they'd committed was that of being Jewish. After being quarantined for ten days due to a typhus epidemic at Stutthof, my father was officially registered as prisoner 95942 at Buchenwald on November 19, 1944, and used as slave labor at the Polte munitions plant. In a 2017 letter to the *Terre Haute Tribune-Star*, he recalled his first days at the camp:

It was a hellhole, a satellite camp of the concentration camp Buchenwald. They put a uniform on me, with black stripes, like I was an Alcatraz prisoner. It was surrounded by a high fence that was topped with barbed wire. I was like a dog in a cage. And I didn't know when this life would end. [20]

One of the Nazis' largest and most feared concentration camps, Buchenwald was established in 1937 and located in a heavily wooded area five miles northwest of the city of Weimar in east-central Germany. Fortified by electrified barbed wire fences, watchtowers, and armed guards, the camp greeted prisoners with a portentous sign reading *"Jedem das Seine."* Translated as "to each his own," the Nazis interpreted the slogan to mean they had a right to disgrace and exterminate their prisoners. Armament production comprised the main labor function at Buchenwald and the camp was also coveted for its clay deposits that could be made into bricks.

Divided into approximately 136 subcamps, Buchenwald was home to thirty-three barracks, a prisoner infirmary, and crematorium. The main camp featured "The Bunker," a block where violators of camp rules were sent and beaten to death. The few female prisoners were forced to become sex slaves at the camp's brothel.

Political prisoners made up a significant percentage of the camp. Ernst Thalmann, former Chairman of the German Communist Party, was one of the more notable captives. Arrested by the Nazis in 1933, Thalmann was executed eleven years later at Buchenwald. The camp was also populated by Jehovah's Witnesses, German military defectors, suspected communists, the mentally and physically disabled, gypsies, sexual deviants, and anyone else whom the Nazis deemed unfit for living.

The camp's population had surged in 1938 following *Kristallnacht*. Occurring on November 9 and 10, *Kristallnacht* was named for the broken glass from the windows of synagogues, homes, and Jewish-owned businesses destroyed throughout Germany and Austria. The two-day reign of terror epitomized Nazi brutality and resulted in more than 100 deaths. Around 10,000 Jews were deported to the Buchenwald camp in the days following the destruction.

In 1942, the Division for Typhus and Virus Research of the Hygiene Institute of the Waffen-SS was established at the camp. In the Institute's labs, Nazi physicians assessed the effectiveness of treatments and vaccines against illnesses including cholera, typhus, and typhoid. Hundreds of prisoners died during the trial. Homosexual prisoners were injected with a male sex gland in order to "cure" them.

Many faces of evil roamed the camps at Buchenwald, but Walter Gerhard Martin Sommer was perhaps the most diabolical. More widely known as the "Hangman of Buchenwald," Sommer took delight in hanging prisoners, their wrists bound behind their backs, from the trees lining the nearby forests. Coined "the singing forest" due to the unceasing, terrifying screams from prisoners left hanging on its branches, the woods of Buchenwald provided an additional killing ground for the Nazis that offset the camp's absence of gas chambers.

Buchenwald was renowned for its sadistic practices, exemplified in the barbaric rituals conducted by Ilse Koch, the "Witch of Buchenwald." The wife of Nazi commandant Karl Otto Koch, Ilse was reputed to have prisoners bearing tattoos executed, in order to use their skins to make decorative objects such as lampshades, book covers, and bindings. She routinely beat prisoners with her riding crop and worked them to the point of exhaustion for her own perverse pleasure.

Like so many other camps, Buchenwald was a place where Jews went to die. Of the 280,000 prisoners who passed through the camp, 56,545 perished. Insufferable conditions accounted for many of the deaths at Buchenwald with Nazi cruelty on full display. The camp was ruled by the *Vernichtung durch Arbeit* ("extermination through work") edict and prisoners were starved to death while doing grueling labor in unbearable conditions. Those deemed unfit to work were hauled off to the Sonnenstein "Killing Factory" in Eastern Germany and executed by phenol injections.

My father arrived at Buchenwald late in 1944, but by the spring of the following year, Allied forces were closing in and he could sense Nazi morale withering. Rumors circulated that the American troops were within sixty miles of Magdeburg and my father remembered the indescribable feeling: "The freedom was so close, I could just about reach it with my hand and yet I didn't know whether or not my eyes were going to be able to see it."[19] In a desperate effort to stave off the Allies, the Nazis forced him and the other laborers to erect roadblocks in the streets. While setting up the blockades, my father repeated to himself, "Nothing can delay those who are right. Nothing can delay those who are fighting against the most barbaric people who ever lived on the earth."[21]

Recognizing that the situation was futile and attempting to conceal their crimes, the Nazis rounded up approximately 28,000 Buchenwald laborers on April 7, 1945. Guards began marching the captives away from the advancing American armed forces, fully intending to execute all who remained. As they began the "Death March," a captive tried to flee and was immediately shot and killed. In all, more than 10,000 captives were killed during the march.

On April 12, 1945, the day of President Franklin D. Roosevelt's death, United States troops crossed the Elbe River near Magdeburg, approximately fifty miles from the German capital. My father, still in the processional, knew he had a choice; either accept his fate or attempt to escape, knowing that immediate gunfire awaited him should he choose the latter. His wheels started to turn:

After spending five years behind barbed wire of concentration camps, my fate was standing at an unknown crossroads: life or death.... These German SS troopers knew that their "great German Reich" was coming to an end. They were mad. Those men knew about the things that were waiting ahead of them. They realized that the things they had done would not be forgotten. Just like wild animals that are about to be shot, these men were in their most dangerous and sadistic condition. They treated me (and the rest of us) worse than they used to. People were tortured to death. The time for us was very critical. Knowing that their case was lost, the only thing was not to leave alive any witnesses behind.

I thought about escaping [in the past], but how can you escape when you are surrounded by a fence with electric power and guards standing all around it? It just couldn't be done, I had to let everything take its course. But my optimistic morale was the biggest part of my body that kept me from collapsing. "No, they can't do this to me, "I thought. Not now, when everything is coming to an end…no, no, no—not now! I kept repeating. The desire to be alive was bigger and stronger than ever. I felt just like an athlete on the track, just a little ways off the finish line. I didn't want to give up, knowing the end was so close.

At night I could hear the steps of columns of people on their last walk to the gas chambers. "Not to leave any witnesses behind"—this sentence kept on repeating in my head, so who knows—maybe I am next on the list. I kept thinking about the crime being done to people but who am I to change it?

I thought about freedom; its opportunities, its fun. I thought about my future. I kept on asking questions, but no answers—nothing. From the stock cage, I used to watch the fires being made by bombs. I was glad to see their cities burning. They must not have known what they asked for when they started this game. I knew that they were going to lose, but my life and the lives of millions were a big question mark. It was a time to be or not to be.

I thought of those terrible past years.… I thought about the torture that history had not seen before. I thought about my mother who had been killed by those…those… those Germans. Every little incident came back to my mind. I started to number them, but I could not draw the total line because I didn't know when the total line was to be drawn, and the main question was whether or not I was going to do it (draw the line). But some unknown voice kept on calling me: "Carry on, Rachmiel. You'll make it. You have to make it! There isn't much longer to wait!"

I started thinking of escaping too. There was not much time to think.… Conclusions had to be made fast and I didn't want to give up the last chance. Freedom was expected any day. The Americans were expected to take the town any day, so if I let myself be taken away, I'd have lost my freedom. If I succeed and escape—I am free. If I don't succeed—then death. These thoughts kept running through my mind. I decided I was going to escape. [22]

With dusk approaching, my father summoned his courage and seized the moment. It was his last chance at freedom.

The guards all around me, we walked towards a direction that was strange to me. The moment for me to act came. There was no time to delay. I began walking close to the curb, but the guard noticed and with the other side of his rifle pushed me in line again. It didn't scare me; nothing could scare me then.

We turned to a street that was caught by a bomb. The buildings along the street were destroyed with bricks and other junk all over the street. I decided that this was the right moment to run…no more thinking…no more conclusions…there was no more time. Just like an automatic toy, I started to run towards those ruins…. I really mean like automatic. My mind didn't work, I didn't think of whether they would see me or not…. I didn't care. I ran, ran…until I hit one of those destroyed buildings. It didn't take more than a minute's time…they must not have seen me. [23]

Bolting from the mass of captives and troops, he darted toward the ruins of the city, sprinting through the rubble and to what he hoped was independence.

Fighting broke out. United States troops had caught up to the processional, and as they battled the Nazis, my father ensconced himself in the ruins, desperately trying to evade capture, the German Shepherds, and the bullets whizzing nearby. After a few hours that, according to my father, seemed "like a lifetime," the deafening sounds of bombs and gunfire ceased, and an eerie silence gave way to a strange sound that my father had never heard—a foreign language. He knew it wasn't Latvian, Russian, or German. Could it be English? He had a glimmer of hope that he might indeed survive:

After two hours the shooting stopped, the town was taken, and I was free. I went out of the hiding place and started to walk to the main street of the town. This was the first time in five years that I walked down the street without an armed guard guarding me. I was drunk with enjoyment. These feelings were indescribable…. It was my personal victory. I hit the finish line; I made it. [24]

After climbing through the rubble, my father exited with his hands up and encountered a squadron of American GIs in a nearby park:

Slowly, units of American armed forces moved into the town. This was the first time in my life that I saw American soldiers. I looked at them and watched their uniforms. I looked at their guns. It was all new to me, so it drew my attention very much. In all those years, Hitler kept on telling Europe all kinds of stories of the American Army and its soldiers. German propaganda kept writing in their newspapers that American soldiers are not well trained, not armored, not loyal, and all kinds of other lies. "Gangsters" was about the only name that Hitler called US soldiers. But when I saw those men with my own eyes, I could tell what kind of liars Hitler and his gang were. These were young men, highly organized, with most modern arms and the best equipment, discipline, and high morale. This was my first view of the American soldiers. [25]

They immediately took my father to be Jewish and could see the starvation on his face and the lice on his clothing. After cleaning him up and outfitting him in a US army uniform, one of the men offered him a Coca-Cola. "You are free!" he said. "How does it feel to be a free man?"

My father couldn't entirely understand what the officer was saying, but he knew he was finally tasting freedom.

CHAPTER

Hope Was in Short Supply

> "For me, there was no room for any thought except survival."
>
> —Eva

My mother and her identical twin sister Miriam were born on January 31, 1934, in the village of Portz in Transylvania, Romania. Alexander Mozes, my maternal grandfather, was a farmer and his wife Jaffa cared for the twins and their older sisters, Edit and Aliz. The Mozes Family resided on a vast farm which included a vineyard and a sprawling orchard that yielded cherries, plums, and apples. They grew wheat, corn, beans, and potatoes and boarded cows, sheep, geese, and chickens. Though the farm lacked a telephone, indoor plumbing, and electricity, it offered an idyllic setting for Alexander and Jaffa to raise their children.

The oldest of the Mozes girls, Edit had a kind demeanor and relished in

Eva (left) and Miriam Mozes.
COURTESY INDIANA HISTORICAL SOCIETY

picking up her younger sisters and twirling them around in the air. Known for her striking good looks, Aliz held a passion for the arts and could often be heard singing around the family acreage. Playing typical twin pranks, my mother and Miriam embellished their identical looks to fool family members and classmates. They looked so much alike that Jaffa had to put tags on them to discern the two. She loved dressing the twins in matching outfits and doted over her youngest daughters, sometimes to the chagrin of Edit and Aliz. When the twins were young, Jaffa would sit them in the large picture window in the front of the house and instruct them to remain still. Passersby took the girls to be dolls.

Alexander yearned for a son and this desire often caused conflict with my mother. "Since I was the younger of the twins and his last child, he often looked at me and said, 'You should have been a boy,'" she recalled in her memoir, *Surviving the Angel of Death*. [26] He was outnumbered five to one, but Alexander's primary motivation in wanting a son was a religious one, as at the time only males could take part in public worship. Exhibiting a strong personality from birth, my mother noted that her fiery disposition was often the only distinguishing feature between her and Miriam. My mother's sharp edges were honed early, the result of many disputes with her father that ultimately prepared her for the battles to come. When any of the Mozes girls misbehaved, Alexander singled out my mother and she endured verbal and, on rare occasion, physical abuse. My mother's paternal grandmother was often her protection.

Jaffa cultivated a competitive spirit in her daughters and routinely handed out a "best helper" award. My mother, ever the competitor, often rose at dawn to water the flowers, hoping to get a leg up on her siblings. With a keen interest in the girls' education, Jaffa taught daily lessons in the subjects of history,

The Village of Portz. COURTESY CANDLES HOLOCAUST MUSEUM

math, and reading. She had a sense of humor as well. During long excursions on the family's horse and buggy, she'd point to a castle in the distance and allude to the Count Dracula legend by playfully warning the girls, "There might be a bad man there, he is a count. Do not ever go into a castle!" Deeply compassionate, Jaffa was a maternal figure in the village and assisted in the delivery of many babies in and around the village. Often helping women who were sick, pregnant, or in need of companionship, her example of caring for the less fortunate made a lasting impression on my mother.

As Hitler rose to power, the Mozes family's blissful home life began to erode. Roughly 100 families lived in Portz but only one—the Mozes family—was Jewish. Like my father, my mother grew up to the shrill sound of Hitler's impassioned orations on the family radio. Attempting to shelter their daughters, Alexander and Jaffa directed the girls into another room but my mother's intuition told her that trouble was on the horizon as she eavesdropped behind the door. Years later, Hitler's animus toward the Jewish people remained a vivid memory:

I never saw Hitler, but I did hear him on the radio. I remember that he seemed

The Mozes Family: (sitting) a cousin, Eva, Jaffa, Miriam; (standing) Aliz, Alexander, Edit, and Luci, a family friend. COURTESY ALEX KOR

like such an angry man. And, he hated Jews so much. I did not understand why he hated Jews so much, but it was scary, because I was a Jew.

As the only Jewish family in town, the Mozes family soon became pariahs and frequent targets of antisemitism.

Though only six years old at the time, my mother had ominous premonitions of what was to come and years later wrote, "Rumors spread that the Hungarian Army would kill Jews and Romanians and set our village on fire.... I knew we were in danger." [27]

The 1940 pact between Hungary, which bordered Romania to the northwest, and Nazi Germany accelerated the anti-Jewish sentiment. Hitler coveted the oil fields across Romania and Hungary and desperately sought to secure them in the event of a Soviet invasion. Also wanting to fortify German military power, he annexed the Hungarian and Romanian armies and successfully negotiated a deal in November to bring Hungary, Romania, and Slovakia into his "axis of evil." The pact called for the immediate Nazi occupation of Romania. My mother remembered the time well:

The town crier came through the village, beating his drum, and he announced that we were all going to the top of the hill to welcome the Hungarian Army. Everything changed overnight.

Following the agreement, school became especially problematic for my mother and her siblings:

We also discovered we had two new Hungarian teachers at school who had been brought in from the city by the Nazis. To my surprise, they brought with them books containing slurs about the Jews. The books also showed cartoon caricatures depicting Jews as clowns with big noses and bulging bellies.... I clearly remember watching the short film called, "How to Catch and Kill a Jew." These propaganda films, something like today's commercials but filled with hatred, were shown before feature films in the theaters in the cities. Imagine watching instructions on how to kill Jews right before a Pixar movie!

Watching these movies and reading these books consumed with antisemitism only inflamed the other students. Our friends, or other children who had been friends, started calling Miriam and me names like "dirty, smelly Jews." Their name-calling really made me angry. Who were they to call us dirty? I knew I was as clean if not cleaner than any of them! Kids began to spit at us and beat us up at every opportunity. One day, our math book contained this problem: "If you had five Jews, and you killed three Jews, how many Jews would be left?" [28]

One act of extreme humiliation left a permanent scar. Falsely accused of placing bird eggs in their teacher's chair, Miriam and my mother were brought before the class and forced to kneel on dry corn kernels for an hour. She recounted the story years later:

The hard kernels dug into the flesh of our knees. But that was not what wounded us the most. What hurt most was our classmates taunting us, leering at us, making ugly, smirking faces at us. Miriam and I were as shocked as we were hurt. [29]

What also stung was Jaffa's concession that nothing could be done. "Children, I am sorry. We are Jews and we just have to take it. There is nothing we can do," she said. [30]

Alexander's words echoed the mindset of acceptance. "For two thousand years, the Jews have believed that if they tried to get along, they would survive. We must obey tradition, just try to get along," he preached. [31]

Alexander and his brother Aaron had combatted antisemitism five years prior when falsely accused of failing to pay their taxes. After serving jail time, they ventured to Palestine to ascertain if the region might provide a better life for their families. Convinced that a brighter future awaited in Palestine, Alexander returned and desperately tried to persuade Jaffa to relocate. His recommendation went unheeded. Not wanting to uproot her four children, especially the young twin girls, Jaffa shuddered at the idea of trading her farm-land for the desert. She also hated the idea of abandoning her own parents, who were in poor health.

My mother later lamented, "I often wondered what our lives would have been like had she [Jaffa] relented." [32]

Following the 1940 agreement, the attacks on the Mozes family increased in frequency and cruelty. Teenage boys pelted the Mozes farm with tomatoes and rocks, the attacks sometimes lasting days, yet Alexander and Jaffa refused to retaliate. My mother later grasped one of the reasons for their passivity:

I could not have known it at the time, but Mama and Papa must have felt that if they tried to stop these juvenile delinquents or fight back, they would have been arrested and taken away from us. At least we were all still together as a family. [33]

An overwhelming sense of isolation enveloped the Mozes family. Rumors were rampant about the atrocities Jews were suffering at the hands of the Nazis, but Jaffa brushed them off. She couldn't apprehend that a small village in Romania would ever be on Hitler's radar, a belief that was reaffirmed after speaking with Hungarian soldiers.

On one occasion, the Mozes family invited Hungarian officers who were passing through Portz into their home for a meal and opened their barn for lodging. During dinner, Alexander and Jaffa exchanged pleasantries with the troops, and there was no hint that imminent danger lay ahead. When the brigade departed the next morning, Jaffa told my mother, "See? There is no truth to the story that they are killing Jews. They are real gentlemen."

Alexander concurred, "You're right. Nazis will never come to a small village like ours." [34]

As traffic in, around, and through Portz increased, guests were common at the farm. Other visitors included slave laborers from Budapest who were in Romania to construct railways. As the laborers had no place to sleep, the Mozes family again offered up their barn for the men, and occasionally their wives, who often gifted toys and books to the Mozes girls in gratitude for the family's kindness.

The feeling of goodwill was short-lived. Prior to the pact between Hungary and Nazi Germany, the Mozes family had not been required to wear the yellow star, an identification mark used in areas more heavily populated by Jews, for one simple reason: in Portz, everyone already knew their heritage. By the fall of 1943 the Nazis, in a further attempt to humiliate them, mandated that every family member wear the "badge of shame."

In late September 1943, outsiders descended upon the Mozes property again. This time, they came in secret and were uninvited, and their appearance disrupted the family's lives forever. Nearly seventy years later, my mother recalled that fateful evening:

Mama and Papa shook us awake, "Eva! Miriam!" they hissed urgently. "Get dressed! Put on your warm clothes, as many as you can get on, with your jacket and boots. Do not light that candle! It has to stay dark, very dark."

"Wha-what are we doing?" I asked sleepily.

"Just do as you are told!" murmured Papa. We piled on our warm clothing and went into the kitchen. By the light of the glowing embers in the fireplace, we saw our older sisters standing there. They were bundled up as well, their faces like stones in the shadows.

Papa gathered the four of us girls together and whispered, "Children, the time has come when we must leave. We are going to try to get over the border to the non-Hungarian side of Romania where we will be safe. Follow us and remember: no noise!" Single file, with Papa in the lead and Mama at the rear, we slipped out of the house and into the darkness. Outside it was cold and windy. But at the time I had only one thought: We were in trouble, big trouble. And we were running away.

Silently we walked, one behind the other, to the back gate of our property at the edge of the orchard. Just beyond the gate lay the railroad tracks. No trains passed at night. It was silent except for the sounds of the crickets and the occasional call of the night bird. If we were to walk along the tracks for an hour or so, we knew we would arrive at the safe part of Romania. When Papa reached the gate at the edge of our property, he leaned over to unlatch it and pushed it open.

"Stop!" shouted a voice, "If you take another step, I'll shoot!"

A Hungarian Nazi youth pointed a gun at us. A group of teenage boys wearing Hungarian Nazi armbands with swastikas and khaki caps had been guarding our farm, stationed there to make sure we did not get away. How long they'd been there was anyone's guess.

We were only six Jews. How could we be so important? I clutched Miriam's hand, not daring to look directly at them, but sneaking side glimpses at the soldiers. Papa closed the gate, and the boys marched us right back to our homes. Our only chance of escape had just vanished. [35]

For more than four months, Nazi guards kept a tight watch on the Mozes farm, though Jaffa was nowhere to be seen. Battling typhoid fever, she was bedridden for weeks, leaving her daughters to manage the household. The Mozes girls were permitted to attend school, but the family remained essentially under house arrest until March 1944. On a brisk morning, two Hungarian police officers pounded on the door and demanded the family gather their belongings immediately. My mother's version of the events reveals the heartbreak, shame, and dejection of being forced from their home:

Mama barely had the strength to get out of bed. Papa and our older sisters bundled up food, bedding, clothing—all the necessities they could think of. Miriam and I wore matching dresses and took two other sets of identical clothes. As the policeman marched us out of our home, everyone in Portz watched us leave on the one road that ran through the village. Neighbors came out of their houses and lined the road. Our classmates from school just stared. No one tried to stop the gendarmes from taking us away. No one said a word. [36]

The Mozes family was transported by horse-drawn wagon from Portz to the town of Simleu Silvaniei, Romania. My mother was awestruck to observe 7,000 people, crammed into a barbed-wire enclosed field, upon her arrival. She soon came to learn that they'd arrived at the Cehei ghetto. Nazi guards informed the Mozes family that the ghetto, situated on the banks of the Bereteu River, was only a temporary stopover and that they'd soon be transferred to a Hungarian labor camp. Captives were forced to sleep in tents and the isolation of the camp allowed for increased Nazi sadism. Hunger abounded, and the Mozes family survived on a diet of beans and little else.

Our entire family stayed in the same tent. Every time the sky darkened, and it began to rain, the commandant barked through a loudspeaker, "Take down the tents! I want them to be built now on the other side." There was no reason for this except simply cruelty. By the time we took down our tents, crossed the bridge, and set up our shelter again in the mud, we were soaked.

The Hungarian in charge, Krasznai, was sadistic. He would wait for us to make our tent, and then force us to tear it down and move it to the opposite side of the area, making fun of and mocking us the entire time, saying, "Look at the Children of Israel living in tents like in the days of Moses." Humiliation and dehumanization were his goals. [37]

My mother and her siblings grew up fast in the ghetto and were often on their own due to the condition of their parents. Jaffa was still battling typhoid fever and Alexander was beaten mercilessly by the Nazis, who charged him with hoarding gold and silver. My mother remembered that his fingernails and toenails were burned off by candle flames. Jaffa's physical suffering was compounded by her mental anguish. If only she'd consented to the move to Palestine, she agonized, her family wouldn't find themselves in this living hell.

My mother mournfully remembered the time, recalling, "Just seeing our parents so powerless, parents that I had always seen as our protectors no longer able to protect our family, had turned any sense of safety I had upside down." [38]

In May 1944, the Germans began evacuating the ghetto, forcing my mother's family and hundreds of others onto cattle cars. The conditions on the train were no better than in the ghetto. Captives were smashed up against each other with barely room to breathe and scant supplies of food and water over the four-day journey:

For days, our train rushed along the tracks, the endless sound of the clacking interrupted by the occasional hoot of a train's horn. Not only did we have no place to sit or lie down, we had no food or water, and no bathrooms.... When the train stopped for refueling on the first day, Papa asked the guard for water. The guard demanded five gold watches in exchange. The grown-ups gathered the watches and then handed them over. Then the guard tossed a bucket of water through the barbed-wire window. Water splashed in uselessly. [39]

Upon hearing the German dialect, my mother realized that they were not headed to Hungary after all and had reached German soil. Their worst fears had come true:

A feeling of horror took hold of us. Up until then, there was hope. Everybody, including me, had understood that as long as we stayed in Hungary, there was some chance that we would go to a labor camp and work. Everyone knew by now that

Germans and Germany meant death to the Jews. Many people started praying. The cattle car filled with the sound of adults barely stifling their crying, children feeding off their exposed despair. Here and there someone attempted to chant the Sh'ma, the Hebrew prayer to God to hear us, save us. [40]

Prayer was all the family had left and Alexander huddled his wife and daughters together as the train rolled into its final destination. "We must pray to God for mercy," he offered, peering into the terrified eyes of his wife and daughters. [41] He begged his family that whoever survived the days ahead would defect to Palestine as soon as possible. I can only imagine my grandmother's guilt upon hearing his directive.

Auschwitz was the largest and deadliest of all the Nazi death camps, and integral to Hitler's plan to exterminate the Jewish population. Opening in the spring of 1940, it was built on a former military base outside Oswiecim, a town in southern Poland near Kraków. In order to construct the camp, the Nazis evicted all the local residents, demolishing more than 1,000 homes in the process. Auschwitz was initially utilized as a detention center for Polish prisoners who were arrested following Germany's 1939 invasion of Poland. Local prisons in Poland were overcrowded, necessitating the need for a larger facility. With nearby railroad lines allowing for the mass transport of detainees and the camp's centrality to other German-occupied European countries, Hitler envisioned Auschwitz as the ideal location to carry out his Final Solution.

Auschwitz ultimately grew to forty subcamps. The original camp, termed Auschwitz I, could hold between 15,000 and 20,000 political prisoners, many of whom were Jews. Communists, Jehovah's Witnesses, artists, gypsies, educators, homosexuals, and anyone else deemed undesirable by Nazi standards were also imprisoned. Over a five-year period, 230,000 children were held captive, and 8,400 workers stationed at Auschwitz. An entrance with the inscription "*Arbeit Macht Frei*" (Work Sets You Free) greeted captives on their arrival and barbed wire encircled the camp, isolating it from the rest of civilization.

Gashouses and crematory ovens were built on the Auschwitz grounds for

The foreboding entrance to Auschwitz. COURTESY YAD VASHEM ARCHIVES

the purpose of mass murder and as a means of accelerating the Final Solution. The gas chambers could hold up to 2,000 prisoners and the crematoriums could incinerate 700 bodies at a time. The chambers were outfitted to look like showers and disguised as disinfection areas, a deception exemplifying the Nazi's cruel deceit. After the emaciated, lice-ridden detainees arrived at the chamber, they were forced to remove their clothing and Zyklon-B poison gas was pumped into the chamber. The SS peered through peepholes to see the horror-stricken victims take their last breaths.

The first gassings took place in 1941 when 600 Soviet prisoners of war and 250 other prisoners were executed. That same year, Heinrich Himmler, the *Reichsführer* (Reich Leader) of the SS, saw the need for an even larger camp and ordered the construction of Auschwitz II. With a capacity of 90,000 prisoners, Auschwitz II, also known as Birkenau, was the largest of the camps. Auschwitz III, known as Monowitz, opened in 1942 and could accommodate up to 10,000 prisoners. As World War II raged on, Nazi barbarity increased as did the death count. At peak times, 6,000 victims were being gassed daily and in 1944, 800 children were gassed in a twenty-four-hour period. The crematoriums were so taxed, that the SS had to dig massive open-air pits to burn bodies, using the victims' own fat for fuel.

Conservative estimates put the Auschwitz death toll at 1.1 million people, but since prisoners considered incapable of working were never officially registered, the count is most likely much higher. Polish historian Franciszek Piper used train arrivals and deportation records to calculate that, of the 1.3 million sent to Auschwitz, 1,082,000 had died.

The selection platform at Auschwitz is what my mother remembered most vividly. After departing the train cars, two lines were formed on the platform: one for older boys and men and the other for women and children. Nazi medical officers then demarcated those suitable for slave labor from those regarded as unworthy of living. Generally, all children younger than sixteen and the elderly were immediately sent to die and roughly 20% of the population selected for slave labor. Those "fortunate" enough to evade death were branded with a tattooed number for registration and used as slave laborers by companies in the manufacturing of munitions and synthetic rubber. Many of the laborers perished from starvation, disease, beatings, individual executions, and the unbearable work conditions. Others lost all hope, and their faith in God, and committed suicide by running through the electrified barbed wire fencing.

Those considered unsuitable for work included women, children, the sick, and the elderly. After being stripped naked, captives were then marched to the gas chambers, their screams permeating the air. Following the gassings, laborers removed teeth, hair, artificial limbs, and glasses before transporting the bodies to the crematoriums. Of the 1.3 million people sent to Auschwitz, roughly 200,000 were chosen for slave labor and 900,000 sent to the gas chambers.

It was this selection platform where my mother and her family found themselves on May 24, 1944, their fate hanging in the balance.

I saw tall barbed-wire fences, cement guard towers everywhere. Soldiers were hanging out of them with barrels of their guns pointed at us. I have no idea how we got from the cattle car to the selection platform. Miriam and I may have jumped or stepped down a wooden ramp. But pretty soon we were standing on the platform in utter terror, two ten-year-olds in matching burgundy dresses.

This place was confusing and noisy. People were yelling. There were screams and confusion, desperation, barking, orders. Crying, crying, crying. The crying of people confused and bewildered. The crying of people who saw the certainty that their nightmares had come true. All together the cries resounded with the ultimate and most unimaginable pain of human loss, emotional grief, and suffering. [42]

My mother likened her first moments at Auschwitz to an out-of-body experience. Menacing German shepherds and Nazi guards along with skeleton-like prisoners roamed the camp to the beat of shrill whistles and mournful cries. Minutes after the Mozes family departed the cattle car, my mother turned to see that her father, Edit, and Aliz were nowhere to be found. Gripping her mother tightly, she heard a guard exclaim, "*Zwillinge! Zwillinge!*"—the German word for twins. Jaffa asked the guard if twins were "a good thing"? He nodded in affirmation and promptly yanked my mother and Miriam away from Jaffa. My mother recalled the heartbreaking scene:

We screamed and cried as we were dragged away. We begged him to let us stay with her. The German guard paid no attention to our pleas. He pulled us across the railroad tracks, away from the selection platform. I turned my head and saw my mother, desperate, her arms outstretched toward us, wailing. A soldier grabbed her and threw her in another direction. My mama disappeared into the crowd.... [43]

It'd be the final time the sisters, only ten years old, would see their mother. They were whisked away and assembled with twelve other sets of twins, leaving my mother bewildered. Why had she and Miriam been separated from their family? Why were they grouped with all these twins? Where were Edit, Aliz, and her father? Miriam and my mother were led to a registration area and given shortly cropped haircuts, showers, clothes with red crosses on their backs, and an anti-lice chemical for their dresses.

Assuming that registration numbers would be imprinted on their clothing, my mother was astounded to see that they were being etched onto captives' arms. A few minutes later, Eva Mozes became prisoner A-7063. Miriam was given A-7064. My mother's fierce temperament, molded after many quarrels with her father, began to surface. While being given her Auschwitz tattoo, she kicked, screamed, bit a guard's arm, and vowed to give the guards "as much trouble as possible."

Her aggression could be verified decades later: while Miriam's tattooed number was very visible, my mother's was quite blurred. Posing for a photo in 1985, my mother marveled at how distinctive Miriam's number was in comparison to hers.

"Eva, you must not remember," replied Miriam, "when we received our numbers, you argued and wrestled with the Nazis. It took four or five of them to hold you down. You even bit one!"

My mother hated tattoos for the rest of her life.

A new home awaited the twin population in Camp II B at Birkenau. The barracks had an acrid stench (my mother described it as a "horrible, thick, chicken feather smell"), and the lack of ventilation made the smell unbearable. Rats scampered about the barracks, circling a twelve-foot-square latrine coated with feces and vomit. Fleas also infested the barracks and prisoners combated lice infestations. The evening meal consisted of a very dark, 2½-inch slice of bread and a brownish liquid purported to be coffee. Though my mother and Miriam hadn't eaten in four days, they refused the bread because it wasn't kosher and offered their portions to two other girls.

Laughing at the naivete of the new prisoners, one of the girls said to my mother and Miriam, "You cannot be fussy here. You have to learn to eat everything if you want to survive." [44]

A fellow captive informed my mother that a crematorium and gas chamber were nearby, and she looked out to see ash and smoke emanating from the chimneys.

"What on earth were these ovens to be used for?" she wondered. She couldn't fathom that anyone could possibly burn a body until a fellow prisoner interjected, "The Nazis do. They want to burn all Jews." [45]

One of the older twins chimed in, "I will show you your parents. See the smoke coming from the chimneys? That's where your parents are." It now struck my mother that she and Miriam may have been separated from their family for good.

I thought of Mama who was so weak after her long illness. I thought of Papa, clutching his prayer book. I thought of our two older sisters. [46]

Near the latrine my mother saw firsthand the magnitude of evil at Auschwitz.

Adjacent to the latrine were the bodies of three dead children. It was at this very moment that she vowed to survive:

I realized that death could happen to Miriam and me. I silently vowed to do everything in my power to make sure that Miriam and I did not end up like those dead children. We were going to be stronger, smarter, whatever it took not to end up that way.

From the moment I left the latrine, I concentrated all my being in one thing: how to survive one more day in this horrible place. From that point forward, in my mind, we were going to walk out of the camp alive. I never permitted fears or doubts to dominate my thoughts. As soon as they entered my mind, I pushed them out forcefully. [47]

She was now familiar with her new surroundings, but my mother remained baffled as to why she and Miriam were there. They'd soon find out.

Nicknamed the "Angel of Death," Josef Mengele was the most notorious physician in the Nazi regime. A student of philosophy and anthropology at the University of Munich in the 1920s, he later earned a medical degree from the University of Frankfurt. Adopting the ideology of Alfred Rosenberg, a promi-

Josef Mengele, aka "The Angel of Death" (center).
COURTESY YAD VASHEM ARCHIVES

nent Nazi theorist, Mengele championed a racial hierarchy assigning the Aryan race to the top of the order with Blacks and Jews on the lowest rung. Otmar von Verschuer, a German-Dutch biologist and geneticist at the University of Münster, served as a mentor for Mengele. Years later, my mother became close friends with von Verschuer's grandson, Michael Worle.

Carrying Rosenberg's torch, Mengele promoted the idea that inferior races were more likely to carry negative traits (i.e., mental and physical deficiencies) than those of superior races. His assertion that Germans were the biologically superior race aligned with Hitler's racist doctrine and he became an essential figure in the Final Solution.

Mengele joined the Nazi party in 1937 and was initially deployed as a battalion medical officer. After being injured in combat in 1942, he was reassigned to Auschwitz a year later, and it was there that he began genetic research on human subjects. Initially assigned as an adjudicator, Mengele decided whether a person qualified as a "pure" German under the Nuremberg Laws, a series of racist and antisemitic edicts passed in 1935. A frequent presence on the selection platform, he was a prominent arbiter of who lived or died at Auschwitz. In May 1943, Mengele had 1,035 gypsies gassed and the following year, he ordered 300 children, who'd arrived by train, to be burned to death.

When not on the platform, Mengele engaged in research that embodied the inhumanity of the Third Reich. Attempting to pinpoint genetic markers that would identify members of a specific race, his work sought to uphold the Nazi's racial ideology and rationalize the mass-murder and sterilization of those deemed unfit to live. To test the effectiveness of specific treatments, he'd infect prisoners with diseases and wait to see how they'd react.

His savagery knew no depths, and as Holocaust scholar Michael Berenbaum put it, "Mengele's ambition was equal to his ruthlessness." [48] Experimenting with mass sterilization, he murdered prisoners for the sole purpose of research and removed organs without the use of an anesthetic. Female twins were given blood transfusions from a male in an attempt to discover ways to change girls into boys. Mengele was once reputed to have sewn twins back-to-back, stitching their organs together. In need of more subjects, he shot approximately 100 children in the back of their heads in 1944.

Mengele's singular obsession was with twins and how Germans might reproduce more of them to expand the Aryan race.

As my mother wrote, "Mengele wanted to discover the secret of twinning. One goal of his experiments was to create blond-haired, blue-eyed babies in multiple numbers to increase the German population."

Performing sadistic trials on more than 1,500 sets of twins, Mengele understood that any differences between twins could only be attributed to behavior and not genetics. Using one twin as a control, he'd experiment with blood transfusions, injections, and amputations on the other. Those that died were dissected and studied and the surviving twin immediately killed and examined. The goal was to delineate between sick and healthy subjects. More often than not, the twins died: of the 3,000 twins known to have been imprisoned at Auschwitz, only 200 survived.

My mother never forgot her first encounter with Mengele:

Dr. Josef Mengele entered the barracks. He was dressed elegantly in an SS uniform and tall, shiny black riding boots. He wore white gloves and carried a baton. My first thought was how handsome he was, like a movie star. He strode through the barracks, counting twins at every bunk, with an entourage of eight people accompanying him.... When Dr. Mengele stopped at the bunks containing the three dead bodies he flew into a rage.

"Why did you let these children die?" he screamed at the nurse and SS guards. "I cannot afford to lose even one child!" Our nurse and the supervisors trembled.

He continued counting until he came to Miriam and me. He stopped and looked at us. I was petrified. Then he moved on. The other children told us he had been on the selection platform the day before when we arrived. He was the one who made the selections of the prisoners with the flick of his baton. To the right meant the gas chamber, to the left, the camp and forced labor. [49]

On a regular basis, my mother, Miriam, and the other sets of twins were led to the blood labs in Birkenau and forced to strip naked. They were then subjected to an array of head and earlobe measurements, x-ray, blood draws, and a meticulous examination of their eyes. She and Miriam were now human guinea pigs:

All of us sat completely naked on benches. Boys were there, too. It was very cold. We had no place to hide. It was embarrassing to be there without any clothes. Some girls crossed their legs and covered hands. Others shook with fear while SS guards pointed at us and laughed... In the afternoon our supervising nurse made us learn a song in German. It went, "I am a little German child. If not, phooey!" She put us in a circle and made one girl stand in the center. We had to walk around that girl and sing, "Phooey, phooey, phooey!"

"Dirty, filthy Jews!" the nurse shouted at us. "Swine!" She loved that song. It meant we, the children, were disgusting. [50]

My mother loathed the physicians, nurses, and cruel experiments, but understood that being twins kept her and Miriam alive. Three days per week, Mengele, who referred to the twins as *Meine Kinde,* meaning "my children," ran various tests on the girls. On the other days, they were in the labs, having blood extracted and given injections with diseases like scarlet fever. My mother hated the shots but knew they were essential to her existence:

On our way back to the barracks, Miriam and I did not talk about the shots. I took those shots as the price we had to pay to survive: we gave them our blood, our bodies, our pride, our dignity, and in turn, they let us live one more day. [51]

In our barrack we, the children, huddled in our filthy beds crawling with lice and rats. We were starved for food, starved for human kindness, and starved for the love of the mothers we once had. We had no rights, but we had a fierce determination to live one more day—to survive one more experiment. No one explained anything to us, nor did anyone try to minimize the risks to our lives. On the contrary, we knew we were there to be subjects of experiments and were totally at the mercy of the Nazi doctors. Our lives depended entirely on the doctors' whims. [52]

As the weeks passed, my mother, only ten-years-old at the time, witnessed the unimaginable. Prisoners, weighing only 70 pounds, with bones protruding from their bodies, strode by her, sets of twins that she'd come to know went missing, and the screams from prisoners en route to the gas chambers became more frequent. Carts of dead bodies rolled by her daily, and she contemplated if her family had been among the pile of the deceased prisoners:

At that moment, I realized that maybe our mother had also gone by on a cart of bodies; we just hadn't seen her. Every day those carts went by. Sometimes the prisoners on them were dead, sometimes mostly dead; regardless they were all being carted away to their final resting place. Until that moment I had stopped thinking about my family. Maybe it was due to the bread we ate each evening that supposedly contained not only saw dust, but a powder called bromide that made us forget memories of home, as a sedative of some kind. Whatever it was or was not, I could not feel sorry for myself, for Miriam, for anyone. I could not think of myself as a victim, or I knew I would perish. It was simple. For me, there was no room for any thought except survival.... I could not think about Mama, Papa, or our older sisters anymore. I had to worry about Miriam and myself. I had to repeat to myself over and over: Just one more day. Just one more experiment. Just one more shot. Just please, please don't let us get sick. [53]

She wouldn't get her wish. Becoming violently ill after Mengele administered yet another shot, she experienced a high fever, chills, a throbbing headache, and burning skin. Red splotches appeared on her bloated arms and legs, and she was beset with fatigue. She veiled her condition, knowing it could mean instant death for both her and Miriam. On two separate occasions, a twin had fallen ill and was sent to the infirmary. Neither returned and the matching twin was executed not long after.

"Why should she die just because I might die," my mother thought of her sister.

Quarantined in what she later referred to as the "barracks of the living dead," my mother was isolated from Miriam for the first time. When neither food nor water arrived, she realized that her situation had grown dire.

"No one here gets anything to eat because people are brought here to die or are taken here to die in the gas chamber," said a fellow prisoner. [54] For two consecutive weeks, my mother had to crawl through filth and sludge to reach a water faucet. During the quarantine, Mengele paid her a visit that further fueled her motivation to survive:

The morning after I arrived, Mengele and a team of four other doctors came to see me. They discussed my case as though they were in a regular hospital. Although they spoke in German, I understood a lot of what they were saying. Dr. Mengele laughed and said about me with a smirk, "Too bad. She is so young and has only two weeks to live."

"How could he know that?" I wondered. They had not run any more tests on me after the poisonous shot. I've since learned that Mengele knew what disease they had infected me with and how it would progress. It might have been beriberi or spotted fever. In all the years since, I have never found out for sure.

As I lay in bed and listened to Mengele and the other doctors, I tried not to let on that I grasped the meaning of their words.

I said to myself, "I am not dead. I refuse to die. I am going to outsmart those doctors, prove Dr. Mengele wrong, and get out of here alive." Above all, I knew I had to get back to Miriam. [55]

She began to regain her strength but was required to show clear signs of recovery before she could return to her barrack. Nurses monitored her fever by placing a thermometer under her armpit. When the nurse looked away, my mother (knowing she wasn't back to full strength) manipulated the thermometer by moving it away from her armpit, allowing for exposure to cooler air. Verifying that her temperature was back to normal, the nurse allowed my mother to reunite with Miriam back in their barrack. My mother later discovered that had she died, Miriam would have been murdered with a shot of chloroform to her heart.

"I spoiled the experiment," she boasted. [56]

Kept in solitary confinement during the separation, Miriam appeared gaunt, weak, and lifeless. When Mengele realized that my mother wouldn't succumb to his experiments, he ordered that Miriam be injected with shots that would permanently stunt the growth of her kidneys. Her spirit grew even weaker as she battled diarrhea and dysentery in the days that followed. With my mother's care, encouragement, and procurement of potatoes (a remedy to treat dysentery), Miriam recovered.

Because we were twins, we clung to each other. Because we were sisters, we depended on each other. Because we were family, we did not let go. At Auschwitz dying was easy, surviving was a full-time job. [57]

My mother's courage and will to live still amazes me. She'd stared death in the eye and not blinked.

In the fall of 1944, Allied bombers began reconnaissance missions over the skies of Auschwitz. Visible from below, the sightings boosted camp morale and offered a glimmer of hope to the prisoners, starving for both food and freedom. Gazing up into the sky, my mother saw a small plane circling the camp and noticed an American flag emblazoned on its side.

"I thought the whole world was one big concentration camp until an airplane appeared over the skies at Auschwitz and flew very low," she recalled, "and I could see the American flag on its wings, and that gave me hope. That somebody was trying to free us, and hope in Auschwitz was in very short supply." [58]

When I first heard her version of events, I asked how she could possibly recognize that this was an American flag.

"Alex," she answered, "while growing up in Portz, I had an aunt in Cleveland, Ohio, and she'd send us letters with a stamp in the form of an American flag." It was hope, barely the size of a postage stamp, but hope, nonetheless.

My mother knew that if she and Miriam could hold on a little longer, they might be saved, but she recognized it wouldn't be easy. Rumors that the camp was going to be blown to bits ran rampant. Like at Buchenwald, the Nazis sought to conceal their crimes by eliminating remaining evidence, and prisoners. Mengele was ordered to send 2,000 medical subjects in his gypsy camp to the gas chambers and onto the crematorium. My mother and Miriam were soon transferred to the gypsy camp where all that remained were blankets and paintings on the walls. The crematorium lay just yards away from the camp. Death seemed even closer.

By early January 1945, it was evident that the Nazis were losing the war, and they began clearing out the barracks and assembling prisoners for a death march.

Back at the barracks, my mother and two other twins, now famished, set out on a mission to pilfer food, and specifically potatoes, from a Nazi kitchen. As they gathered their feast, the blaring sound of a jeep pierced the air, signaling a Nazi return. Potatoes in hand, my mother and the two others wheeled around to see two gun barrels pointed at them. The guards began spraying bullets and the three girls fell to the ground. As the Nazis left the barrack, my mother rose up and recalled feeling like "she was in heaven." Miraculously, she'd fainted as the bullets whizzed by and the guards had assumed her to be dead. She reached over to discover that the other girls were ice cold, leaving her the unenviable task of informing their twins that they had died.

The girls, along with 8,200 other prisoners, were marched from Birkenau that evening. The Mengele twins were spared execution but warned that they'd be shot if they fell or tried to escape. In one hour, 1,200 people were executed and only 7,000 returned to the barracks at Auschwitz.

Once there, my mother, Miriam, and a small group of prisoners were alone again and left to scavenge food in the bitter cold. Returning once more to Nazi quarters, they were ecstatic to find a table stocked with food, but an ominous feeling superseded my mother's hunger, and she bypassed the rations.

"Why would the Nazis leave this food here," she thought, later learning that the Nazis had poisoned the food before departing the camp.

The pack of twins eventually found sauerkraut and bread and then procured water from the Vistula River. Gazing across the river, my mother witnessed a young girl heading to school. It marked the first time in a year that she had observed life beyond the barbed wire of Auschwitz:

I froze. I could not believe that there was a world out there where people were clean, and girls wore braids with ribbons and nice dresses and went to school! Once, I had been that girl in nice clothes with ribbons in my hair, on my way to school. Until that moment, I thought everyone had been in a concentration camp like us. But I realized then that was not true.

The girl stared at me. I looked down at myself wearing ragged clothes swarming with lice and a coat and shoes many sizes too big for me.... I do not know what she thought, but as I looked up at her, I could feel the fire of anger rising in me. I felt betrayed. Miriam and I had done nothing wrong! We were just little girls like her. Why were we in this situation while she was over there looking so pretty and clean and living a perfectly normal life? It was so wrong, so inconceivable to me. But there she was. And there I was. [59]

With the Red Army nearing Kraków, the Nazis began their evacuation of Auschwitz, destroying evidence of their atrocities in the process. Warehouses were obliterated and records destroyed. Mengele gathered all evidence of his monstrous experimentation and fled the camp. Sixty thousand prisoners were assembled and marched in sub-zero temperatures westward toward German territory. Those too feeble to walk were executed on the spot, and 15,000 captives died during the march.

As the chaos ensued, my mother and Miriam—who were both to remain at the camp—became separated, and each thought the other to have perished. After searching for an entire day, my mother finally found Miriam and recalled her elation:

I had the strongest feeling of relief and love that I have ever felt in my whole life. I pulled away to look at her scrawny face and then put my arms around her again, holding her tight. Those twenty-four hours of searching for her had felt like

forever. The more I held onto her, the more I felt sure we would never be parted again.
"I am so glad I found you," I told her, filled with more emotion than I could express…. Our hands tightly entwined, our bodies close for comfort, we shut our weary eyes. No matter what happened next, we knew we had each other. [60]

On January 27, 1945, four days before my mother's birthday, soldiers from the 322nd Rifle Division of the Red Army descended upon Auschwitz. My mother, Miriam, and the remaining prisoners hid in the barracks, praying they'd be spared from gunfire and bombshells enveloping them. The Red Army platoon suffered 231 casualties before finally driving out the remaining Nazi forces.

Upon entering the camp, the Soviet troops were stunned. A search of the premises revealed more than 600 corpses, 837,000 articles of women's clothing, 44,000 pairs of shoes, and 7.7 tons of human hair (a portion containing hydrogen cyanide). Six warehouses held hundreds of thousands of women's dresses, men's suits, and shoes. Layers of excrement coated the floors of the barracks. Approximately 7,000 prisoners—many starved, withered, and sick—remained at Auschwitz.

At about 4:00 p.m., my mother heard a woman bellowing out, "We are free! We are free! We are free!" My mother was wary:

About twenty feet away, we saw Soviet soldiers emerging through the snow, approaching us in snow-covered capes and suits. They did not speak as they crunched through the snow. As they came closer, they looked at us like they were smiling. Were those smirks or smiles? I peered closely. Yes, those were smiles. Real smiles. Joy and hope welled up inside of us. We were safe. We were free!

Crying and laughing, we ran up to the soldiers, crowding them. A shout rose from the crowd: "We are free! We are free!" There was laughter and wails of relief all mixed together in a jumble of sounds. Laughing themselves, some with tears in their eyes, the Soviet soldiers hugged us back. They handed us cookies and chocolate—delicious. We were not only starved for food, but we were starved for human kindness.

It was our first taste of freedom. And I realized that my silent pledge the first night in the latrine to survive and walk out of the camp alive with Miriam by my side had become a reality. [61]

My mother and Miriam (at front) liberated by Red Army with other Mengele twins.
COURTESY ALEX KOR

In the aftermath, Soviet troops, aided by local residents and the Polish Red Cross, set up makeshift hospitals to treat the hordes of ailing people. The number of sick captives overwhelmed the small medical team even as they worked eighteen-hour shifts, and 2,200 prisoners were cared for by just a few doctors and nurses. Many of the patients were starved and suffering from tuberculosis and diarrhea, their psyches also decimated. Ultimately 7,500 people, including my mother and Miriam, made it out alive, having overcome nearly impossible odds.

My mother and Miriam were two of only 180 children to survive. They were detained in the barracks for two weeks, until a safer location could be secured. Despite how they'd been treated by their neighbors, despite the way they had been singled out and imprisoned and made to march to their presumed death between rows of cold, unblinking eyes, my mother thought of Portz:

Memories of home filled my eyes. The sounds of the farm echoed in my ears: chopping wood, chickens clucking, cows bellowing. The smells of ripe fruits in the orchard filled my nose…. I stated [to Miriam], I want to go home. [62]

The Soviets returned several weeks later with cameras and lights in order to stage the liberation for propaganda purposes. The Nazis had excluded twins from having to wear uniforms, so for the first time Miriam and my mother were dressed in prison garb and strategically placed in front of the assemblage of liberated prisoners.

"What are we, movie stars or something?" my mother queried. [63] By the sixth take, my mother, like any eleven-year-old child, stuck out her tongue, showing her displeasure with the multiple tapings. Following the filming, she and Miriam exited the gates of Auschwitz, free at last.

CHAPTER

Love Language

> "We needed to move on."
>
> —Eva

F ollowing the war, my parents' paths diverged. Within a few days after his liberation, my father met a soldier who would forever alter his life's trajectory. A Terre Haute, Indiana, native, Lt. Colonel Andrew Nehf was the commanding officer of the 250th Engineer Combat Battalion of the 7th Army, a unit charged with building bridges over German rivers. Though my father knew no English, Nehf soon realized that his knowledge of the area and fluency in German and Russian could come in handy. The two became fast friends and could often be found sitting together atop Nehf's military jeep, their strong rapport drawing the envy of the other recently liberated captives. Nehf would soon leave Germany but ensured that my father would remain on

Lt. Colonel Andrew Nehf (seated) with the 250th. COURTESY ALEX KOR

as a translator. "His loyalty is irreproachable," Nehf wrote. "It is with regret that I must leave him behind." [64]

The battalion, with my father in tow, left Magdeburg for Vienna in early May. Fearing that he might end up in the hands of Russian troops, the battalion kept a tight watch on their new "recruit." Ensuring that he was dressed in fatigues at all times, the 250th kept him out of sight and made sure that he was well fed. Nehf's departure left nineteen-year-old Wendell Cox, a private first class from Oklahoma, responsible for my father's well-being. Cox developed a great fondness for my father, as did the entire 250th—so much so that they declared him to be their "mascot."

In the summer of 1945, my father was transferred to Frankfurt, Germany, and deployed as a translator. Immersing himself in the GI culture, he taught himself English by reading *Stars and Stripes,* the official US military newspaper for the Armed Forces personnel stationed overseas. He still had no clue as to the fate of his brothers but was certain of where he wanted to go next.

His devotion to Nehf coupled with a desire to start all over were the driving forces for his hope to go to America. He expressed his wishes in a letter published on September 20, 1945, in *The Forward,* an American Jewish newspaper that was assisting liberated captives in seeking asylum and tracking down their relatives:

At the age of 12½ years [editor's note: my father was actually older, likely 16, when this event occurred] *the Nazis murdered my family in a cold-blooded manner before my very eyes, including my mother, my father, and my three brothers. I am now alone in the world, and not knowing where to turn. I am looking forward to whatever advice and help may be extended to me, in helping me gain a foothold in the future to come. Now that time has progressed, I want to forget the terrible past. I look forward to the future and the hope that somehow, I will be given the opportunity of entering the country of the United States of America and become a most useful citizen.*

I've come to you for whatever help and advice you may be able to give. It is my way of hope in entreating you and see what action can be taken in having entered the glorious union of the United States of America. It is my expressed hope and feeling of beginning life anew. I want to become a credit to mankind and

My father in 1945 following his liberation in Magdeburg. COURTESY ALEX KOR

not a liability. I await your reply and will appreciate whatever help and advice that you may afford me. I thank you from the bottom of my heart. [65]

He'd previously made his ambitions known to Nehf, declaring, "I want to go where you guys come from." After Nehf departed Germany, my father followed up with a letter in broken English, updating the Lieutenant Colonel on his status. The letter bounced around and ultimately made its way to Nehf's wife Caroline in America.

"You need to help that boy," she wrote to her husband in a telegram. [66] Nehf knew that my father would have to speak better English to enroll in high school in America. In the hopes that he'd become more fluent, he ordered my father to "hang out" with the group of GIs that had liberated him.

Meanwhile, Nehf began arranging for my father's emigration to the United States. Looking homeward, Nehf coordinated for the Kaplan family in Terre Haute to house my father and convinced State Lab High School (now on the campus of Indiana State University) to accept him. On May 11, 1946, my father boarded the SS *Marine Flasher*, bound for the United States, in Bremerhaven, Germany. The ship had formerly been used in the war as a Navy transporter in the Pacific. In December 1945, President Harry S. Truman had issued an executive order mandating that immigration quotas be designated for displaced persons. The 867 passengers onboard the *Flasher*, including more than 650 Holocaust survivors and 70 orphaned children, were the first refugees granted admission through Truman's edict. My father was ecstatic; he was leaving five years of darkness behind for what he hoped would be a brighter future in America.

Upon boarding, he immediately went to the top deck and felt a noticeable difference: The US soldiers treated him as a human being, not an animal. A band booming out patriotic music greeted the passengers, and an army official wished them good luck on their journey to America, and to freedom. Given that many passengers had never sailed on a vessel of this magnitude, seasickness was prevalent, but a minor inconvenience compared with what they had endured. The exuberance was so great that dancing among the passengers broke out, though my father didn't partake, later acknowledging that he "did not know how to dance!"

On the morning of May 21, 1946, the *Marine Flasher* arrived in the Port of New York.

On May 20th we arrived in the bay of New York, and it was a very interesting view—there were millions of lights! The boat anchored there so we could move to the port in the morning. Only four more miles to New York Harbor! In the morning we started out and after a little sailing, we saw the Statue of Liberty. At nine o'clock the boat docked, my voyage from Europe to the USA was over. [67]

From New York, my father traveled to Terre Haute, Indiana. In addition to acquiring his freedom, he also received a new name. Either the 250th or his newfound circle of friends in Terre Haute began referring to him as "Mickey," a name that stuck with him for the rest of his life.

At the ripe old age of twenty-one, my father enrolled at State Lab High School in Terre Haute where he was active in the Latin and book clubs. He served as vice president of the Student Council and, inspired by the Red Cross's benevolence in the war's aftermath, volunteered for the school's local chapter. In his initial and only year at State Lab, he was recognized as the best English student in his class and won the "Quiz Kid" competition—quite a feat given that he'd just begun to learn the language two years prior. Described as "lots of fun" in the school yearbook, his classmates also noted that he loved to dance despite being too shy to "look at girls." His favorite phrase was "Hubba, Hubba," and he listed his career objective as Chief Justice of the United

The SS *Marine Flasher*. COURTESY ALEX KOR

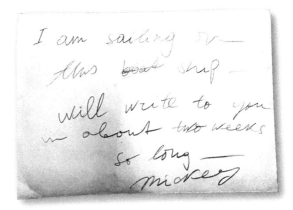

Note written by my father while on board the SS *Marine Flasher*. COURTESY ALEX KOR

States. A year to the day of his coming to the United States, his classmates threw him a party with ice cream and a cake adorned with a single candle to mark his one year of residency.

He remained in close contact with the Nehf family and taught himself to play the piano at their nearby home. As a means of earning money, he worked at a local pharmacy and saw a future in it. He quickly embraced his adopted hometown and years later recalled his first few days in the country: "Every day was like a painting by the American icon Norman Rockwell on the cover of the magazine the *Saturday Evening Post*. I fell in love with the American way of life." [68]

Following his graduation from high school, he enrolled at Indiana State Teachers College (now Indiana State University) where he remained for two

The State Lab High School Yearbook, 1947. COURTESY ALEX KOR

My father's Indiana State Teacher's College identification card. COURTESY ALEX KOR

years. Initially denied entry, he finally gained admission into Purdue University's pharmacy program and completed his degree in 1952. His love for basketball was honed at Purdue, where he split his time between the library and Lambert Fieldhouse, home of the Boilermaker basketball team.

The Korean War was raging, and he was soon drafted into the US Armed Forces and sent to Fort Sill, Oklahoma. After finishing his basic training, he worked as a pharmacist at a military hospital in Osaka, Japan. My father took considerable pride in serving his country, later reflecting, "I don't have enough words from the English lexicon to describe my feelings about this: at one time, I wore the uniform of a prisoner, and then, I wore the stripes of a PFC in the American Army. I get tears in my eyes when I think about it." [69]

Upon fulfilling his military obligations, my father yearned to be closer to family and so eyed West Hartford, Connecticut, where his brother Leib had settled after also surviving the death march in Magdeburg and finding his way to the United States. It had taken the two of them nearly a full year after the conclusion of the war to learn that each other had survived, but now they would be together again as my father joined Leib and his young family in Connecticut. He began his career as a pharmacist and aspired to meet a young, Jewish woman to build a family of his own. While his career flourished, his search for a future mate proved futile. Longing for his friends and beloved Purdue Boilermaker sports teams, he soon headed back to the Midwest in 1954.

My father on duty in Osaka. COURTESY ALEX KOR

Returning to Terre Haute, my father was hired by the M&C Pharmacy and immersed himself in his work. He took up tennis, cheered on his Boilermakers, and attended every social gathering he could find. His dry sense of humor and accent, a hybrid of Hoosier English and Latvian, drew attention, but his "unique" driving style left the most memorable impression. Bob Rimstidt, his former coworker, remembers how my father would accelerate for a few seconds and then suddenly release the pressure on the gas pedal. Whether driving around the block or to Indianapolis, he'd employ this technique despite the honks and colorful gestures it inspired from fellow drivers.

I still remember that when other cars whizzed by him, he'd say, "There goes Mario Andretti!"

Years later, the mayor of Terre Haute once remarked to me, "Everyone in town knows when your dad is driving. He's the only one who goes under the speed limit!"

My father was elated to be home, but had no luck in meeting women. At the urging of Shlomo, his other living brother who had escaped to Israel during the war, my father traveled to Tel Aviv, hoping to improve his fortunes.

Reunification was overdue as the brothers hadn't seen each other in years, but the chance to meet a single, Jewish female was the driving force behind my father's overseas excursion.

Meanwhile, my mother took a more circuitous route to Israel. After her liberation from Auschwitz, the Soviets, in coordination with the Jewish Refugee Association, placed her and Miriam in an orphanage at a Catholic convent operated by the Sisters of Saint Jadwiga in Katowice, Poland, where they stayed from March to May 1945. The girls were provided hot meals and toys upon their arrival and were stunned to see beds with clean sheets and floors without rats. Worried she'd mess the sheets up, my mother slept on the floor on the first night. Though only fifty-one miles from Kraków, they were now a world away from Auschwitz. My mother's yearning for home had only intensified after her liberation and she pleaded with the nuns to send her and Miriam back to Portz. She had no answer, however, when asked about her parents' whereabouts. The girls were ordered to remain at the orphanage and told they'd eventually be deported to Palestine.

Yet, my mother's wheels were always turning. She had discovered that Rosalita Csengari, her mother's friend from Simleu Silvaniei, whose twin girls were in the same Auschwitz barrack with her and Miriam, was at a displaced persons camp nearby. My mother and Miriam, afforded a free ride if they showed their tattoos, hopped on a streetcar and made their way across town to the camp. My mother convinced Mrs. Csengari to masquerade as the twins' aunt, which in turn allowed for their release from the orphanage. For a month and a half, the girls bunked at the camp with Mrs. Csengari and her two female twins. Their old family friend provided nourishment and care, washing the twins' clothes, sewing them dresses, and ridding them of their dreaded lice. Several weeks later, Mrs. Csengari led her daughters, my mother, and Miriam to a railway station where they hopped aboard another cattle car. Yet again, my mother was perplexed as to her destination.

Outfitted with bunk beds, mattresses, and even windows, this cattle car proved much snugger than the last. As the train wound through Romania, my mother observed scores of bombed-out villages and stewed over Portz's fate and that of her family. Arriving in Czernowitz, Poland, a border town between Romania and Moldova, the twins disembarked at a former labor camp where they would stop over for nearly two months. In July 1945, the twins and the Csengari family boarded another train that they presumed was bound for Romania. To their dismay, the train bypassed Romania and rolled further east into the Soviet Union. My mother recalled that a handful of passengers jumped off the rail cars and rolled down hillsides in a desperate attempt to escape communist rule. Arriving near the demolished city of Minsk, the survivors were led to a refugee camp in Slutz where they'd remain for several more months. My mother and Miriam spent their days at the local fruit market and on a nearby hill where they picked red poppies, which they gifted to Mrs. Csengari as a token of their appreciation. She appreciated the gesture but forbade the girls from ever returning. It had been the site where more than 1,000 Jews had been murdered, some buried alive after the Germans had run out of ammunition.

In October 1945, my mother and Miriam, along with other displaced persons, were transported by cattle car to a Jewish refugee center in Oradea, Romania, and housed there for three days. They then accompanied Mrs. Csengari to her home in Simleu Silvaniei, where they stayed for several days before boarding a train bound for their home village of Portz. It was finally time for the twins and their benevolent guardian to say goodbye.

As they exchanged hugs, Mrs. Csengari whispered, "When I get back, I will tell the world what they have done to us." The girls would never see her again. My mother and Miriam arrived in Portz several days later, clinging to hope that they'd find their family:

As we approached the house, my heart beat so hard I could hear it thumping.... My memories of the house were of nice things and good times: warm beds and clothes that fit, a mother who cooked for us, a father who provided. My family.

But none of that was left. Nothing but the untilled land and the bare walls of the empty house. Everything looked neglected. Abandoned. I realized immediately that Mama and Papa had not returned. They would have never let the weeds grow so high. They would never have let the house get run down.

It was at that moment that we knew, Miriam and I, that we were all that were left of the Mozes family. Grandma and Grandpa Hersh—our mother's primary reason for not escaping to Palestine were also gone. There was nobody else.

Still holding hands, Miriam and I went inside. We were surprised when Mama's dog Lily, a little red Dachshund, ran out to greet us, barking and wagging her tail. All this time and there she was! She seemed to recognize us, and when we reached out to pet her, she licked our hands. I guess Jewish dogs were not taken to concentration camps, only Jewish people. [70]

Little was left in the Mozes home, which had been looted by the Nazis. One of the precious few exceptions were three family photographs. Mournfully glancing at pictures of her parents, Edit, and Aliz, my mother confronted the unbearable reality that they were dead. Just a few years prior, they'd all lived in tranquility in this quaint Romanian farmhouse and now, only agonizing nostalgia remained. My mother's grandparents had also been murdered by the Nazis. In total, she and Miriam lost more than 119 family members during the Holocaust. Their lives had been completely uprooted; the twins were now on their own:

I did not feel comfortable in the house even though it was ours. I did not feel as though I belonged there anymore. Miriam and I had no home, no parents, no sisters. But we still had each other. [71]

A short while later, the girls were picked up by their cousin Shmilu, a fellow Auschwitz survivor and son of Irena, Alexander's sister. He drove the girls to the Portz train station, and they were informed of their terminus—they were off to live with their Aunt Irena in Cluj, Romania.

For the next five years, my mother and Miriam lived in Cluj. They'd previously visited the city, but it had changed dramatically since coming under communist rule. Government officials confiscated land, committed election fraud, and imprisoned anyone opposing communist ideology.

Enrolled at the Queen Mary Gymnasium for Girls on a probationary term of one semester, my mother and Miriam struggled academically. Their grades gradually improved, and they learned the Romanian language over the next few months. My mother was appointed as Head of the Communist Youth Party whose platform stood for brotherhood, equality, and freedom. The ideals all sounded rather good to a sixteen-year-old who'd just emerged from captivity.

Foraging for food in Cluj proved to be nearly as exhausting as it had been at Auschwitz. My mother and Miriam, still malnourished, scrounged for meals at a local orphanage and often had to stand in line for hours for a single loaf of bread. They quickly grasped that "freedom" wasn't all that it was cracked up to be.

The twins were bereft of material possessions, but more than anything they lacked emotional support. Having lost both her husband and a son in a concentration camp, Irena was emotionally taxed and incapable of providing warmth and affection to the girls. Now teenagers, my mother and Miriam required comfort and reassurance, but like food and clothing, they were nowhere to be found in Cluj. One thing that hadn't changed was rampant antisemitism. My mother and Miriam were the only Jews at school and once again subject to cruel slights. They even fended off rumors that a Jewish vampire was harassing Christian girls and sucking their blood. She wondered if the vampire would know that they were Jewish, and thus not harm them.

In addition to their mental anguish, the twins battled frequent physical ailments as a result of Mengele's experimentation. Painful sores that progressed into scars enveloped their bodies and they were often plagued by colds and fatigue. Terrifying memories of Auschwitz continued to torment my mother:

Every night I had nightmares. I dreamed of rats the size of cats, dead bodies, and needles stuck into me. After we found out that the Nazis had made soap out of Jewish fat, I dreamed that soap bars spoke to me in the voices of my parents and sisters, asking me, "Why are you washing with us?" [72]

By 1950, communist persecution, unremitting antisemitism, and a dearth of basic resources pushed Irena, Miriam, and my mother to the brink.

Never forgetting her father's directive to move to Palestine (now the State of Israel) upon survival, my mother recalled, "I began to think it would be a privilege to live in a place where my father had dreamed of living." The twins had remained in contact with their Uncle Aaron, and he'd pledged to help them relocate. My mother had less noble motivations as well. "We wrote to him and asked if there was chocolate in Israel," she later admitted, "He replied, telling us that we could eat all the chocolate we wanted and all the oranges we wanted, too. He would take care of us. We thought Israel sounded like paradise!"[73] It's not surprising that I never had trouble finding sweets in our home while growing up.

My mother and Miriam suffered an agonizing two-year wait before finally being allowed to leave Romania. Dependent on young people to revitalize the country, Romanian officials were reluctant to grant visas. Before departing, the girls were required to sign their farmland (little remained after being granted to peasants) over to the country, officially severing their final tie to Portz. Originally told that they could take their material possessions, the girls were ultimately allowed to depart with only the clothes on their backs. My mother wore three dresses and a winter coat that she'd stood in line for twenty hours to receive. Nonetheless, her emotions were high as she and Miriam boarded the ironically named ship, *The Transylvania*, bound for Haifa, Israel:

As we pulled away from shore, I knew there was nothing left for Miriam and me in Romania. During the past five years I had continued to hope that our sisters or parents might come back. The Jewish Red Cross had posted lists of people returning. I had checked the lists at the orphanage where we ate dinner every night, but there was no sign of any member of my family. Miriam and I were sixteen years old. We needed to move on. [74]

Not afforded the luxury of a cabin, the girls remained on the deck of the ship, crammed with more than 3,000 passengers, for three days. For what the vessel lacked in comfort, it made up for in sanguinity. Dreams of a new life lay ahead for so many who had narrowly evaded death. The choppy seas and claustrophobic quarters couldn't quell the twins' euphoria and they relished their time on the Black Sea, even spotting dolphins along the way. The ship finally docked in Haifa on June 25, 1950:

As the boat docked, we stood on the deck and watched the sun rise over Mount Carmel, Israel. It was one of the most beautiful sights I had ever seen. The land of freedom. Most of the passengers on the ship were Holocaust survivors like us. Everybody burst into the Israeli national anthem, "Hatikvah." We were crying and singing with joy.

As we disembarked at the port, we searched for a person looking for us. Uncle Aaron finally spotted us, yelling our names and waving his arms so we would be sure to see him. We hugged, and he kissed us. We cried in his arms. It had been so long since my sister and I had received any real love from anyone besides each other.

My twin sister and I, in our matching rust-colored coats and layers of matching dresses, felt at last that we had come home. [75]

The Youth Aliyah was a Jewish organization charged with resettling displaced children from the Holocaust. Establishing kibbutzim (communal settlements) and youth villages in Palestine, the communities served as both a school and residence. My mother and Miriam joined 300 other youth at a large Youth Aliyah Village with acres of farmland, and they split their time between attending class and performing farm chores, the former no doubt evoking memories of Portz. Psychological services were provided, and the refugees were assigned an "old timer" who helped look after them. They learned Hebrew, history, and the Bible, the latter of which my mother flunked three times. She and Miriam developed friendships with children who hailed from many different countries. Dancing and singing were nightly rituals, and the village offered a familial environment. "Miriam and I were finally part of a new, large, welcoming family," my mother remembered. Slowly, she also began healing from the trauma of the last decade:

For the first time since leaving Auschwitz, I would sleep without having nightmares. I would no longer have to worry about our physical safety or survival. There was no antisemitism, and we would be allowed, indeed even encouraged to celebrate our Jewish heritage. Our hurts and suffering would slowly begin to heal in those youth villages. [76]

Military service was mandatory in Israel, so in 1952, my mother and Miriam enlisted in the Israeli army. My mother trained to become a draftsperson, ultimately rising to the rank of sergeant major, while Miriam studied nursing. The twins dated frequently in their early twenties and my mother (apparently keeping her options open!), learned to say "I love you" in ten different languages. Still pranksters, they never disclosed to their dates that they had a twin sister. Their deception came in handy at a time when Miriam was seeing a young man whom she likened to an octopus, with hands everywhere. One evening Miriam

My mother (left) and Miriam in Israel.
COURTESY INDIANA HISTORICAL SOCIETY

and my mother switched places, and when he leaned in to kiss whom he thought was Miriam, my mother scared the young man half-to-death and made him understand that "no means no." He exited their apartment and was never seen again.

By the age of twenty-six, my mother began dating a *sabra* (native-born Israeli) who hailed from a sizable family. Miriam was dating a young man named Kuti Czaigher, also a sabra, whom she eventually married. While happy for her sister, my mother felt like an "old hag" and pined for a ring of her own. She was crushed when her boyfriend's mother questioned his involvement with a Holocaust survivor. His mother desired that her son marry into a large family and my mother had none to speak of. Her boyfriend cared deeply for her, but lacked the *chutzpah* (nerve) to stand up to his family and they ended the relationship. Fifteen years had passed since her liberation, but my mother was still affected by the echoes of Auschwitz.

Employed at *Maariv*, a prestigious Israeli newspaper, my Uncle Shlomo wasted no time in accelerating his brother's search for a mate upon his arrival in 1960. After placing an advertisement in the personals section on behalf of my father, he received an immediate response from a young Israeli draftswoman named Eva Mozes. There was one problem: My father spoke minimal Hebrew and my mother spoke even less English. Armed with dictionaries and optimism, the twosome went on three dates over the coming weeks. My

My parents on their wedding day. COURTESY INDIANA HISTORICAL SOCIETY

father was attracted to my mother's beauty and found it very appealing that she was in uniform. She found him humorous--though she probably had no idea what he was talking about! Shlomo and his family had no qualms with my mother's background, which also helped cement their relationship. Still dependent on dictionaries on their third date, my father asked my mother "something" (her words) and she replied, "yes." They'd just gotten engaged! Sometimes the language of love requires few words.

On April 27, 1960, Mickey Kor and Eva Mozes were married at a synagogue on Dizengoff Street in Tel Aviv. Members of the Kor family along with Miriam and Kuti were present to celebrate the union of two survivors, who in their darkest hours never envisioned this day would come. I've still yet to confirm if the Rabbi relied on a dictionary for their nuptials.

There was no time for a honeymoon as my father had to return to work in Indiana and my mother needed to fulfill her military commitments. Over the next few months, the newlyweds were not only separated by two different dialects but by an ocean as well.

CONNECTICUT JEWISH LEDGER

New Relative Of Kors Here From Israel

MRS. EVA KOR

WEST HARTFORD — An Israeli woman who married an American is visiting her husband's family here this week. Mrs. Eva Kor, wife of Michael Kor, is staying with her husband's brother and sister-

Connecticut Jewish Ledger announces my mother's arrival in America.

In the summer of 1960, my mother bid farewell to her Uncle Aaron and Miriam, and to her adopted home country of Israel as she boarded a plane destined for New York. My uncle Leib, his wife Ruth, and an Israeli cousin of my mother's greeted her at New York International Airport. Upon their meeting, Ruth applied a corsage to the lapel of my mother's jacket. She later recalled her bewilderment at the gesture and the immediate trials in her new home:

Although this [gesture] was greatly appreciated, I was not familiar with this American custom and asked [in Hebrew], "What is this flower doing here?"

My cousin responded, "Do not take it off. You will insult your in-laws. When you get to the restaurant, tell everyone that you are hot and take the jacket off." Once at the restaurant, I removed the jacket and wished to appear very debonair by looking at the menu. Obviously, I couldn't read any of the options and so when the remainder of the table all ordered steak, I did so as well. When asked how I wanted it cooked, I copied the others at the table and said, "Well, well." My steak arrived the texture of a brick.

My Uncle Leib and Aunt Ruth hosted my mother for a few days before she departed for Terre Haute. Her stay offered another moment of great levity.

Upon my arrival in Connecticut, Mickey called me and said, "Eva, everyone in Terre Haute is very excited."

I pulled out my dictionary and looked up the word 'excited.' This was a good thing. He then said, "Eva, my friends, their wives want to give you a 'shower.'"

I again referenced my dictionary and turned very red in my face. Unsure if my new husband was referring to a mikvah, *a Jewish religious ritual involving an oversized bathtub, I responded, "Mickey, thank you very much, but tell your friends, I take shower alone."*

My parents were happy and free, having overcome the most formidable circumstances imaginable. They couldn't wait to start a family and begin their life anew. Their future looked promising, but new challenges lay ahead.

CHAPTER

The Unlikeliest of Destinations

> "It was like going to the moon."
>
> —Eva

Founded in the early nineteenth century, Terre Haute, Indiana, is situated in Vigo County, five miles east of the Illinois border and seventy-five miles to the west of Indianapolis. The city's roots trace back to French Canadian explorers who christened its name (*Terre Haute* translates as "highland" in French) due to its perch atop the Wabash River. Farming was the region's dominant means of industry upon its founding, later augmented by iron and steel mills, breweries, and distilleries. The region's bountiful cornfields buoyed the food and alcoholic beverage industry and coal companies emerged to support the burgeoning railroad transit. Today, Terre Haute's economy relies heavily on manufacturing in the areas of food, steel, and plastics.

Terre Haute lays claim to a number of prominent leaders, including Eugene Debs, a five-time candidate of the Socialist Party of America for President of the United States. It's also the birthplace of former United States Senator Birch Bayh and Robert Greenleaf, an AT&T executive who pioneered the servant leadership movement. Basketball has long been a religion in the Hoosier state and Terre Haute has produced some of the sports' giants, including Hall of Famers Clyde Lovellette and Bobby "Slick" Leonard. Its favorite son, however, is Larry Bird. Though he grew up two hours to the southeast in French Lick, Bird led Indiana State University to the 1979 NCAA championship game before embarking on a legendary NBA career. For years, he owned a hotel in Terre Haute where patrons came to pay homage to his greatness, and a fifteen-foot bronze statue of Bird stands at the corners of Eighth and Cherry Streets.

Nearly 60,000 people now call Terre Haute home, and its makeup is a microcosm of the state's demographic population. Eighty percent of its residents are White and only 10% African American. Approximately 0.1% of Terre Haute residents identify as Jewish. Terre Haute also happens to lie in a state that was once a hotbed for the Ku Klux Klan (KKK).

Established in 1915, the Indiana Klan, a branch of the KKK, gained prominence following World War I and espoused racial superiority against African Americans, Chinese Americans, Catholics, and Jews. The Indiana Klan preyed on the fears of the state's large, White Protestant base who felt threatened by the day's social and political issues, foremost among them immigration laws that allowed for a substantial influx of European immigrants. By 1922, Indiana boasted the largest national chapter, and its membership increased dramatically under the leadership of Grand Dragon D. C. Stephenson. Stephenson's coercive leadership and intimidating tactics (he once proclaimed, "I am the law in Indiana.") resulted in a massive upsurge in Klan membership.

From July 1922 to July 1923, the Indiana Klan amassed 2,000 new members per week and membership swelled to nearly 250,000, or about one third of all White males in the state. Indiana Historian James Madison, author of *A Lynching in the Heartland: Race and Memory in America*, noted that the

Klan's members "were mainline, mainstream people — 'good Hoosiers' in their view, they ranged from bankers to doctors, farmers and churchgoers. They deemed themselves patriots on a moral crusade, rather than bigoted racists." [77] Winning higher office also required backing from the KKK, and by 1925 over half the elected members of the Indiana General Assembly, Governor Edward L. Jackson, and many other high-ranking officials in local and state government were Klan members.

An incident in 1901 laid the foundation for the Klan's later infiltration into Vigo County. On February 26, 1901, a mob of Terre Haute residents lynched George Ward, a Black man, for the suspected murder of a White woman. The execution drew more than 1,000 White onlookers who watched as Ward was dragged from his jail cell, bludgeoned with a sledgehammer, hanged from a bridge, and burned. His toes and the hobnails from his boots were collected as souvenirs. A grand jury was convened but failed to charge anyone with Ward's murder. In Vigo County, more than 24% of the population belonged to the Klan during the 1920s, but it wasn't a KKK stronghold. Prohibition was a major tenet of the Klan's agenda, one that didn't play well in Terre Haute where the farming industry relied upon alcohol consumption and where booze was readily available in local speakeasies. Following Grand Dragon Stephenson's 1925 conviction of the rape and murder of schoolteacher Madge Oberholtzer, the Indiana Klan's power eroded, but its stain on the state has never been completely expunged. Pockets of Klan activity and sporadic rallies have remained throughout the past century along with other incidents indicative of the state's ignominious history with discrimination.

In March 1907, Governor Frank Hanley approved the first eugenics law in the United States, making sterilization mandatory for "criminals, idiots, rapists, and imbeciles in state custody." The law became the catalyst for the United States eugenic program, later the inspiration for Hitler's public health laws targeting Jews and non-Aryan Germans.

It was Indiana, a state possessing both midwestern charm and a sordid history of intolerance, which would become the unlikeliest of destinations for two Holocaust survivors.

My father and me at the piano.

I was born on April 15, 1961, the same day fifteen years earlier when my father escaped the Nazis in Magdeburg. My parents named me in memory of my maternal grandfather, bucking a friend's suggestion that they bestow me with the first name, "Peace." I'm glad they won out.

I commanded my parents' attention until my sister Rina came along two years later. Initially angry that I'd have to cede the spotlight, I was grateful for a sibling and have always tried to display my love for her. On the weekends, I enjoyed taking drives (assuming my mother was commanding the wheel!) with Rina and my parents. A casual observer might perceive us to be the average American family, not knowing the harrowing journey my parents had endured to get to the United States, nor the personal torment they still carried.

From 1964 to 1973, we lived in a very modest, three-bedroom apartment at 2732 Park Street in Terre Haute. The Bilyeu Family lived behind us, and I befriended their son Kris. We played a lot together and I even taught him a few words of Hebrew, which I predominantly spoke in my early years. We had a nice backyard and a carport where my dad installed a basketball hoop, practically mandatory in Indiana. The rim was a little more than five feet high, and I became extremely popular since all the neighborhood kids wanted to come play at the Kor home.

Although my parents grew up in devoutly Jewish households, they were not, themselves, overly religious. Yet, because they valued our heritage, we attended synagogue regularly, and they demanded that Rina and I identify ourselves as Jewish. It would have been easy for them to cloak themselves in anonymity given where we lived, but they were proud of their Jewish heritage and expected us to be as well. I attended Hebrew School at the United Hebrew Congregation every

Sunday until my bar mitzvah.

We didn't have a lot of money and lacked some of the creature comforts other families enjoyed. I once asked my parents for a designer tennis shirt which was rather expensive for the time.

"Alex, when I was your age, I was lucky to have one shirt, let alone several," my mother responded. It was a humbling lesson for a twelve-year-old.

Rina and I loved grilled cheese sandwiches, but my parents couldn't afford a stove top griddle to toast them in. Undeterred, my mother came up with the ingenious idea of using her iron to prepare them! "Iron sandwiches" became a mainstay on Sundays, and many of my friends would venture over for this delicacy.

A young Mario Andretti. COURTESY ALEX KOR

During family dinners, we'd hover around the TV and watch the local and national news. My parents took great interest in what was happening both locally and abroad and instilled in us the importance of keeping up with world events. They often debated Israeli policy issues and I'd occasionally attempt to moderate without much success. My father took pride when he'd see a Jewish news anchor or movie star on the television, and it was a thrill for him years later when actors Ed Asner and Elliott Gould became family friends.

My father worked as a pharmacist at M&C Pharmacy, the AP&S Clinic, Hook's Drugs, and later CVS. He had a reputation for repeating instructions many times over when filling a prescription. I eagerly awaited his return home every night. We had a big picture window and I'd often yell *"Abba ba! Abba ba!"* which means "Father is coming" in Hebrew. He loved music and would often sing as he roamed through our home. I became knowledgeable of the era's famous crooners, and it was quite humorous listening to him belt out

Dean Martin tunes in a Latvian accent and broken English.

My mother had several jobs. Trained as draftswoman in the Israeli army, she pursued a career as an architect and worked for years at a local engineering firm. When we purchased a home in a nicer neighborhood, she took an interest in real estate. The state realtor exam was a major hurdle and she flunked it at least three times. Her limited grasp of the English language proved to be a barrier and agencies feared that clients wouldn't be able to understand her. A small company eventually hired her, and no one outworked her. Her boss often referred to her as a "bulldog" because she was so persistent.

Over the years, I've had countless patients and friends share, "You know your mom sold us our first house. She was the best and was relentless in finding us our dream home." My parents both impressed upon me a strong work ethic that I still carry to this day in my work as a podiatrist.

My parents preached a healthy lifestyle, with a notable exception of the "iron grilled cheeses," and maintained that sports could instill invaluable lessons in their children. Every morning, my mother began her day by lifting dumbbells to the beat of *The Jack LaLanne Show* on TV, and my father developed a keen interest in handball. Our Friday nights were often spent at the local YMCA pool where we'd swim as a family. Bereft of these opportunities during their own childhoods, my parents cherished their time with Rina and me, and sport offered ample occasions to do so.

I inherited a passion for sports mainly from my father. Unrecognizable unless wearing his Purdue Boilermaker garb, he was glued to the television whenever Purdue played. My heroes growing up included Rick Mount, the great marksman who led the Boilermakers to the 1969 NCAA championship game. Purdue lost that game to Lew Alcindor (later Kareem Abdul-Jabbar) and the powerhouse UCLA Bruins, and it took us months to recover. The loss was perhaps softened a bit by the identity of the coach on the opposing sideline.

During a Bruin game once, my father had pointed to UCLA Coach John Wooden and said, "There is my gym teacher." Baffled, I came to learn that Wooden was my father's physical education teacher at Indiana State University. My father later wrote to Coach Wooden and began receiving letters from him every preseason.

I quickly figured out that the referee controlled all the action during football and basketball games, so my mother bought me a referee shirt and, much to the consternation of our neighbors, a whistle. During games, I'd don the zebra stripes and blow the whistle when I thought there was a bad call. My tennis opponents

Playing catch with "Bart Starr."
COURTESY ALEX KOR

will tell you that I still embrace the role of referee when we compete. My father and I played a lot of sports in our backyard. One of my favorite photos is of me decked out in Green Bay Packers gear while my father is tossing footballs to me. He cherished his time playing the role of Bart Starr while I pretended to be flanker Carroll Dale. My father didn't understand baseball but tried to teach me basketball (he had learned from John Wooden, of course!) on our outdoor court. He took up tennis and rose to the level of city champion in the late 1950s. He taught me tennis as well, but I had no interest. I loved baseball and wanted to be the next Johnny Bench, but later realized that tennis was a better option when I stopped growing.

My parents had different perspectives when it came to the importance of sports.

I can still hear my mother shouting, "They are just playing a game.... Do not take it so seriously!"

After a tough loss in tennis, she'd always remind me, "Just try to have fun and don't worry about the result." On one occasion though, she did take an active role in my athletic endeavors.

At the age of thirteen, I faced my first major athletic setback. Although I'd been named an All- Star Little League baseball player the year before, I was cut from making the Babe Ruth League. It was rumored that if your parents volunteered to coach, you'd be assured of a roster spot. My mother immediately called the league director and offered to coach a sport she knew nothing about!

Conversely, sports provided an escape for my dad who was still tormented by his memories of the Holocaust. He took every loss, be it one of my games or Purdue's, extremely hard. By the eighth grade, I had developed into a good tennis player and played a match against Cam Cameron.

Something of a local legend, Cameron was the best athlete in Terre Haute and later matriculated to Indiana University where he played both football and basketball. He enjoyed a long coaching career, which included a stint as the head coach of the Miami Dolphins.

I was in control of the match when Cameron made a controversial call. From out of nowhere, I heard my father holler, "Quit hooking my son! That ball was in!" I was really embarrassed but went on to win the match.

In 1978, the NBC miniseries *Holocaust* debuted on national television and the Terre Haute affiliate invited our family to the studio to watch the final episode. In the last scene, a little boy is shown kicking a soccer ball and as I looked over at my dad, I noticed that he was crying hysterically. He'd played soccer as a youth and saw himself in the boy's image. From that moment on, I knew I needed to help him deal with his past and encourage my mother to speak up more about her own experiences. I was only seventeen at the time.

Sports also provided an opportunity for a Jewish kid living in Indiana to assimilate into the Hoosier culture, and the natural place to start was the basketball court. In my quest to one day play point guard for Purdue, I competed in three separate leagues.

Despite being vertically challenged, I was named a starter on my ninth-grade basketball squad. Our season culminated in the annual county tournament, and we made it all the way to the tourney finals. Unfortunately, our best player was suspended for disciplinary reasons prior to the title game, and no one gave us a chance against a heated rival. The game was nip and tuck the whole way, and we found ourselves down by two points with just ten seconds to play. During a timeout, our coach drew up a play for Ralph Wagle, our second-best player. The play called for Wagle to flash to the free-throw line where I'd pass him the ball for a game-tying shot. After receiving the inbounds pass, I noticed that Wagle was double-teamed, and I couldn't find anyone else open. As the clock ticked down, I did my best Rick Mount impersonation and heaved a 25-footer. Nothing but net. The game went to overtime, and we went on to capture the county championship. Andy Amey, a local sports reporter, wrote a wonderful column in the following morning's paper, emphasizing that I was the shortest player on the court. My parents beamed with pride. They'd been underdogs their whole lives as well.

Despite my love for hoops, my height limited future opportunities. My father suggested I take up tennis, and I enrolled in the summer tennis program at Woodrow Wilson Junior High School. Under the tutelage of coach Bob Fischer, I developed into a skilled player, paving the way for my high school and college tennis careers. Making honorable mention All-State as a senior, I received scholarship offers from the University of Evansville and the University of Kentucky before committing to Butler University. Tennis taught me a number of life lessons and exposed me to people who educated me in areas well beyond the realm of sport.

I've enjoyed many close friendships through the game of tennis, but one of the first was with Mark Hord. Having previously battled on the YMCA basketball courts, Mark and I ended up as teammates on the tennis and basketball squads at Woodrow Wilson. We shared a love for both sports and we became fast friends. During the summers, we'd spend hours on the tennis courts where we'd play epic seven-set matches. What made our friendship unique is that Mark is African American. Even though the Civil Rights Act of 1964 had passed just a decade prior, friendships between Blacks and Whites were sometimes frowned upon in Terre Haute. Despite our ethnic differences, we shared many commonalities. Both of us came from middle class families, and his parents had also overcome many obstacles. Mark, who had two other siblings, had more financial hardship than me, but we both grew up without some of the luxuries our friends enjoyed.

Mark recently reflected, "Growing up in a different neighborhood with a different background, I was a young Black male who was blessed to forge this friendship with Alex. I was also embraced by his parents who would include me in family trips to see professional basketball and tennis events in Indiana." Mark and I both went on to play college tennis and remain close friends to this day.

My parents taught me from an early age, often referencing their own histories, to never judge others based on their nationality, religion, or race. I was five years old when I first became aware of discrimination. While on a family outing in Louisville, Kentucky, I noticed that there were bathrooms designated for "Whites" and "Coloreds."

"Why do they have different bathrooms?" I asked my mother.

"Alex, unfortunately we live in a world where some people judge others' by their skin color," she replied.

I vividly remember riding with several friends to a game at the United Hebrew Congregation when my friend's father turned to me and inquired, "Alex, what kind of car will you drive when you get your driver's license?"

We were discussing several potential options, including foreign-made automobiles, when another friend chimed in.

"Well, I will never buy or drive a car made in Germany! Why would you buy a German car, Alex? You're Jewish." he said.

With gumption, I immediately shot back, "That's crazy, why wouldn't you buy a German car if it were the best one?"

I was only eleven years old at the time and only thirty years prior, my father had been held captive in a concentration camp in Germany. We had two families of German descent in our neighborhood. My parents openly embraced them and encouraged Rina and me to do the same.

Despite being naturalized citizens, my father in 1948 and my mother in 1965, my parents were very active in American politics and in their local community. My father, in particular, valued freedom and the American way. Indebted to the United States army for liberating him, he was fiercely loyal to his adopted country. Both he and my mother were immensely proud to vote and even when his health later prevented him from voting in person, he made sure that Rina or I secured an absentee ballot for him. On June 7, 1968, one day after his assassination, my father wrote a message of support for Senator Robert F. Kennedy that appeared in *Time* magazine, landing on the same page as letters from Elizabeth Taylor and Gregory Peck:

Sir: To those of us who voted for him in the Indiana primary, Robert F. Kennedy represents honesty, imagination, courage, and leadership. These, in my

My father with Senator Robert Kennedy in Terre Haute. COURTESY ALEX KOR

opinion, constitute the ingredients that Presidents are made of.

He also wrote numerous letters to the *Indianapolis Star* and *Terre Haute Tribune*. If his letter got published, he'd make copies at the library and have my mother send them out to politicians and media members.

Both my parents were great admirers of Kennedy and had high hopes for him in the 1968 presidential election. Kennedy's scheduled appearance in Terre Haute prior to the May primary brought great anticipation to our household. While attending a fundraising dinner, my father had his picture taken with Senator Kennedy and the following morning, my mother helped the League of Women Voters host a breakfast for him. I had the privilege of meeting Senator Kennedy and got an autograph, which I still keep to this day.

On June 6, 1968, the night of the California Democratic primary, I went to bed around 8 p.m. and was later awakened by my mother, who was crying hysterically.

"What happened Mom? Why are you crying?" I shouted. I was stunned when she informed me that Kennedy had been shot. I'd met him just two months prior and had never known anyone who had died. It was my first realization at how fleeting life can be.

After Kennedy's assassination, legislation was brought forward in Indiana calling for stronger gun control. Rina and I owned water guns and in a symbolic gesture, turned them in at city hall. Nearly fifty years later, it makes me sad that gun violence remains such a scourge on society.

Upon arriving in the United States, my mother was initially naive to racism, but quickly ascertained that her new home had serious issues with discrimination. After Martin Luther King Jr. was assassinated, she organized, sponsored, and oversaw a daycare center in Terre Haute for underprivileged children.

Rina and I supported her efforts and the experience helped foster my appreciation for diverse cultures, races, and religions. Despite my mother's good intentions, many African American men in the area took exception to the fact that a White woman, from the other side of the tracks, was teaching their children. On one occasion, an aggrieved parent showed up with a baseball bat and threatened to "knock her out." Never one to be intimidated, she stood at a distance and challenged the man to hit her. He backed down. Apparently, her courage won him over. For the next eighteen months, she ran the center, which eventually became the Head Start program.

I first became aware that my parents were survivors of the Holocaust at the age of five. My mother, more vocal than my father, offered age-appropriate information about her past to me and my sister. Rina was also five when she realized that our mother had a unique background. While at her friend Jill's, Rina noticed that Jill's mom had no number on her arm like our mother did.

"How come you don't have a number on your left arm like Mommy?" inquired Rina.

Caught off guard by the query, Mrs. Baker suggested that Rina ask her mother.

Rina ran back to our house and immediately asked my mother, "How come Mrs. Baker does not have a number like you?"

Without hesitation, she responded, "Rina, remember that your father and I told you and your brother that some bad people did some bad things to us. One of those things was that they tattooed a number on my arm."

Other periodic episodes suggested that my parents were different. At a family dinner at Red Lobster, my father suffered a panic attack after seeing fish jumping for food in a nearby tank. The image triggered the agonizing memory of being crammed into the hull of the ship bound for Danzig.

"I don't want to talk about it, Alex!" he cried after I asked what had upset him.

From an early age, I felt that I was special. My parents, especially my mother, showered Rina and me with love and affection. I also came to realize that I was a miracle. What if my grandmother hadn't forced my father to hide when the Nazis came for them? What if he hadn't found shelter on the death march? What if my mother hadn't been a twin? What if Mengele decided my mother didn't deserve to live following his cruel experimentation on her and Miriam? I didn't dwell on those questions often, but I never took for granted how fortunate I was to be alive.

People often ask me what it was like growing up in Terre Haute, Indiana, as the son of Holocaust survivors. It's a simple question, but not easy to answer. Following the surrender of Nazi Germany, 11 million people sought refuge after being displaced by the war. Aided by the Allied Forces and the United Nations Relief and Rehabilitation Administration, 7 million people were able to return to their home countries. Thousands of others emigrated to Palestine and approximately 140,000 settled in the United States, most of whom were between the ages of twenty and forty, a painful reminder of how many very young children and older adults perished in the Holocaust. Many of these survivors sought refuge in large cities like New York, Chicago, and Los Angeles. New York even had its own association, the New York Association for New Americans, to assist the plethora of survivors seeking refuge there. These cities offered resources to help the displaced, significant Jewish populations, and provided relative anonymity for those who wanted to cope in isolation after experiencing the unthinkable. Terre Haute provided none of these opportunities.

Growing up in Terre Haute was difficult for many reasons. Having two parents with thick accents was a significant challenge for me. My father had lived in Terre Haute since 1947 and could speak broken English but my mother, having just moved to the United States in 1960, lagged far behind. Even by the late 1960s, her accent was hard to decipher, and her knowledge of the English language was limited. Hebrew translators were few and far between in Indiana, so she learned English by watching soap operas. As a third grader, I attended a PTA meeting where I had to translate my teacher's English into Hebrew so my mother could understand. I learned this could be advantageous and translated my teacher's mediocre assessment of me into a glowing report of my academic prowess!

Besides Rina and me, there were only two or three other Jewish kids at our elementary school and Holocaust Education wasn't a major priority. Each December, our elementary school put on a Christmas play and every student was required to participate. I wasn't comfortable with singing Christmas hymns, and not just because I was out of key and a mediocre singer. In the third grade, I was selected to be an angel and the experience was so awkward that my mother and I both requested I not have to do this again. In place of participating the following year, I drafted a report on the meaning of Hanukkah, and I imagine this was the first such report done in school history.

Our class was afforded a brief lesson on the Holocaust when my mother gave her very first lecture at our school. She wasn't a polished speaker and wept throughout the talk. After obtaining her high school diploma, she began taking classes at Indiana State University. Insecure with her English, she chose a course where she'd at least have familiarity with the subject matter—a class on the Holocaust. On the first day of class, she approached the professor and introduced herself.

"Dr. Perard, my name is Eva Kor," she said. "I sure hope that I pass your class. It would be embarrassing to flunk your course and pass the real thing!" Just as she did at Auschwitz, she passed with flying colors.

Dating was (and still is!) a challenge for me in Terre Haute. Many assume that my parents wanted me to solely date Jewish girls, but that was my preference. However, with a Jewish population of less than 5%, my options in Terre Haute were extremely limited. It was imperative to me that my dates have a knowledge and appreciation of my parents' backgrounds. I once took a non-Jewish girl to a Holocaust Museum where she was aloof and uninterested.

It was the last time we went out on a date. I will admit that when my mother lectured, she often surveyed the crowd for attractive Jewish females who fit my criteria, but she just wanted me to be happy, regardless of who I was dating.

I credit my parents for their openness, yet after both of them passing away, finding a Jewish girl has not been as critical to me.

Another hurdle for us was that we had no other family around. Growing up, I began meeting the grandparents, aunts and uncles, and cousins of my friends. It dawned on me that I had no extended family in Terre Haute nor had I heard my parents mention much about other relatives except for my Aunt Miriam and a cousin who lived in Connecticut.

My Aunt Miriam, or "Doda" as I called her, was an overly sweet lady. Given what they experienced at Auschwitz, my mother and Miriam remained very close, and we traveled to Israel every few years to visit Miriam and her three daughters. Miriam worked as a nurse and her husband Kuti, who was related to former CNN talk show host Larry King, was an administrative manager for the city of Afridar. I have warm memories of staying with Miriam where I was able to hear her memories of Auschwitz while eating her delicious cucumbers.

After completing my freshman year at Butler University, I spent three

Aunt Miriam, with husband Kuti, pointing at the liberation photo of her and my mother as they exit Auschwitz. COURTESY ALEX KOR

weeks in Israel with Miriam. On the Butler University tennis team at the time, I was itching to get on the courts and asked Miriam if there were any nearby. Her neighbor's son Shlomo played tennis and she encouraged me to challenge him to a match.

"I played number four singles at Butler this past season, I don't want to waste some time with a novice!" I declared.

Unbeknownst to me, the son of Miriam's neighbor was a 6-foot-1, 200-pound, twenty-two-year-old and looked like a linebacker in tennis shorts. It turned out that he was Israel's version of Roger Federer. Hitting every shot just over the net and a foot from the baseline, Shlomo destroyed me 6-1 in the first set. My one win was a game that Shlomo generously "donated" to me.

As we exited the court, I said, "Wow, you are a great player! What's your last name?"

He replied that it was Glickstein, and shared that he'd just finished a tour of duty with the Israeli army. Adding that he was the number one player in Israel, Shlomo briefed me on his plans to play on the Association of Tennis Professionals tour.

A year later, he played at Wimbledon and lost to Bjorn Borg in the first round in five close sets.

I had severely underestimated Aunt Miriam's judgement of talent! Shlomo and I kept in touch and we played against each other in the mixed doubles finals in the Maccabiah Games (the Jewish Olympics) in 2005.

As noted previously, my mother lost more than 100 family members during the Holocaust, and my father lost nearly as many. Not having grandparents has been a major void in my life, but growing up I didn't know any better. The Nehf family lived around the corner and my parents told Rina and I that they were our "pretend grandparents."

The holidays were particularly difficult for us. My mother and father did their best to make up for the fact that we had no extended family around by showering us with gifts and love, but it was hard watching my friends celebrate with their grandparents, aunts, uncles, and cousins. Hanukkah was significantly overshadowed by Christmas in Terre Haute and going back to Israel to celebrate with Miriam was simply not possible.

I would have loved to have grandparents, but it's hard to miss something that you've never had and unfortunately, I never got to meet my maternal or paternal grandparents. My parents instilled in me and my sister not to dwell on the negative but instead to appreciate what we did have.

I enjoyed growing up in Terre Haute. It had nice neighborhoods and an array of courts and ballfields for sports-crazed kids like me. In reality it was all I knew. I had no clue what lay beyond the borders of Terre Haute, and even cities like Chicago (only a three-hour drive) were foreign to me.

One of the challenges we faced is that very few people could relate to our past. Most of my friends and their parents couldn't fathom what my parents had endured. My classmates and neighborhood buddies never asked questions of me, and their parents were reluctant to bring up the Holocaust to my parents.

In my college years, a tennis teammate once said, "Alex, I'm really surprised your mom is out there lecturing about her experiences. I would think that you would want to forget those experiences." I discovered during my childhood that there were many experiences I wished to forget as well.

My first encounter with antisemitism occurred on Halloween night in 1972. Several classmates came through the neighborhood and began pelting our house with bushels of corn before scrawling "GO HOME DIRTY JEW" on our windows. My mother started chasing the boys through the neighborhood. She called the kids' parents, who acted with indifference and responded that these were children who were "just having a little fun."

I was filled with shame following the incident, but mostly enraged at my mother. I couldn't understand why she would chase my peers, mere kids, around the yard. Why did she feel so compelled to do this?

On the other hand, my father reacted by turning out his lights and dozing off. "Let's leave them alone, they won't do it again," he'd argue.

I was extremely embarrassed by my mother, and many times uttered, "Mom, I'm so ashamed of you. Why can't you be like other mothers?"

The incident, the first in a string of antisemitic attacks on Halloween, was an early revelation that she was dealing with some severe anger issues. When these incidents occurred, her thoughts would immediately revert to 1944 when the Nazis would harass the Mozes family.

Years later, I was the one who felt terrible that I couldn't relate to what my mother was going through.

In 2013, she was lecturing in Gainesville, Florida, when a lady approached her following the lecture and said, "Mrs. Kor, I was one of those kids that tormented you and your family. I am so sorry. I had no idea. Will you forgive me?"

Of course, she did.

Around the same time, I attended a swimming party for our fifth-grade class at the local YMCA. Two brothers charged after me, roughed me up, and screamed antisemitic slurs at me. Confused, I failed to understand why I was attacked for being Jewish. I'd never encountered an act of hate like this but soon realized that the only thing that I'd done wrong was be Jewish. My parents apprised school officials and the two boys received punishment. And while I later received an apology, I never felt it to be sincere.

My sister Rina and I have always had a complex relationship, in part due to the circumstances of our parents' pasts. Growing up, we attempted to understand our family history while navigating our own issues. She might disagree, but I don't believe Rina experienced the same level of discrimination I faced.

The stream of threatening letters and death threats we received pushed my parents to the brink of relocation. They once contemplated moving us to Las Vegas given its robust Jewish population, but my mother's job offer fell through and my father couldn't imagine himself so far from his beloved Purdue sports teams. Concerned for my safety, they enrolled me in self-defense classes and reacted to the antisemitic episodes with great sadness. Especially troubling was that these incidents occurred in America, a country my mother and father genuinely believed to be "the land of the free and the home of the brave." They had escaped the most grotesque environments of hatred imaginable and were experiencing it all over again.

CHAPTER

My Toughest Match

> "Alex, my motek, this is your
> Auschwitz! You need to fight!"
>
> —Eva

I cry very easily, especially when watching certain movies. In 1971, the movie *Brian's Song* premiered, chronicling the real-life relationship between Chicago Bears teammates Gale Sayers and Brian Piccolo. Piccolo, played by James Caan, and Sayers, played by Billy Dee Williams, became the first interracial roommates in the history of the National Football League and their relationship reminded me of my friendship with Mark Hord. In the film, Piccolo is diagnosed with embryonal cell carcinoma, an aggressive form of germ cell testicular cancer, and ultimately succumbs to the disease at the age of twenty-six. Over the years I've seen the movie more than twenty times, and I always sob. After viewing it for the first time as a kid in Terre Haute, I had a premonition that, at some point in my life, my own fortitude would be tested. My parents' journeys had always inspired me, but I also had a gut feeling that they were preparing me for my own challenges.

In the fall of 1986, I entered my second year of podiatry school at the Scholl College of Podiatric Medicine in Chicago. That year, a medical journal article circulated around the school suggesting that male podiatry students had very high rates of testicular cancer. I remember thinking the rumors to be ridiculous and laughed off the periodical's findings.

I lived a pretty mundane life in podiatry school, essentially spending my days eating, attending class, and sleeping. I didn't know many people and my dating life was stagnant. Exercise has always been an escape for me and so I spent many hours in the gym. In February 1987, I experienced pain in my lower abdomen and assumed it to be just a strain or hernia incurred from lifting weights. Driven to stay on track academically, I ignored the issue but by April, I couldn't cross my legs without experiencing severe pain in my right testicle. I continued to ignore the discomfort and told no one, including my parents.

After finishing my final exams in May, I returned to Terre Haute to visit my parents. At some point I broke my silence, divulging to my mother that I suspected I'd suffered a hernia and needed to see a doctor. I went in for a consultation with Dr. Werner Lowenstein, a family friend and my mother's doctor, and I was confident that a quick visit would confirm my suspicion.

After a thorough examination, Dr. Lowenstein turned to me and asked, "Alex, how long have you noticed this lump?" I replied that it'd been there for two to three months. The uneasy look in his eyes told me this was no hernia.

"Alex, you do me a favor," Dr. Lowenstein said, "Next week, when you get back to Chicago, see a urologist immediately."

In denial, I put off seeing a doctor upon returning to Chicago. My father, an incessant worrier, knew nothing about my predicament but my mother continued to nag me about going to a specialist. Finally heeding her advice, I went to the Northwestern Medical Hospital in Chicago where a doctor examined me, ordered blood tests, and conducted an ultrasound of my testicles.

A few hours later, he uttered the words that so many of us dread: "Alex, you have cancer—testicular cancer."

With tears running down my face, I called my mother and gave her the terrible news. All kinds of thoughts raced through my mind: Would I live? Should I quit podiatry school? When do I tell my dad? Why did this happen to me? Will I ever have children?

My mother attempted to comfort me by phone, but all I could do was cry. I repeatedly hung up on her, but she kept phoning to offer encouragement. Her words rang hollow as I only wanted to dwell in self-pity.

She called one final time and said, "Alexander! You listen to me now. Look, I am a survivor. Your dad is a survivor. You will be a survivor! Alex, my *motek*, this is your Auschwitz! You need to fight!"

Once again, I hung up on her. I was twenty-six years old, the exact age as Brian Piccolo when he died. Inconsolable, I feared that life would never be the same.

The next day, I called her back and affirmed, "I understand now. Your words have motivated me. I will survive. I need to tell Dad."

She summoned my father, still in the dark regarding my diagnosis, to the phone. With surprising composure, I shared my diagnosis. From the shakiness in his voice, I could tell that he feared the worst—he'd always associated the word "cancer" with death.

Armed with my mother's confidence, I attempted to quell his anxiety and shared, "Dad, I know that you think I will not make it, but after I survive this, I need you to do me a favor. I want you to be more positive and worry less!"

He promised that he would and replied, "Ok, I will do that for you. I will do anything for you. Anything!"

My surgery was scheduled for the following week in Chicago and my mother flew in to be with me. I don't recall much about the surgery but remember that my mother and the surgeon were there to greet me when I came to.

"Everything went well," the doctor said, "but there is one part that looked a little unusual. You might need some radiation, but this will not be a big deal." However, the words "one part that looked a little unusual" concerned me, and I'd never associated the phrase "not a big deal" with cancer.

A day later the urologist called, informing me that I needed some chest x-rays, and again I thought this to be odd. I had that pit-in-the-stomach feeling that my parents must have had when they boarded trains, bound for unknown destinations during the Holocaust.

My mother and me during my battle with cancer.
COURTESY ALEX KOR

I was trying to stay positive, but a voicemail later that same day deflated me.

"Alex," came the voice on the other end, "your cancer may have spread to your lungs. You need a CT scan now." I was panicked and couldn't fathom how the cancer could have reached my lungs.

I phoned Mike Bush, a tennis partner, medical student at Indiana University, and most importantly, someone whom I trusted.

"If the cancer has spread to my lungs wouldn't I have some breathing or lung issues?" I contested.

Very diplomatically, Mike replied, "Not necessarily. It could have spread to your lungs and have no symptoms." This was not the answer I had hoped for, but I suspected he was correct. He then added that a doctor in Indianapolis by the name of Larry Einhorn was a world-renowned oncologist for his success in treating testicular cancer. "He is the best," Mike declared. "If you want to see him, I can help."

Despondent, I confessed to my classmate and close friend John Hester, "John, I may not be around for much longer."

Back at Northwestern the next day for the CT scan, I was instructed to call the urologist's office two hours later. It's now been thirty-seven years, but I can still recall being on the third floor of the podiatry school when I made the call and learned that the cancer had indeed spread to my lungs and retroperitoneal lymph nodes. I needed chemotherapy treatments right away. My mother was right: this was my personal Auschwitz. I wasn't sure I was going to survive it.

Mike Bush delivered on his promise and connected me with Dr. Einhorn, who instructed me to fly to Indianapolis and bring my recent chest x-rays and CT scans. Hours later, I landed in Indianapolis and was greeted by my father at the airport. Still in denial, he said, "Alex, you look great. Are they sure that you have cancer?" Apparently, my directive that he stay positive was working.

At the IU hospital, I learned that my chemo would begin immediately and that I'd been selected for a clinical trial program involving three new drugs: VP-16, Bleomycin, and Cisplatin. In addition, I'd be assigned to multiple courses of chemotherapy. The prescribed treatment plan was daunting, but I did my best to listen to my mother's reassurance rather than the negative voices ringing in my brain.

My mother arrived a few hours later and was incredibly upbeat; her positive spirit immediately lifted my mood. She spent hours at my side because she loved me, but I suspect that she felt an extra sense of obligation since her parents couldn't help her during her own time of trial at Auschwitz. She encouraged me to stick with podiatry school and I decided that I would, fearing that if I took leave I'd never return. I studied before, during, and after my chemo sessions, taking the national board exams between my second and third rounds of chemo. If my parents could survive the most inhumane conditions imaginable, I could power through my classes while fighting cancer.

The treatments were extremely unpleasant, as was the news that my hair would soon begin to fall out. I'd had a full head of thick curly hair as a teenager and dreaded the thought of losing all my locks. Losing my hair wasn't a painful process, but it did remind me of how close I was to death.

More hurdles were to come as I started my second course of chemotherapy. While an in-patient and during a routine CT scan, I began sneezing uncontrollably and my face swelled up. Doctors rushed into the room and immediately realized that I was having an anaphylactic reaction to the dye.

"Give him some epinephrine!" they ordered the nurses.

I'd had an allergic reaction and was fine upon receiving some adrenaline. I returned to my room and was greeted by my parents. My mother's zeal hadn't entirely rubbed off on my father, but he grinned at me nonetheless.

With each passing day, I lost more hair and hated looking at myself in the mirror, so much so that I covered it with tape. I was fitted for a wig and was told by friends that I bore a resemblance to either Ted Koppel or singer Bobby Goldsboro. I would have preferred Tom Cruise.

Back in Chicago, I was walking near the Water Tower when a throng of pedestrians began chuckling at me. I just assumed that I'd slept well and looked particularly chipper. My friend John greeted me a few minutes later and burst out laughing.

"You might want to check out your rug in the bathroom!" he chuckled. In my haste to get out the door, I had applied the wig as if it were a beret, leaving half my head uncovered. This explained all the giggles on Michigan Avenue.

These moments of levity were few and far between. Back in Indianapolis, I began my third round of chemotherapy. In their own attempt to lift my "spirits," friends from Butler University snuck a keg of beer into my hospital room. (There was a reason our group was referred to as "The Zoo.") My final round of chemotherapy went well, and I felt privileged to have been part of the experimental trial. Still sporting the wig, I began my third year of podiatry school.

I was eager to start but also cognizant of an especially important CT scan on the horizon. If the scan still revealed cancer in my lymph nodes, I'd need an additional surgery, which would likely make me infertile.

Back in Terre Haute with my parents, I received a phone call informing me that the lymph nodes were void of any cancer. We were jubilant, and I immediately thought back to that awful day in June 1987 when I learned that I had cancer. My mother was right—I was going to beat this.

My elation quickly evaporated, however, upon receiving the results of my national boards exam. I'd passed all sections except for Gross Anatomy, the one section I'd failed to study for, and couldn't believe it. I was at the goal line of beating cancer, but my test scores looked likely to impede my chances for a desirable residency.

By Halloween of 1987, my hair had grown back to a suitable length, and I could finally see a light at the end of the tunnel. When a friend asked to borrow the wig for a Halloween costume, I happily obliged. I hoped I'd never have to wear it again. More scans, chest rays, and blood tests were still to come, but I began to put cancer in the rear-view mirror—and even removed the tape from my own mirrors. I also reframed the entire experience. Overcoming cancer was now a source of strength for me and would pay dividends for the rest of my life.

By February 1988, much like my parents after their liberation and resettlement, I began to think once more about companionship. I'd finally met someone in Chicago and planned a date for the two of us to attend the Bulls-Pacers game. Back when I was growing up in Terre Haute, I'd enjoyed a stint as a ball boy for the Pacers. As fate would have it, I was working an exhibition game between the Pacers and Milwaukee Bucks when Ernie Grunfeld, the only NBA player ever whose parents survived the Holocaust, played in one of his first games in the NBA.

It was still early in the relationship, and I wasn't prepared to disclose my bout with cancer to my date. My friend David Craig, the trainer for the Pacers, scored us great seats, so I was looking forward to a fun, carefree evening rooting on my home state team. Unfortunately, the Bulls, with a young Michael Jordan and a rookie named Scottie Pippen, defeated the Pacers but we had a great time nonetheless.

After the game, David invited us back to the team hotel where we ran into Pacer players Stuart Gray and Greg Dreiling. Greg had visited me while I was hospitalized in Indianapolis.

"I hope things are going well with your cancer," he offered. His intention was good, but my date was suddenly full of questions and the evening spiraled downhill from there. It was my first realization that there is a stigma with having cancer, even after you've beaten it. I never saw her again and will never know if my cancer scared her away.

The stigma spread into my professional life as well. Having retaken and finally passed the Gross Anatomy section of the boards, I began interviewing for residencies. During an interview in South Bend, Indiana, the podiatrist in charge of the search said to me, "You are near the top of your class, but I see that you failed Gross Anatomy the first time. What the heck happened there?"

I explained that the chemo treatments had impacted my preparation, and he responded in an angry tone, "So, you are kind of a liability. We could select you and you could die during your residency."

Biting my tongue, I said, "Sir, I have been told that I am in the 90th percentile for a cure. All of my tests are looking good."

Over the next decade, I had no more health concerns and enjoyed my career in podiatry. A teammate of mine at the Maccabiah Games referred me to a position in Denver, and I moved there in 1996. While working in Colorado, I developed a winter cold and cough that persisted for more than a week and decided to get checked out.

Since my battle with cancer, I'd had pulmonary fibrosis (scar tissue) on a lobe of my lungs. While I knew this, my provider didn't and said, "I know that you had cancer. Your chest x-rays show something, and the radiologist thinks you may have cancer again." I attempted to explain the pulmonary fibrosis condition, but he was ardent in his opinion. My second scan showed no change from the previous one, and I sent the scans to Dr. Einhorn back in Indianapolis. To my relief and elation, he informed me that this was the same scar tissue as before and after a brief scare, I was fine. For the past thirty-seven years, I've had a clean bill of health and am fortunate that I've been "liberated" from cancer, my "own Auschwitz."

From the time that I was a child, both of my parents emphasized that hard work, determination, and perseverance were qualities that would endure. Thus, when I had to battle cancer at the age of twenty-six, I knew that I was being tested. I had to overcome this adversity, and defeating cancer has made me a stronger person. Now, nearly four decades later, I know that I am one of the lucky ones. When I encounter difficult situations, I always remind myself that I am, indeed, a survivor. This inner strength is my legacy.

Yet, inner strength and tears often go hand-in-hand. We all cry. Sometimes it wells up in us and comes out when we least expect it. Other times, we know it's there, and we can choose to let it out or hold it back for another time. Yet, we all cry. We have to. I learned this too from my mother. During an interview in the early 2000s, she spoke about my cancer fight and her experience in supporting me.

"I wanted my son to see me being very positive," she said. "So, every time I saw my son in the hospital, I smiled a lot and tried to cheer him on. But I cried all the way to the hospital and all of the way back. I could not let him see me that way. I was scared too, but he was not going to know."

Several decades ago, I was invited to attend a meeting for second generation descendants of Holocaust survivors. During the panel discussion, each participant was asked to share their experiences as the child of Holocaust survivors. To my astonishment, each panelist admitted that they had, at one time, entertained suicidal thoughts. When my turn came, I underscored that my life circumstances had only been positive and referenced my cancer diagnosis as an example. Every day my parents fought their own demons, and their example of resilience inspired me to conquer cancer. My parents' past has never been a burden; it was, and still remains, a blessing.

CHAPTER

For Herself

> "I'm free inside and out. I am healed."
>
> —Eva

G eorge H. W. Bush had seen a lot, but even he was aghast at the scene unfolding in front of him in the Capitol Rotunda. Attending the 1986 Holocaust Remembrance Day ceremony, Bush, along with a stunned audience, gasped as three police officers struggled to drag my mother off the premises.

As Elie Wiesel, a Romanian survivor of Auschwitz, addressed the crowd, my mother hoisted a sign reading, "MENGELE TWINS SUPPORT HOUSE OF REPRESENTATIVES BILL 255."

The bill sought reparations for the victims of Mengele's experiments, compensation long overdue in her opinion. Her outrage at what she believed to be complete apathy for the plight of the Mengele twins had boiled over and was on full display on that May afternoon. Working his very first assignment, Capitol policeman David Wells raced over and demanded to see her permit.

Flashing her Auschwitz number tattoo, my mother exploded, "Here's my permit!" As Wells and his fellow officers forcibly escorted her out of the building, she screamed bloody murder. The incident made headlines nationwide, but more importantly it represented a turning point in my mother's long journey to forgiveness.

Following her 1978 interview on a local television affiliate after the airing of the NBC miniseries *Holocaust,* my mother began to lecture more. Thanks in no small part to the soap opera *As the World Turns,* she grew more self-assured in her English and had more time on her hands after I'd enrolled at Butler University in the fall of 1979. Developing a commanding stage presence, she crafted a lecture that amalgamated her experiences at Auschwitz with motivation and humor. To lighten the mood, she'd conclude her speeches with, "Congratulations, you *survived* my lecture!" She had a gift for building an emotional connection with her audience, and her talks often moved people to tears.

I was proud of her for having the courage to address her past, but began to notice a disturbing trend. The more she lectured, the angrier and more frustrated she became. At national and international Holocaust survivor gatherings, she grew infuriated when denied the opportunity to speak, often snubbed in favor of historians who weren't survivors themselves. When she sought to integrate details of Mengele's research into her lectures, the scarcity of historical evidence enraged her. She had only her memory to rely on when it came to laying bare the atrocities of Mengele's experiments. If she could track down other Mengele twins, their shared memories could contribute to a historical record, but she hadn't the faintest idea of where to look. She penned hundreds of letters to newspaper editors, urging them to publish an appeal for other Mengele survivors to contact her. Not wanting to leave a stone unturned, she even reached out to celebrities like Carol Burnett to help promote her cause. Despite her doggedness, my mother's efforts were met with scant response.

Though the last Halloween prank in Terre Haute had occurred years ago, she still seethed over it. If only people knew more about her history, she reasoned, they'd understand and let her and my family be:

Those tricks reminded me of the days when the Nazis harassed us in Portz, days when I was helpless and could not defend myself. But this time I lived in this great country of the USA where I did not have to put up with it.... I thought if I could tell my story of what happened to me as a child, the kids would understand and leave me alone to live in peace in my home. But as a victim of such atrocities, I did not know how to accomplish this. [78]

Growing up, I sensed that my mother was completely overwhelmed. An ocean away from Miriam, she served as the primary caretaker for two young children and remained engaged in an incessant battle with her own inner demons. Her transition to Terre Haute wasn't easy and she once remarked that the only commonality between Terre Haute and Tel Aviv was that both started with the letter "T."

She later admitted, "I had a difficult time in the United States. I was a sergeant major in the Israeli Army and became a sergeant major in diaper changing." [79] She eventually sought out a therapist but didn't initially make known her Holocaust past.

After several sessions, she finally divulged her childhood, leaving her dumbfounded therapist to exclaim, "What? Oh my gosh, you're doing great! You will be fine. For you to have a family, a good job, and ambition—you do not need to see a therapist!" And so, she never saw one again.

My mother had also developed an unhealthy obsession with tracking down Mengele. Following the liberation of Auschwitz, he evaded capture until being taken as a prisoner of war by American troops in June 1945. Though he used his own name, Mengele, who did not have an SS tattoo, benefitted from a muddled list of most-wanted Nazis. He was overlooked and released. Under the alias "Fritz Hollmann," he found work on a farm near Rosenheim, Germany. Fearing immediate execution if captured, he fled Germany with the aid of his family and SS officers in April 1949 and sailed to Argentina. In June 1960, Mengele was indicted in Germany on suspicion of murder and attempted murder, and German authorities unsuccessfully tried to extradite him from Argentina. He'd already fled to Paraguay by this point and in late 1960, using the name "Peter Hochbichler," he relocated to Brazil. Mengele hadn't been seen since but remained a permanent fixture in my mother's head.

"I do not want him executed," she told *The New York Times*, "He should be put in isolation to listen to the screams of his victims for the rest of his life."[80]

In 1984, my mother met a fellow Mengele twin named Marc Berkowitz at a reunion of survivors in Philadelphia. He knew of other Mengele twins living in New York, and the two developed a plan to generate more publicity for the victims. Formally naming their new program CANDLES (Children of Auschwitz Nazi Deadly Lab Experiments Survivors), they aspired to create a database of living Mengele twins. My mother named herself president and appointed Miriam vice president. A formal title would command respect in her opinion, and she'd no longer have to take a backseat to anyone. It'd been nearly forty years since she'd been liberated, but her need to control her own destiny was as fervent as ever.

Over the next few months, my mother, Miriam, my uncle Shlomo, and Berkowitz collaborated on an effort to track down Mengele twins. Shlomo, a newspaper executive in Tel Aviv, put out an ad asking for others to come forward, and the result yielded more than fifty sets of twins. In all, 122 Mengele twins were located, scattered across the globe in places like Israel, Australia, Austria, Canada, and the United States. In early 1985, more than fifty Mengele twins, many experiencing significant health issues, participated in "J'Accuse," a mock trial and the first international conference of Auschwitz twin survivors, in Jerusalem. CANDLES hoped the trial, held at Yad Vashem, the World Holocaust Remembrance Center, would spark more awareness and aid them in locating both Mengele and his research records. They'd soon get their wish, but not in the manner desired.

On May 31, 1985, West German police, acting on a tip, raided the home of Hans Sedlmeier, a lifelong friend of Mengele, in Gunzburg, West Germany. Inside, they uncovered a coded address book and correspondence between Sedlmeier and Mengele. One of the letters, written by Wolfram Bossert of São Paulo, Brazil, had notified Sedlmeier of Mengele's death. West German officials contacted São Paulo authorities, who in turn were able to locate Bossert; he led them to a grave at the Our Lady of the Rosary cemetery in Embu, Brazil. On June 6, 1985, authorities exhumed a corpse from a grave marked "Wolfgang Gerhard." After analyzing handwriting samples, uncovering evidence of injuries consistent with Mengele's medical history, and employing a technique called skull-face superimposition, a team of six forensic scientists announced "within a reasonable scientific certainty" the corpse to be that of Mengele. [81] Four days later, his son Rolf expressed "no doubt" that the body was that of his father. According to Rolf, his father had drowned in 1979 and he'd kept silent for six years "out of consideration" for those victimized by his father.

Skepticism abounded, and several experts felt that there wasn't sufficient evidence to make a positive identification. Brazilian Federal Police Chief Romeu Tuma announced, "This confirms testimony we have obtained in Brazil, but it does not impede or suspend our investigations, which will continue on all fronts." [82] Famed Nazi hunter Simon Wiesenthal was most dubious of the findings and contended, "It's not a matter of believing. It's a matter of closing a case or not closing a case. A man who was silent six years after the death of his father cannot be enough. We need the confirmation through the forensic medicine expertise." [83] Back in Israel, Gideon Hausner, the prosecutor who'd convicted Nazi war criminal Adolf Eichmann, said, "This is just a very elegant way to move away from public interest in a matter which is not too pleasant for [the family]." [84]

My mother, along with other Mengele twins, couldn't believe the news. As a child, Mengele had suffered from hematogenous osteomyelitis, an infection of the bone marrow, in his femur, but the examination revealed no such evidence. Fingerprint samples and comparable teeth x-rays were unavailable for analysis, which compounded the suspicion. When asked to provide blood samples, Rolf and Irene Hackenjos (Mengele's first wife) refused to cooperate.

Just when the world press was picking up on Mengele's diabolical past, he'd been conveniently found dead. Refusing to accept the verdict, my mother, who referred to the bones as "phony baloney," took out a second mortgage on our home to finance an inquest of the findings. She announced her investigation at Terre Haute's 9,000-seat Hulman Center, though few people attended.

With her funding, a panel of experts in law, forensics, and history convened in Terre Haute for a three-day hearing billed as the "CANDLES Inquest: The Truth About Mengele." Several Mengele twins who were unable to attend the mock trial in Jerusalem were also given an opportunity to testify. At the probe's conclusion, the panel issued a statement denouncing the conclusions from Embu and called on the German government to address the issue of compensation for Mengele's victims. "Today they suffer a series of medical problems," the report read, "including but not limited to kidney ailments, cardiac difficulties, degenerating spines and recurring infections, among other chronic conditions." [85] My mother mailed the report to every member of Congress, requesting that an open hearing be held. She received two letters in return.

The press too paid little attention; their indifference only further incensed my mother, as did a statement by Rabbi Marvin Hier, Dean of the Wiesenthal Center. "I find it difficult to accept what CANDLES is saying…(but) maybe they are entitled to that hope. They live with these dreams. Mengele is alive in them. The Mengele who appears every night in their dreams, he has become a living person even if the scientists tell us he's dead." [86]

Determined to uncover the truth, my mother traveled to Israel in 1987 to meet with Israeli officials. There, she met Lieutenant Colonel Menachem Russek, the head of the national police department's Nazi crimes unit. A fellow Auschwitz survivor, Russek was present in São Paulo when Mengele's supposed remains were excavated and shared my mother's incertitude. Russek expressed his doubts to the Israeli government in a report that was chock-full of questions about the examination. Despite my mother's dogged pursuit to read his conclusion, the report remained classified.

It took four years, but in 1991 she obtained a leaked copy of Russek's report. The document outlined numerous inconsistencies in the autopsy along with Russek's allegations of a cover-up. Russek questioned the many discrepancies

My mother and Miriam protest outside the Mengele family factory in Günzburg, Germany. COURTESY ALEX KOR

between Mengele's Nazi file and the coroner's report. For instance, the Embu man's right leg was 1.5 centimeters longer than his left. More than likely, this individual would have walked with a limp, but Mengele was never observed to have had difficulty walking. Russek also intimated that the Bossert family had covered up key facts in the case.

A press conference was held in Tel Aviv in May 1991 and my mother released Russek's report to the Israeli media. Russek, who'd retired the previous year, attended the briefing but offered no comments. Three months later, my mother and three other twins staged a protest at the Mengele family factory in Gunzburg. They circled the plant for hours with posters that read, "We had to give lots of blood in Auschwitz. We demand that Rolf give one drop of blood for a DNA test and the truth!"[87] She'd lobbied the international media to cover the demonstration, but only a freelance crew from CNN showed up.

In the years that followed, both the United States and German governments attempted to use DNA to verify the identity of the remains. DNA testing was still in its infancy and scientists from both countries were unsuccessful in withdrawing DNA from the bones. In 1990, Dr. Alec Jeffreys and Dr. Erika

Hagelberg, two British scientists, were able to extract trace amounts of DNA from a section of the femur and humerus and placed the samples in storage. The sample was a major breakthrough, but there remained nothing to compare it to.

For years, Rolf Mengele refused to provide a DNA sample, but when a German prosecutor threatened to dig up the graves of other Mengele family members in 1991, Rolf and Irene Hackenjos finally relented. In February 1992, Jeffreys compared Rolf's sample to that of the Embu man and concluded "beyond reasonable doubt" that the two were father and son. [88]

The findings were sufficient for the Israeli government who closed the case, and the German and United States governments soon followed suit. The US Department of Justice released a 197-page report, asserting that the remains found in Embu were indeed that of Josef Mengele.

My mother was crushed. She returned to Terre Haute and resumed her real estate career but remained indignant about the Mengele autopsy. That the final report had curiously not been released until seven years after the discovery of the body only added to her disgust.

The incident at the Capitol occurred one year after Brazilian authorities exhumed the body from the grave in Embu. In many ways, it was the culmination of a storm that had raged inside her for decades. She was angry at the Nazis for stealing her childhood and her parents. She was angry at her parents for not protecting her and her siblings from the Nazis. She was angry at Mengele for all the physical and psychological damage he'd inflicted on her and Miriam. She was angry that she still had to deal with antisemitism in her own backyard. She was angry at the dubious results in the identification of Mengele's body and the fact that few seemed to care. In short, she was angry at the world.

After her eviction from the Capitol grounds, Officer Wells led my mother back to his command post and tried in vain to calm her down. Fearing that he was going to kill her, she fought to regain control of her emotions. Though not Jewish, Wells wore a Star of David that had been gifted to him as a young child. He pulled it out for her to see, and she finally began to relax. Years later, Wells speculated that my mother had experienced a flashback during Wiesel's speech that had triggered her fury.

She immediately flew back to Indiana, both paranoid and dejected. Before getting in her car at the airport, she inspected it to see if a bomb had been planted. After the Capitol story made national news, she expected to receive calls asking for her side of the story, but none came. Numerous articles portrayed her as a crazed Holocaust survivor while others condemned her behavior. Despondent, she called me upon reaching Terre Haute.

"Alex," she cried, "I can't believe that in the 'land of the free and the home of the brave' that I would be treated this way." I was embarrassed by the incident, but simultaneously genuinely concerned about her well-being. My father disdained confrontation and, often working double shifts, wasn't there to help, while my sister was finishing up school at Purdue. As my mother's sole sounding board, I suggested she give up on the idea of helping the Mengele twins.

"Mom," I suggested, "maybe it's time to close the Mengele chapter and just focus on real estate." She'd recently turned fifty-two and was facing a most daunting midlife crisis.

On top of my mother's personal struggles, her loved ones faced their own trials. My cancer diagnosis came the following year. As my mother helped me to navigate this crisis, Miriam was diagnosed with kidney failure and given two options: start dialysis in Israel or have a kidney transplant. My mother had always been there for Miriam and this time would be no different.

"I have two kidneys and only one sister," she pointed out before flying to Israel.

Tests confirmed her to be an exact match for Miriam, and surgery was scheduled for a few days later. After removing Miriam's kidney, doctors discovered that it had not developed beyond the age of a ten-year-old—her exact age while at Auschwitz. Though never confirmed, the abnormality was most likely the result of Mengele's invasive tests. A successful transplant took place the following day, and my mother and Miriam were released a few weeks later.

Just when she perceived that life was returning to some level of normalcy, Miriam was diagnosed with urinary bladder cancer. Since the transplant, she'd experienced urinary tract polyps and a recent test revealed a cancerous tumor. Given the advanced stage of the cancer, which had metastasized to her lungs, Israel's national health system wouldn't cover any curative measures, leaving palliative care as her only option. Dr. Larry Einhorn, the Indiana University oncologist who'd treated me, had recently asked my mother to lecture at the IU Medical Center. She called Dr. Einhorn and inquired if he'd be willing to treat Miriam. Though Miriam didn't have adequate insurance, he agreed to see her and never charged the family for his services.

By the time she arrived in the United States, Miriam's cancer had spread and she was in dire condition. Dr. Einhorn informed us that they'd try chemotherapy but was candid that her prognosis was grim. As she'd done with me, my mother visited Miriam daily and gave her overwhelming support during the grueling chemo treatments. After four weeks of chemo, Miriam's lung fields were clear and we temporarily rejoiced, still knowing she was in for an arduous battle. Miriam returned to Israel and her chemo continued for the next six months.

In April 1993, I traveled to Israel and stayed with Miriam. Her treatments had concluded, and she'd resumed work as a nurse.

One morning at breakfast, she bellowed, "Alex, I had a nightmare last night. My cancer is back!"

I reassured her that this was unlikely, though she didn't seem her upbeat self. The conversation would be one of our last. On June 6, my mother received a voicemail from Miriam's husband Kuti notifying her of her sister's death and that the funeral would be held immediately. Devastated, she called and begged her brother-in-law to delay the services. She'd lost her parents and siblings and had never been able to say a proper goodbye.

"I have never buried a family member, *please*!!" she cried out. Her plea went unheard, and the funeral was held a few hours later. For months, my mother grieved the loss of her twin and her nightmares returned. Drowning in despair, she confided, "Alex, not only did I lose my sister, my best friend on the whole earth, but my kidney went with her as well."

I'm not sure how my mother persevered during this period. She'd been ridiculed and arrested. She and my father were financially strapped after their investment in the Mengele investigation. And now, she'd lost her closest companion. Having invested so much energy in supporting Miriam and me in our cancer battles, she was emotionally spent. She'd hit rock bottom.

Amid her personal struggles, my mother constantly emboldened those around her to turn a negative into a positive and in the fall of 1993, just a few months after Miriam's passing, she was given an opportunity to practice what she preached. Dr. John Michalczyk, a physician from Boston University with a concentration in medical ethics, invited her to attend an upcoming ethics conference. He asked if she'd be interested in speaking and added a peculiar request: would she bring a Nazi physician with her?

"Where do you think I can find one of the guys," my mother sarcastically replied, "the last time I looked they were not advertising in the yellow pages!"

She was intrigued with the invitation but unsure how to proceed. Could she turn this into a positive? If she could track down a Nazi doctor, perhaps he could divulge more information about Mengele's experiments and help other twins avoid Miriam's fate. With little to go on, she remembered that she and Miriam had been co-consultants for a documentary for the German television network ZDF. A Nazi doctor had also been interviewed for the film.

On December 22, 1947, a Polish court sentenced 40 of 41 Nazi defendants to death for their war crimes. Dr. Hans Münch was the one man spared. Münch was recruited by the Nazis as a scientist and deployed at the Hygiene Institute of the Waffen-SS, a laboratory for hygienic and bacteriological work, located just a short distance from Auschwitz. He inspected the camps, conducted bacteriological research in Mengele's labs, and ultimately left a complex legacy. At his trial in 1947, nineteen former inmates testified to his innocence. The court's ruling was made, "not only because he did not commit any crime of harm against the camp prisoners, but because he had a benevolent attitude toward them and helped them, while he had to carry the responsibility." Many contend that he refused to partake in the selection process and mass executions, earning him the nickname, "The Good Man of Auschwitz." It is well-documented that Münch made up fictitious experiments to fool his superiors and keep his subjects, many who were Jewish doctors, alive. According to author Robert Jay Lifton, Münch "was the only physician whose commitment to the Hippocratic oath proved stronger than that to the SS."[89]

Others, however, paint Münch in a darker light. Imre Gonczy, an Auschwitz prisoner, claimed that Münch did indeed take part in the selection process and even accused Münch of using the flesh from dead bodies to cook a broth used as a medium for his microbes. In a 1998 interview with *Der Spiegel*, Münch defended his work at Auschwitz, remarking, "I could make experiments with human beings, otherwise only possible with rabbits. This was very important scientific work."[90] His son Dirk later asserted that his father, soon to be diagnosed with dementia, was not of clear mind when he gave the interview. The French government charged him with war crimes but withdrew them, ruling that his mental state made him unfit for trial.

As fate would have it, Münch was the doctor who had been interviewed for the ZDF documentary. My mother contacted ZDF by fax and requested, in Miriam's memory, if they'd share Münch's contact information. The information arrived shortly thereafter, but she was perplexed as to how to proceed. Susanne Severeid, whom my mother had met a year before, and her husband

My mother interviewing Hans Münch at his Bavarian Home in 1994.
COURTESY SUSANNE SEVEREID

Tony Van Runtergran, who'd been in the Dutch underground during World War II, had a vast international network and had previously tried to track down Mengele's whereabouts. With Susanne as the intermediary, my mother learned a few days later that Münch had consented to an interview with one caveat: he would not go to Boston. My mother had to come to him.

In October 1993, my mother, accompanied by Susanne, Tony, and a Dutch TV crew, flew to Germany for the interview. Once on the ground, her apprehension grew as the crew approached Münch's Bavarian home. Her last experiences with Nazi doctors hadn't been pleasant ones.

"How would I feel if he treated me like a nothing—the way I was treated in Auschwitz?" she pondered. Reminding herself that she was doing this in Miriam's memory and to help the living Mengele twins, she mustered the courage to approach the house. Münch greeted the party with a smile and escorted them to his porch. As she sat down, my mother's back flared up and Münch, sensing her discomfort, offered her pillows to ease her pain. "I've never experienced a Nazi doctor who made me feel better," she said to Münch.

She began grilling Münch, now eighty-two years old, on what he knew about the Mengele experiments.

"Maybe if we know what was injected, we can save the lives of other twins and help them avoid the fate of my sister," she pleaded. With a look of resignation, he replied that Mengele concealed everything from the other physicians and that only Mengele himself could answer her question. His response was met with a look of grave disappointment.

She also inquired as to how Münch's conscience allowed him to take part in the inner workings of Auschwitz.

"As a human being there, how did you live your life?" she asked. "When work was done how did you cope?"

Münch disclosed that many of the Nazis at Auschwitz got drunk every night in order to numb themselves from their involvement in the mass executions. Münch claimed that neither he nor Mengele drank, and that Mengele justified his experiments, rationalizing, "They would have been murdered anyway—I will at least keep them alive for a while." [91]

As they continued their conversation, Münch admitted that he suffered from nightmares.

"What do you mean?" my mother uttered. "I thought we were the only ones with nightmares. Why do you have nightmares?"

Münch insisted that his role at the Hygiene Institute had precluded him from making selections on the platform. Maintaining that he'd had Jewish friends as a youth, he recounted that he'd even saved a former acquaintance from being gassed. His night terrors, according to Münch, were the result of his assignment at the gas chambers. Periodically required to stand outside the chambers, Münch was responsible for ensuring that the Zyklon B gas was effective. Peering through the peephole, he'd wait until all the bodies were lifeless before signing one death certificate for all.

"It's my problem," professed Munch. "This is the nightmare I live with." [92]

She sat in stunned silence as Münch disclosed all the grotesque details of the gas chamber operation. She then exhorted, "Dr. Münch, the world needs to know what you just told me! For all the revisionists that say there was no Holocaust and no Auschwitz and 6 million is an exaggeration, you need to tell the world!" The 50th anniversary of the liberation of Auschwitz was to take place on January 27, 1995. Would he accompany her and other Mengele twins to Auschwitz and tell the world what he'd just conceded?

Without hesitation, Münch agreed.

Upon returning from Germany, my mother called, and I inquired how the trip went.

"We had a great meeting!" she exclaimed of her time with Münch. "Unfortunately, he knew nothing about Mengele's experiments, but he and his family are joining us for the 50th anniversary to document the existence of Auschwitz and the Holocaust." In disbelief, I interrupted her and warned her that this was a terrible idea.

"You should not do this!" I protested. "The Mengele twins in Israel will not approve!"

"He is doing the world a favor with this gesture," she countered. I knew

My mother, joined by Münch, declaring her forgiveness at Auschwitz in 1995.
COURTESY INDIANA HISTORICAL SOCIETY

her decision would be met with great disapproval, and I was concerned that Miriam wouldn't be there to shield her from the condemnation from other survivors. My advice fell upon deaf ears.

I was unaware of the plans for the 50th anniversary but knew Münch would likely be criticized by the neo-Nazi community for taking part in the ceremony. My mother understood this as well and felt obligated to find him a gift as a token of appreciation for his commitment.

"What do you buy a former Nazi physician?" she thought. Her first stop was at a Terre Haute liquor store, but she didn't purchase anything. She next tried a local Hallmark boutique, but in her words, "couldn't find a card appropriate for a Nazi." When the clerk asked if they could help, she left the store in embarrassment.

After a year of introspection, she finally had an epiphany: she would write, in her name only, a letter forgiving Münch for being a Nazi. From her perspective, this was the highest honor she could bestow upon him and surely, she thought, he'd appreciate the gesture. In doing so, she had no idea what the act would do for her. "Then the idea of a forgiveness letter came to my mind," she later recalled. "I knew it would be a meaningful gift, but it became a gift to myself as well, because I realized I was not a hopeless, powerless victim."

My mother struggled for four months to compose the letter, later commenting, "I had to work through a lot of my pain—I had to mean it." Concerned about her spelling and grammar, she tasked Dr. Susan Kaufman, her former professor, to help write the letter.

"The letter is very good," said Dr. Kaufman, "but you should really think about forgiving Dr. Mengele. He is your problem."

My mother emphatically refused. "No, I just want to forgive Dr. Münch. I'm not ready to forgive Mengele."

Armed with her declaration of amnesty, she and a few Mengele twins met Dr. Münch and his family at Auschwitz on a snowy day on January 27, 1995. At the ruins of one of the gas chambers, he repented and read a statement admitting his role in the gas chamber operation. My mother then declared her forgiveness, in her name only, to Münch, making clear that her pardon was not conditional. Her declaration granted amnesty to all Nazis who participated directly or indirectly in the Holocaust and "to all governments who protected Nazi criminals for fifty years, then covered up their acts, and covered up their cover up." Her critics later contended that she'd made a previous arrangement granting Münch clemency only in exchange for his admissions of guilt. This is unequivocally false.

Following the ceremony, my mother and Münch walked arm-in-arm through the camp grounds. Fifty years earlier, they'd strolled this same site separately, one as a ten-year-old captive and the other as a Nazi. A few hours later, the CANDLES group held a ceremony in one of the gas chambers and lit a candle for loved ones who'd perished at the camp. Not wanting Münch to feel uncomfortable (the height of irony), my mother didn't offer him a candle.

Toward the end of the ceremony, Münch asked, "Where is my candle?" My mother handed him one and as onlookers sobbed, he followed suit and dedicated a candle as well.

A press conference followed, and reporters interviewed both my mother and Münch.

She declared, "I no longer have this weight on my shoulders. I'm free inside and out. I am healed.... Forgive your worst enemy. It will heal your soul and set you free." She added, "I am healed inside; therefore it gives me no joy to see any Nazi criminal in jail, nor do I want to see any harm come to Josef Mengele, the Mengele family or their business corporations. I urge all former Nazis to come forward and testify to the crimes they have committed without any fear of further prosecution. Here in Auschwitz, I hope in some small way to send the world a message of forgiveness, a message of peace, a message of hope, a message of understanding."

In an interview years later, she reflected on her emotions that day. "I immediately felt very free, emotionally liberated by the idea that even I have power over Joseph Mengele, and he cannot do a single thing to change that." For the rest of her life, she kept Münch's written account of the Holocaust in her purse, never hesitating to pull it out when encountering a Holocaust denier.

Fifty years had passed since her release, but as my mother exited the Auschwitz grounds, she was liberated once more, this time from the anger and resentment that had crippled her for so many years. Forgiveness had set her free.

CHAPTER

It's Not the Critic Who Counts

"I decide when I forgive."

—Eva

In the months following her declaration, I observed a noticeable change in my mother. She laughed more and, for the first time in years, appeared to enjoy life. Her witty sense of humor returned on occasion and her anger seemed to dissipate. Her healing process entailed making amends to others she'd felt wronged by, including her family.

"When I forgave the Nazis I forgave my parents, too," she later wrote. "I forgave them for things they didn't do. My father wanted to emigrate to Palestine in 1935 with my uncle Aaron. They spent a month there to see if they could find a way to make a living. My mother had four little girls under five. She refused to go, so we remained. I had to forgive my mother for not going."[93]

In addition to the letter she composed to Münch, years later my mother wrote a letter of forgiveness to her father as well. Alexander's lament that she was born a girl had wounded her for many years, but she granted him forgiveness and exonerated him for not demanding that the family exit Romania prior to their capture. She even credited him with cultivating her strong will, imperative in her survival at Auschwitz.

She was a new person, though Dr. Kaufman's suggestion about forgiving Mengele lingered. She eventually found the strength to not only forgive Mengele, but to exonerate all the Nazis.

"At first I was adamant that I could never forgive Dr. Mengele," she acknowledged, "but then I realized I had the power now…the power to forgive. It was my right to use it. No one could take it away." [94] When later interrogated as to why she adopted her stance, my mother offered a simple answer that subtly paid tribute to both Miriam and me. "Forgiveness is as personal as chemotherapy," she declared, "I do it for myself." [95]

Prior to 1995, my mother's lectures centered around the theme of "never giving up." She'd awe audiences with her moving tale of survival and encourage them to overcome their own hurdles. Her delivery was stoic, yet effective. With her burden lifted, she gradually began incorporating forgiveness into her talks. Often crying, she chronicled her path to forgiveness: from her initial encounter with Dr. Münch to her public declaration in 1995. Her story was already remarkable, but adding a chapter on forgiving the Nazis made it even more enthralling. The inclusion of forgiveness also made her story more relatable. Few could fathom what life was like at Auschwitz, but everyone had a person in their lives whom they were struggling to forgive.

Her newly crafted lecture was also a more personal narrative. Millions had been held captive at concentration camps, but she was the first concentration camp survivor, to my knowledge, who'd publicly forgiven the Nazis. Her embracement of forgiveness transformed her disposition, which in turn amplified her talks. She no longer had that chip, more akin to a log, on her shoulder and stopped viewing herself as a Mengele victim. In full control of her emotions, she now spoke freely about her experiences and how forgiveness had empowered her.

During my high school years, I was often apprehensive that she'd embarrass herself when lecturing, but things changed in the 1990s. Now a practicing podiatrist in Evansville, Indiana, I rarely accompanied her when she lectured outside of Terre Haute and hadn't heard her speak in years. In the mid-1990s, she was invited to present at a middle school in Indianapolis and asked if I'd give her a ride. I thought it'd be a routine trip, yet the experience completely altered my viewpoint. We arrived at the school auditorium to find 300 seemingly uninterested eighth graders who were talking amongst themselves. They barely noticed my mother's entrance and I feared they'd have even less interest in her words. Once again, I thought she'd humiliate herself, and I counted the minutes until we'd be back on the road.

As soon as she took the stage, you could hear a pin drop. Commanding the attention of the room, she remained in complete control of her emotions. Her thick accent was no longer an issue and there was no crying. I was flabbergasted. Speaking in the first person, she described her life's journey, emphasizing both perseverance and forgiveness. Tears began to flow, but this time, they were mine. My shame morphed into immense pride as she mesmerized the crowd. Hopping into the car, my mother asked me to assess her performance.

Weeping, I proudly proclaimed, "You were amazing!"

As word got out on her forgiveness, people began flocking to her for advice.

"I know that you forgave the Nazis, but how did you really do this? I need to forgive someone who hurt me," they'd press. She'd look the individual in the eye and prescribe her preferred methodology:

The first thing you need to do is find a private room and grab a paper and pen. Pretend that the person that you want to forgive is in the room sitting across from you. Start thinking and writing. When I did this the first time with Mengele, I had to get a dictionary to look up curse words. I wrote, "Dr. Mengele, you no-good, despicable human being who treated me and millions of others like a piece of dirt...." I tried to write every curse word and awful words directed at him. At the end, I wrote, "Despite all these terrible things, I have chosen to forgive you. I am forgiving you not because you deserve to be forgiven, but because I deserve to live the rest of my life free of the pain that you caused me." When you are done, you do not need to keep that letter! Never, ever give that letter to the person who you are forgiving. It is for you and not that person. Forgive your worst enemy and it will set you free!

Her message touched people of all ages. She counseled teenagers who were contemplating suicide and older people who'd held decades-long grudges. Those who felt wronged by their parents, spouses, and bosses came to her for advice. She even counseled a former White supremacist. Thomas Adams, who was originally born in Germany, had relatives who'd served in the SS; as a youth he had adopted Nazi beliefs, even going so far as to have swastikas tattooed on his back. Later in life, he'd become a Christian and was still in the process of forgiving himself for his past. Thomas approached my mother before her lecture in Billings, Montana.

Commenting to the *Billings Gazette*, Adams remarked, "She never met me before, but I know she loved me. She just has a presence about her." [96] In each case, she had an uncanny ability to listen intently and, with a dose of tough love, offer a roadmap to forgiveness.

Her credibility bolstered the message. Many of those seeking advice grasped that if she could forgive Mengele and the Nazis, they could surely find a way to make amends to a family member, friend, or coworker. Two anonymous testimonials offer a glimpse into the impact she had on others:

But perhaps even more important to me is Eva Kor's message of "Forgiveness"—I remember hearing her say so many times that in order for her to heal she had to forgive the people that did those awful things to her. Unfortunately, I am not there yet…but I am trying. If Eva Mozes Kor could forgive the Nazis for what was done to her, I have to find a way to forgive myself, my family and God. —Anonymous [97]

Forgiveness is a simple word but a complicated challenge. Eva changed the paradigm for me. By forgiving, we take the power back from those who have wronged us. We take the power back for ourselves so we can move on from that burden: the grudge I held for decades against the attending physician who belittled me to the point of tears during medical school because he was "teaching"; the colleagues at work who created upheaval in my life without compassion. Forgiveness is for me, not for them. Eva showed me that I no longer have to let my bitterness weigh me down. —Anonymous [98]

She reiterated to her audiences, large and small, that her decision to forgive was in her name only and had nothing to do with religion. Her form of forgiveness appealed to people of many faiths as well to those who were agnostic or atheist. She was a nonthreatening presence and refused to judge, even though she was facing much scrutiny herself.

———————————————

My mother's stance was not universally accepted. From the moment she and Münch stood in unison at the gas chambers, opposition lined up. The Israeli Mengele twins were furious with her, and with Miriam now gone she no longer had an ally to defend her. Several Mengele twins in the United States also voiced displeasure.

In the 2006 documentary *Forgiving Dr. Mengele,* Jona Laks, a Mengele twin, and my mother engaged in a heated exchange that was caught on camera.

"How can I forgive?" Laks demanded. "I do not have the permission to forgive. My parents, who were killed by the Nazis, would not want me to forgive. I do not have the right to forgive. I am unable to smile." [99]

"Who needs to give you the right?" my mother shot back. [100] Laks wasn't buying it and the two failed to reach a resolution.

In 2001, my mother arranged a visit to the Max Planck Society in Germany where she and fellow Mengele twins received a public apology. Dr. Hubert Markl, President of the Planck Society, asked the twins if they could bring themselves to forgive the German people. A number of twins grew outraged at the question and my mother's restatement of forgiveness that morning only fueled their ire.

"I was a pariah wherever I turned," she later recalled. [101]

In public my mother reiterated that she didn't need anyone's affirmation, but privately she hoped another Mengele twin would support her. She also wondered if there was a better way to articulate her reasoning. She later sent me an email reflecting this desire:

Dear Alex:

For years, I have been thinking of a new way to talk about forgiveness so the survivors would not misunderstand me. I often call it self healing. We have chemotherapy, physical therapy, logotherapy, psychotherapy. Why not self-therapy? What do you think? I mean SELF-THERAPY through forgiveness.

Love, Mom

She tried different approaches to explain her rationale, even referencing her parents, whom she'd harbored so much resentment towards. "For most people there is a big obstacle to forgiveness because society expects revenge," she wrote. "It seems we need to honor our victims, but I always wonder if my dead loved ones would want me to live with pain and anger until the end of my life." [102] Though she could never know for certain, my mother felt confident that her parents would not have wanted her to hold on to the pain.

She also continued to draw the comparison between chemotherapy and forgiveness. "If you are diagnosed with cancer and are treated with chemotherapy, you, the patient hopefully will benefit from the chemotherapy," she'd proclaim. "Your husband or brother cannot take the chemotherapy for you. You, the patient, must take your own chemotherapy. Forgiveness is really no different. If you are tired of being mad at the world or only think about revenge, you, not your husband or brother, can forgive. You must forgive the person that hurt you. No one else can do this. If you decide to forgive and feel no more pain but want the pain back, you have that right to do this as well." [103]

My mother's definition of forgiveness, no matter how she explained it, didn't deter her critics. Some in the Jewish community condemned her, citing that forgiveness under Jewish doctrine had to be earned.

"Mengele had done nothing to earn this," they asserted.

My mother refused to back down. "Do I remain a victim for the rest of my life?" she countered. "It gives the perpetrator power and I have no power over my life. That is absurd. I decide when I forgive. Maybe this Jewish tradition should be changed. We should never wait for the perpetrator to ask for forgiveness. It is the victim's right to forgive whenever they want." [104]

Many in the survivor community pointed out that the Nazis had not atoned for their crimes and weren't deserving of forgiveness. Why should they make amends to those who had no remorse for their actions? Others knocked her for her outspokenness, depicting her as an aggrieved attention-seeker. Fellow survivors expressed anger over her ability to see humanity in the Nazis, and when she later led tours to Auschwitz, they failed to comprehend how she could possibly smile and dance at the former death camp.

Others denounced my mother's advice as being naive. In a piece entitled, "Reasons to Forgive - or Not to Forgive," Marjorie Ingall and Susan McCarthy, writers for *The Tablet* magazine, wrote, "Make no mistake, choosing to forgive can absolutely be therapeutic. Kor's strategy of writing a letter to someone who harmed you, calling them all kinds of names, and then never sending the letter could work beautifully for some people. But her insistence that it *will* work is simplistic." [105] Mengele twins who'd previously admired my mother now refused to speak to her. Even those who had profound respect for her took issue with her conviction.

Michael Berenbaum, a famed Holocaust scholar, enjoyed a lengthy friendship with my mother, but disagreed with her views. "I demand gestures, deeds, and acts of enormous significance. I disagree with cheap grace. I understand where Eva is coming from but it seems formulaic," explained Berenbaum. [106]

I was living in Washington, DC, at the time of her declaration and was a member of The Generations After, Inc., an organization of children of Holocaust survivors. During a program on forgiveness, I was tasked with leading a panel discussion and, not wanting to be a distraction, hid my nametag behind the lapel of my sports coat. A participant led off the discussion by framing the controversy around forgiveness post-Holocaust.

Someone else immediately chimed in, "Look, I don't know what you are talking about, but if you are referring to the crazy lady in Indiana who forgave Mengele, I want no part of this discussion." Compelled to say something, I made my nametag visible and asked why he thought she was crazy. He could only muster that he had "no use for her." I informed him that this crazed woman was my mother, which drew a look of both astonishment and embarrassment. He was apologetic and swore that he didn't mean to insult me. It was the first, but far from the last time, that such harsh criticism of my mother would be levied before me.

I can understand why some chose to criticize her, especially with regard to her decision to extend her forgiveness to all Nazis. It is fair to ask if she had the right forgive those who didn't harm her directly, but who did harm others. I can't necessarily disagree with that. But, I understand where my mom was coming from in wanting to forgive everyone— Münch, Mengele, herself, her mother and father, and all Nazis—and move on. Her list was so encompassing because she wanted a clean slate. Her forgiveness to all was not negotiable and she didn't want to revisit the list in the future. Furthermore, I can also rationalize that her forgiveness was more symbolic than practical.

Lost in the controversy over my mother's views was her role in lending validity to the atrocities committed by the Nazis. Convincing Münch to join her at Auschwitz and publicly admit to what he witnessed was a significant accomplishment. His letter was the first and, to my knowledge, only written admission of guilt by a Nazi and helped undermine the baseless claims of Holocaust deniers.

Her tireless efforts to track down former Mengele twins and advocate for their rights were overlooked as well. She received little credit for all the time, money, and energy she invested in uncovering the details of Mengele's research, information that she hoped might save lives. Even as she forgave, she still demonstrated a willingness to hold others accountable for their actions, which was on full display as the turn of the century approached.

In February 1999, my mother filed a lawsuit against Bayer, alleging that the German pharmaceutical company, which at the time of World War II had been one of six companies in the chemical and pharmaceutical conglomerate IG Farben, abetted Mengele's research at Auschwitz. In the first known lawsuit in the United States to take aim at Mengele's experiments, my mother's attorneys contended that Bayer had supplied Mengele with its drugs in order to test their effectiveness. The suit sought punitive damages and the restitution of profits Bayer reaped from Mengele's research.

Not long before my mother brought the suit, Bayer had admitted to having used slave labor during World War II, and, along with twelve other German corporations, agreed to contribute to a $1 billion reparations fund. In addition to an admission of guilt and fair compensation, my mother demanded Bayer apologize to all of the Mengele twins.

"After fifty-four years, it is time that Bayer takes responsibility for their actions," she pronounced. "That means that they should give proper restitution, say they are sorry for what they have done and say they will never use another human being as a guinea pig. This represents the worst example of individual and corporate evil." [107]

When Bayer executives refused to apologize, my mother moved forward with her lawsuit.

Elan Steinberg, executive director of the World Jewish Congress, surmised that it was the first case of Nazi medical atrocities to reach a court of law since the Nuremberg Trials held in 1945. "In the last few years, we've been focusing on Nazi financial crimes, slave labor, and the Swiss banks issue, but Mrs. Kor's case is different," said Steinberg. [108]

The case hinged on the prosecution's argument that Bayer had paid the Nazis in exchange for access to the victims' records for research and development purposes. Long refuting allegations of involvement with Mengele, Bayer had previously spurned requests to disclose their records and compensate the victims. Company spokesman Thomas Reinert stated that similar claims had been levied against Bayer's predecessor, IG Farben, during the Nuremberg trials. Reinert reminded the court that the allegations had been rejected as false and maintained that Bayer was not a legal successor to IG Farben.

The prosecution, led by Irwin B. Levin, alleged that Dr. Helmuth Vetter, who'd been affiliated with the Bayer corporation, had experimented at Auschwitz with drugs on healthy captives who'd fallen ill after having been given pills, injections, and powders. In 1947, Vetter was sentenced to death by a United States military court and executed two years later. Levin also identified a Bayer physician, known only as "Dr. Koenig," as an accomplice to Mengele. According to Levin, Bayer furnished Mengele with toxic chemicals to be used on the victims. After documenting the results, Koenig submitted the findings to Bayer.

The parties reached a settlement that resulted in the establishment of a $5 billion fund for the Foundation Remembrance, Responsibility and Future, a German organization charged with making financial compensation available to former slave laborers and others "affected by other injustices from the National Socialist period."

Through all of the criticism and advocacy, my mother continued taking advantage of every possible opportunity to lecture, paying special attention to school-aged audiences. As she crisscrossed the United States delivering talks, one particular visit to Mahomet, Illinois, proved most memorable.

In 1996, Kevin Daugherty and Jane Fisk, teachers at Mahomet-Seymour Junior High, were flummoxed. They'd booked my mother to speak to their classes the following spring, and they were struggling to help their seventh graders fathom the number of people killed in the Holocaust. Daugherty had recently come across an article chronicling an East Coast school's attempt to recycle 11 million cans. While driving to work one morning, Daugherty popped off the tab of his Diet Coke can and presented it to Fisk. "Let's collect pop tabs!" he exclaimed. Could an assemblage of that magnitude, the approximate number of Holocaust victims, be gathered in Mahomet? Daugherty wasn't certain, but was determined to find out.

After hearing about the initiative, my mother visited Mahomet and donated 119 tabs—one for each of the relatives she'd lost in the Holocaust—to the cause. After congratulating the students for their persistence, she plopped down onto the gym floor and counted off all 119 of the soda tabs. The students, now aware of the significance of the number, sat in stunned silence. Months later, they were tasked with counting the mountain of tabs by hand. Daugherty, who was assisting in the effort, reached in and filled his hand with as many tabs as possible. Improbably, the number in hand came out to be 119 on the nose.

Energized by my mother's visit and by reading Holocaust-denial accounts, the Mahomet students achieved their goal, collecting 11 million tabs over the course of the 1996–97 school year. Six million of the allotment represented the number of Jews who had perished in the Holocaust while the additional 5 million memorialized gypsies, political dissenters, pacifists, homosexuals, the disabled, and those who abetted the persecuted. Several of the students composed poems that verbalized their array of emotions over the months-long drive.

The national media picked up on their heartwarming effort which resulted in boxes of tabs flooding in from all fifty states. ABC Nightly News paid a visit to Mahomet and snared footage of my mother's interactions with the students.

"They have learned, and they can teach now, the lessons of the Holocaust," she told a national audience. On Holocaust Remembrance Day in 1997, and with camera crews from all over the country present, the Mahomet-Seymour students dumped 6 million tabs onto the school gymnasium floor and lined the perimeter with shopping bags containing the additional 5 million tabs.

The story caught the attention of Jeffrey Schrier, an artist who'd recently completed a memorial project in honor of Raoul Wallenberg, a Swedish humanitarian credited with saving thousands of Hungarian Jews during the Holocaust. Moved by the Mahomet students' accomplishment, Schrier envisioned that the tabs might be utilized for another commemorative sculpture. Totaling nearly five tons, the tabs had already been sent to be recycled, but Robert Silverman, then Executive Director of the Champaign-Urbana Jewish Federation, called on the recycling plant to halt production.

After five months, Schrier constructed a wing-like, feather structure consisting of the tabs, wire, and a two-foot aluminum rod. The shape was inspired by "The Butterfly," a poem written by Czechoslovakian poet Pavel Friedmann, who'd been executed at Auschwitz. Dubbed "WINGS of WITNESS," Schrier's work has been featured at multiple art and Holocaust museums across the country. Since 1997, approximately 60,000 participants from twenty-three states and Canada have erected pop-tab feathers for ten site-specific variations of WINGS of WITNESS.

In 2023, Daugherty was in the process of donating tabs to the WINGS of WITNESS archive. Once more he grabbed a handful of pop tabs, counted them out, and landed on 119. I later received an email from him that read, "It still worked…so another sign your mom is still with us in this program!"

By a conservative count, my mother gave more than 5,000 talks on forgiveness in her lifetime and continued to speak up until her death. As the visit to Mahomet illustrates, the size of the venue didn't matter: she'd travel to the end of the earth to get her message across. She spoke everywhere from Cape Town, South Africa, with Desmond Tutu in attendance, to the Leaning Tower of Pisa.

Günzburg, Germany, the birthplace of Josef Mengele, was the site of one of her most unique lectures. During her address, she was interrupted by one of Mengele's grade school classmates who shouted, "You are wrong! He did nothing wrong!" My mother paused and requested to shake the man's hand, but he was promptly removed by security. No matter the size of the audience, she considered her lecture a success if even one person was moved to forgive.

Even when stateside, she was still always on the move. On one occasion, she spoke at Cedar Sinai Hospital in Los Angeles and flew home that evening, arriving in Terre Haute after midnight. The following morning, I caught her as she bolted out the door.

"Where are you going Mom?" I yelled.

She replied that she was headed to catch another flight bound for Montana, where she was to lecture that evening. Astounded, I pressed her on why she'd come home for just a couple of hours.

"Alex, my dear," she replied. "I wanted to sleep in my own bed."

CHAPTER

A Permanent Reminder

> "I knew I would do something in her memory."
>
> —Eva

The CANDLES organization, once a one-woman operation, had grown in scope and influence by the mid-1990s. My mother's declaration of forgiveness garnered worldwide attention and shed more light on the predicament of the living Mengele twins. Now delivering more than 100 lectures annually, she never missed an opportunity to educate the public about CANDLES and its mission. Steven Spielberg's blockbuster film *Schindler's List* premiered in 1994 and sparked a renewed interest in the Holocaust. The momentum bolstered CANDLES' reputation and afforded it a bigger platform. After eleven years, it was finally being recognized as a credible organization, but my mother wanted more.

The CANDLES Holocaust Museum and Education Center in Terre Haute.

COURTESY CANDLES HOLOCAUST MUSEUM

With Mengele in the rear-view mirror, my mother flourished. Her real estate business was thriving, and she was ebullient that Rina and I were establishing ourselves in our chosen fields. Yet, one void remained: Miriam was gone, and my mother had yet to come to grips with her passing. For several years, she'd contemplated how to appropriately memorialize her sister. Long pining for a physical space for CANDLES, she arrived at the idea of a museum to be dedicated in Miriam's memory. My parents' garage, once the site of many epic ping pong matches, was now chock-full of literature, photos, and archival records from the Holocaust and required a new home. A museum could offer space for these artifacts, a venue for lectures and guest speakers, and a locale where patrons of all ages could learn about the Holocaust. The notion of a Holocaust Museum in Indiana may have seemed preposterous to some, but my mother thought it to be the ideal place to pay tribute to her late sister.

Leveraging her real estate contacts, she began searching for potential locations in Terre Haute. A retail strip center, barren besides a travel agency, had a vacancy and she scooped it up, relying on personal funds after refinancing their home. The site, near Interstate 70, was underwhelming to say the least. Roughly the size of a tennis court, it was outdated and had little in the way of amenities. In the *Forgiving Dr. Mengele* documentary, my sister Rina pegged the location as "laughable" and neither my father nor I were optimistic about its long-term prospects. Indianapolis, with more diversity and a population of over 1 million, made more sense, but my mother never considered it. Despite the numerous antisemitic episodes over the years, Terre Haute had become home for her, and it would be for her museum as well.

In early May 1995, the CANDLES Holocaust Museum and Education Center opened. I emceed the event and my mother, Terre Haute Mayor Pete Chalos, and several survivors from Chicago all spoke about the importance of Holocaust education. Members of Terre Haute's Jewish community beamed with pride during the ribbon cutting ceremony, but no one was more joyous than my mother. Thrilled that her vision to honor Miriam had come to fruition, she was determined to extend her twin's legacy by ensuring the museum's success.

———————

The CANDLES Museum began as a barebones operation and had no funding for support staff. My mother worked tirelessly to promote the museum, balancing her real estate obligations and lecture schedule in the process. She spent hours decorating the space with photos using thumb tacks and scotch tape and meticulously produced handmade posters detailing her time at Auschwitz. Images of the Kor Family, including the well-known picture of my mother and Miriam exiting Auschwitz upon their liberation, lined the walls along with a timeline depicting my mother's long and laborious path from Transylvania to Tel Aviv to Terre Haute. In anticipation of the emotions her lectures would often trigger, she always kept an ample supply of Kleenex on hand.

My father's retirement as a pharmacist coincided with the museum's opening. His visions of traveling up to West Lafayette for Purdue games were quickly dashed by my mother, who immediately put him to work at the museum.

"I don't care what you do there," she ordered. "You can listen to your political shows on the radio, but if someone comes in, please show them around."

While she could comfortably narrate her Holocaust past to crowds of thousands, my father remained reluctant to open up. He made it clear that recounting his past would not be included in the job description.

"Eva, I do not lecture on my experiences. It is too painful," he maintained. Eventually, they reached a compromise: he'd volunteer two days per week, but only in the role of a guide. In return, she'd allow him an "excused absence" for Purdue basketball games.

In 1997, however, his role expanded, due in part to a visit from a local high school class. Mike Lunsford, an acquaintance of my father's, was a substitute teacher and wrote a sports column in the Sunday edition of the *Terre Haute Tribune Star.* Lunsford had scheduled a visit to the museum so that his students could hear my mother speak.

Eagerly anticipating her talk, the class was disheartened to learn that she had to cancel due to an unexpected appointment. Sensing their dejection, my father volunteered to fill in.

"Mike, I can lecture to your students today," he offered. "I normally don't talk about my past, but I will do it for your students and for you."

Lunsford was flabbergasted. After all this time, he had no idea that my father was a survivor.

"Mike, I never told you. I survived four years of concentration camps," my father admitted.

My father wowed the students with a stirring account that climaxed with the Coca-Cola story.

"When he told his story about how he was found," Lunsford shared. "And how Colonel Nehf helped him, and how he eventually came to this country, I realized that in many ways his life was just as remarkable as your mother's."

My father won over his young audience and left an indelible impression not only on the students, but on his longtime friend as well. Lunsford later penned a column on the lecture, dropping in a classic quote from my father on his love for Purdue basketball.

"If the Nazis had gotten their way," he'd told the students, "there would be one open seat at Mackey Arena. But I survived and can now enjoy my Boilermakers!"

To the surprise of my mother, my father became a fixture at the museum, and he began delivering two lectures per week.

"You know, your dad is now lecturing at the museum," she informed me. "He tells people that he does not like to speak, but then two hours later, he's still talking! I think he actually likes it."

She was right: he loved to engage in playful banter with visitors, even when on the receiving end of a barb. A teenaged guest once told my father that he

My father on the piano at the museum. COURTESY ALEX KOR

was "the unluckiest man" that he'd ever met.

When my father asked why, the young man responded, "You were a Jew in Germany, and now you're a Purdue fan in Indiana University territory!"

He revealed to me that while still reluctant to disclose his past, he enjoyed answering intelligent questions from his audiences. To spice up his talks, he added a piano performance at the conclusion of each lecture, including music from *Schindler's List* and numbers from his favorite singers like Bing Crosby. He judged his performance by the number of tears shed during his presentations. The music was his litmus test.

I've received countless notes over the years like the following that demonstrate my father's lasting effect on museum visitors:

My most treasured memory of your dad was the kindness he showed to my dad and me one time when I was visiting from Milwaukee with my son (maybe ten years old?). I had heard about the CANDLES museum and was eager to see it and share it with my son, so my dad called your dad to ask if we might be able to see it, even though it was not a normal day to be open. Not only did he graciously meet us, show us through the museum, tell us his story, and play the piano for us, but he spoke sincerely about how glad he was to have my dad as a friend. It was lovely to watch the warmth between them. My son, now in his 40s, and I have enjoyed sharing the memory of how many emotions we felt that day.

My parents especially embraced children on their visits to CANDLES. They knew that younger audiences would have difficulty comprehending their narratives, so they were thoughtful in their approach. A ten-year-old boy, with a quizzical look on his face, once cornered my mother after her lecture.

"Mrs. Kor, who taught you how to survive at Auschwitz?" he asked. She immediately walked up and got right in his face, easy for her to do given that she was 5-foot-1 on a good day. He immediately retreated and my mother asked, "Why did you do that?" The boy apologized, explaining that she'd gotten too close to him. "That is how I survived," she revealed. "I just reacted. I did not think or reason. Everything was pure instinct."

My parents weren't the sole Holocaust survivors integral in educating museum guests. Walter Sommers, a Terre Haute resident, was also recruited to lecture. Born in Frankfurt, Germany, in 1920, Sommers was raised in economically depressed, post-World War I Germany. Despite their financial hardships, his parents ensured that their son was well-educated and enrolled him in English, French, and Spanish classes. On November 9, 1938, Sommers was on his way to work at a shipping yard in Hamburg, Germany when he spotted Jewish businesses and homes being vandalized and looted by the Nazis during Kristallnacht. That night, all but one of his father's stores was destroyed. Sommers and his family fled Germany before being taken from their home, and he ultimately settled in Terre Haute. Covering the events of Kristallnacht and Hitler's rise to power, Sommers lectured at the museum for many years before passing away at the age of 101.

With three Holocaust lecturers, each with their own captivating account, in tow along with other guest speakers, the museum grew in popularity and size. My mother bought out the adjoining travel agency, allowing for more space at the museum, and finally hired additional help. Kiel Majewski, a student at Indiana State University, was hired as the museum's first employee and played a pivotal role in the museum's growth. With a photographic memory, Majewski assisted in organizing my mother's lecture schedule and provided a vital link between the museum and the academic community at ISU. A board of directors was established, and my mother built a loyal army of volunteers who provided support, guidance, and energy. Every year, she presented the "Eternal Light Award" to an individual or group of individuals who helped tell the museum's story.

As word got out about CANDLES, more and more visitors flocked to Terre Haute, including some notable guests. Ed Asner, the seven-time Emmy Award winner who starred in *The Mary Tyler Moore Show*, made a memorable appearance in 2011. He had come to support my mother's fundraiser and expressed a keen interest in seeing the museum and my mother "in action." On the afternoon of the event, I walked into the museum to find her speaking before a packed house. Asner sat intently in the audience, his eyes locked on my mother's and hanging on her every word. Following the lecture, he approached me and asked if I'd drive him to a gas station.

"Ed, I have plenty of gas," I replied. "I don't need to go to a gas station."

With an inquisitive look, he demanded, "Alex, I need you to buy me cigarettes!" I'd never purchased cigarettes and pleaded my case. "I will teach you how!" Asner sarcastically replied. Because he was the star of the evening fundraiser, he got his cigarettes.

The museum has also played host to many athletes and teams over the years. In 2014, the Saint Louis University basketball team, in town to play Indiana State, took a day trip to the museum. At the conclusion of the team's tour, my parents requested to take a picture with Calbert Cheaney, an assistant coach with the team and the all-time leading scorer in Indiana University basketball history. When Cheaney saw my father's Purdue hat, he jokingly refused the photo op. My parents got their wish (the 6-foot-7 Cheaney towers over my parents in the picture) and the Billikens went on to defeat Indiana State that night.

In 2018, Rachael Denhollander, a star USA gymnast and the first woman to publicly accuse Larry Nassar, the former Michigan State University and USA Gymnastics doctor, of sexual assault, came to the museum. She and my mother spoke later that evening, both talking about their paths from victimhood to empowerment to forgiveness.

"I release bitterness and anger and a desire for personal vengeance. It does not mean that I minimize or mitigate or excuse what he has done. It does not mean that I pursue justice on earth any less zealously. It simply means that I release personal vengeance against him [Nassar]," Denhollander later wrote.

One of the more interesting visits took place in 2017. Ted Green, an Indianapolis filmmaker, was making a documentary on my mother and had tracked down David Wells, the officer who'd escorted her out of the Capitol in 1986, for an interview. Wells had long wondered about my mother's fate and was stunned to hear that she was still alive. Following his interview with Green, Wells requested to come see her in Terre Haute. I was touched by his gesture and offered to pay for his travel expenses, though he declined. Their meeting would bring closure to the 1986 incident, I surmised, but I was unsure of how my mother would react.

Working in Milwaukee at the time, I traveled back to Terre Haute and had dinner with Green, Wells, and Wells' wife. Following dinner, I drove over to see my mother.

"I need to tell you something and I'm not sure how you will respond," I began. "Officer David Wells is in town and would like to see you." She was surprised but agreed to meet him.

The museum was empty when they gathered the next day. For a couple of hours, the two sat and revisited the Capitol incident.

"I thought you were going to kill me," she professed with tears in her eyes. Wells had sensed her fear.

"I know you were scared," he acknowledged. "And I think that you had a flashback. You might have thought I was a Nazi." She gave Wells a tour and they embraced at the conclusion of their reunion. As per usual, she presented Wells with a signed copy of her memoir.

On the drive back to his home in Baltimore, Wells pulled over and read the inscription. Never missing an opportunity for humor, she'd written, "To Officer David Wells, my arresting officer. Forgive and heal."

Through generous contributions, the museum has significantly expanded its collection of photos, artifacts, and rare documents, including letters from Mengele to his wife Irene. In 2016, my mother joined twelve other Holocaust survivors who participated in Dimensions in Testimony (DIT), an initiative sponsored by the University of Southern California Shoah Foundation, which was funded by Steven Spielberg. Employing multiple-angle, green-screen filming technology, natural language processing, and voice recognition software, the DIT initiative produced a vivid projection of each survivor and allowed for the avatar to respond to questions. The museum added a small theater in 2018 featuring my mother's hologram, ensuring that her voice will live well beyond her passing.

In 2025, CANDLES will celebrate its 30th anniversary. More than 30,000 patrons have been through the museum, and 8,000 school-age children continue to visit annually. The museum's longevity is a testament to my mother's drive, persistence, and belief that anything is possible. Despite his initial reluctance to make public his past, my father was integral in the museum's success as well, and found a second calling there following his retirement.

"I was in a lot of pain," my mother said as she reflected on the days before the museum's opening. "I'd wake up many nights suffocating. I could feel how Miriam died when the cancer filled her lungs. I knew I would do something in her memory, and I opened CANDLES Holocaust Museum and Education Center and the nightmares stopped." Just as with her championing of forgiveness, the museum not only benefited her but also aided thousands of others in search of their own healing. Most meaningful to my mother, she'd established a permanent reminder of both the Holocaust and of Miriam. Indiana was long overdue for a repository on the Holocaust, and she was gratified that her vision materialized in her adopted hometown. Now, visitors to Terre Haute could get an authentic glimpse of what life at Auschwitz was really like. But, that wasn't enough for my mother. She still wanted them to see the real thing.

CHAPTER

You Can Go Home Again

> "I want to go home."
>
> —Eva

Though my mother was liberated in 1945, she struggled for decades to truly escape Auschwitz. For years, distressing memories of the selection platform, the gas chambers, and Mengele tormented her. Often contemplating the fate of that hell on earth, a myriad of questions stayed with her for years. Were the barracks still there? What had become of the gas chambers? Was there a monument in remembrance of the victims?

From the inception of the CANDLES organization, she'd yearned for a reunion of the Mengele twins at Auschwitz. A gathering would generate media attention and, in her view, expose Mengele's murderous practices and help unearth his medical records. Many of the Mengele twins, who were approaching middle age, were reporting health issues, and identifying what they'd been injected with was essential. My mother envisioned the reunion as critical to bolstering CANDLES' credibility, but she needed to see Auschwitz, once again, before proceeding further. In the spring of 1984, she decided to return.

———————

In 1944, my mother had been accompanied to Auschwitz by her parents and three siblings, but this time, she'd make the journey alone. My father, Rina, and I were very apprehensive about the trip. Her courage was admirable, but what ramifications would result in her visit? Hadn't she suffered enough? Why must she go alone?

We weren't the only ones disconcerted. My mother suffered a panic attack at 35,000 feet while on board her Lufthansa flight to Poland. It'd been thirty-nine years since she'd heard German, and the airline attendants' native dialect triggered flashbacks. Regaining her composure, she arrived at Auschwitz a day later. With a tape recorder in hand and joined only by a tour guide, she roamed the remains of the camp for several hours while capturing her thoughts on tape. Every step evoked agonizing memories of the past:

Mom and Dad: I remember this place and am as scared now as I was in 1944. Here I am in Birkenau—the closest place to Hell on this Earth. I am standing here at the entrance to the camps. And I am trying to think what.... Oh God... Oh God.... Where did she vanish? Mom: I will tell our story because the world must know. [109]

The camp's physical layout hadn't changed much, but my mother picked up on things that she'd never previously noticed. The infamous sign at the camp entrance reading *Arbeit Macht Frei* (Work Makes You Free) was one of the hallmarks at Auschwitz, but she never remembered it. She was also surprised to learn that an orchestra, composed of Jewish captives, played music for the Nazis' enjoyment and to lull new detainees into a sense of safety just beyond the entrance. I postulate that she was so laser-focused on survival that all else represented an unwelcome distraction. She had blinders on to everything but freedom.

Revisiting the guard tower and the remnants of the barracks proved especially excruciating. Her life was forever altered on this soil and thirty-nine years later, the pain still permeated her entire being. In 1944, she'd at least had Miriam at her side, but this time she was alone. It was by choice. Still obstinate about relying on the support of others, she had to make this expedition by herself. For her, there was no other alternative.

———————

My mother's return to Indiana was met with great trepidation. Assuming that the visit had been traumatic, I feared it would only augment her preoccupation with Mengele. Expecting the worst, Rina and I met her upon her return and were pleasantly surprised to see a smile on her face as she exited the security gate.

"I have presents for you both!" she shouted. Sporting a Cheshire grin, she pulled out two sweatshirts and presented them to Rina and me. The front bore the iconic photo of my mother and Miriam exiting Auschwitz and the back read, "My Mom Survived Auschwitz and All I Got Was This Lousy Sweatshirt!" She'd made it out of Auschwitz again and somehow kept her humor intact.

Back in the States, my mother set her sights on the Mengele twin reunion to be held in conjunction with the 40th anniversary of the liberation. As mentioned previously, with my Uncle Shlomo's assistance, more than 100 twins responded to an advertisement in the Israeli newspaper. From her kitchen, my mother launched a massive public relations campaign and lobbied major media outlets to provide coverage of the upcoming reunion. She called television stations and sent hundreds of letters to newspapers, but her efforts generated no interest.

With the reunion only months away, out of the blue a reporter from *Parade* magazine phoned my mother. Her name was Lucette Lagnado; she'd received one of the letters and was intrigued by the story. On September 4, 1984, *Parade* published Lagnado's article entitled, "The Twins of Auschwitz

Today." The piece proved to be a ninth inning, pinch hit home run and prompted a favorable reaction from the Mengele twins in the States.

Following the advertisement in Israel and the *Parade* magazine article, several sets of twins came forward with an interest in attending the reunion. Their response, coupled with my mother's tenacious PR efforts, inspired the addition of a mock trial to be held one week later in Israel. Dubbed "J'Accuse," the Mengele twins would testify to Mengele's crimes at Yad Vashem, The World Holocaust Remembrance Center, in Jerusalem.

From the time I was five, my mother had been readying me for my first trek to Auschwitz. Without going into detail, she laid the groundwork by sharing age-appropriate information about her time at the camp. While other kids were listening to Doctor Seuss rhymes, I heard narratives of cattle car rides and barbed-wire encampments. By the age of ten, I'd been privy to all the stories that she'd later share with thousands. There were no photos of Auschwitz in our home (few existed until the 1980s), so I conjured up images of what life might have resembled at the camp. By my teenage years, one mention of Auschwitz elicited visions of barking dogs, large rats, and diabolical doctors. Despite my "formative education" on the Holocaust, I was apprehensive about my toughest exam yet: an in-person visit to Auschwitz, where my emotions would be tested to the limit.

January 1985 marked both the 40th anniversary of the liberation and my initial trip to this mysterious locality that had long piqued my curiosity and haunted my imagination. Brimming with anticipation, a million questions ran through my mind as I boarded a plane bound for Kraków. Would my mother be able to contain her emotions and successfully lead this expedition? Would she be able to find meaning in the trip? How would I respond to the experience?

In contrast to her most recent visit to Auschwitz, she'd be accompanied on this pilgrimage by a large traveling party that included Rina, me, Miriam, and eight other Mengele twins and their relatives; journalists from the *New*

York Times and *Los Angeles Times*, who had learned about the reunion through the *Parade* magazine article; and seventeen camera crews. Given that my father was never held captive at Auschwitz, he saw no reason to go and, at that juncture, wasn't emotionally prepared to revisit any concentration camp.

My own apprehension was compounded by the meticulous planning involved. Charged with ensuring all passengers were on the bus to and from Auschwitz, I also served as my mother's press agent and set up media interviews for her and the other twins. Hours of work went into mapping out the details for our journey, but I was uncertain that things would run smoothly. I also had doubts from an emotional perspective. Did I have the mental toughness to do this? Could I be a source of strength for my mother if she needed me? I'd find out soon enough.

◆

A chilling wind greeted us as we departed our hotel in Kraków and boarded a bus destined for Auschwitz. Despite my three layers of winter gear, the temperatures, which hovered in the teens, made life miserable for me and all the attendees that January morning. It dawned on me that my mother, Miriam, and thousands of others had somehow outlasted the mercilessly frigid winter of 1945 at Auschwitz. With minimal protection from the cold, they'd not only survived the most arduous of outdoor conditions but had overcome insufficient rations, psychological and physical torture, and, for some, Mengele's grotesque experiments.

The gravity of our visit gripped me as we disembarked from the bus. As I ambled toward the distinctive and still menacing guard tower, an eerie feeling that I'd been here before enveloped me. The images that had percolated in my mind for the past twenty-four years were now real and right before my eyes.

I immediately recognized two familiar faces: *ABC News*'s Peter Jennings and Holocaust survivor Elie Wiesel, who were both there to film a news segment. Their presence was an auspicious sign that there'd be sufficient coverage of the reunion. My mother's years of scratching and clawing for

My first visit to Auschwitz, 1985. COURTESY ALEX KOR

publicity had finally paid off and she hoped the world would soon know the truth about Mengele and what had really transpired at Auschwitz.

When we reached the selection platform, I thought of my grandparents and my mother's older sisters Edit and Aliz. Forty years earlier, the Mozes family spent their final moments together at this very location.

After chronicling that fateful day to our group, my mother looked skyward and pronounced, "Mom and Dad, meet Alex and Rina. They are your grandchildren. We have finally come to say goodbye to you. We have never forgotten you, and we will never let the world forget what was here." Her words rippled through the frigid air, causing me to sob uncontrollably. As tears poured down my face, I again had an intuitive feeling that I'd stood on this very platform once before.

Following my mother's lead, we made a short walk down the train tracks which terminated at the ruins of the gas chambers.

A reporter called out, "Eva, during your time at Auschwitz, were you ever here?"

Without hesitation, she yelled, "If I was here [pointing to the gas chamber], I would *never* be here! So, *no!*"

Our next stop was the twins' barracks at Birkenau. Much of the site had been reduced to rubble, but the layout remained seared in my mother's consciousness. Motioning to the front of the barracks, she identified this as the area where she had "lived" from May 1944 to January 1945. The Nazis had burned these barracks to the ground and all that remained was a modest memorial dedicated to the Mengele twins.

Pausing at the monument, my mother recounted two stories to her audience, by now already emotionally raw from the tour.

Gesturing to the far end of the barracks, she declared, "This is where Miriam and I went to the latrine floor on the first night and saw the scattered corpses of two twins who had died. Right here, I made up my mind that we would not end up on that filthy floor. This is also where we were told that the flames in the distance were our parents. We did not want to believe that."

Recalling a more joyous moment, she pointed near the memorial and noted, "This is the spot in August 1944 when I looked up to the sky to see a small plane, with smoke billowing out, circling Auschwitz. When I looked even closer, I saw an American flag on the side of the plane. I found out years later that this reconnaissance plane was marking Auschwitz so that the Allies would not bomb the camp."

The CANDLES organization later placed a wreath and its memorial pledge near the selection platform:

We, CANDLES, are the voices of the children saved from the ashes. We pledge to do the following:

We will not let the world forget what happened here in Auschwitz.

We will remember that a part of humanity perished here. This soil is soaked with the blood, the tears, and the ashes of our mothers and fathers, sisters and brothers.

We will show our children where their grandparents hugged us for the very last time.

We will work together to eliminate prejudice from the face of the earth.

We will not rest until Dr. Josef Mengele is caught and brought to justice.

We will appeal to the conscience of the world never to let this happen again.

Standing alongside my mother, Miriam, and a handful of other Mengele twins overwhelmed me. It dawned on me how close my mother and aunt had been to death. I realized that my presence that day was nothing short of miraculous.

Reflecting on the day's events, my mother told the Associated Press, "I thought it was a wonderful feeling to walk the same streets because I had never walked them before as a free human being. Forty years ago, I could never imagine that I would be singing Jewish songs in Auschwitz." [110]

———————————————

From Auschwitz, we flew to Jerusalem for the mock trial of Mengele. The hearing, held at the Hashmonaim Hall at Yad Vashem, attracted press outlets from all over the world along with more than 100 survivors, their family members and friends, and scholars. Approximately fifty Mengele twins, most of whom hailed from Israel, were given the opportunity to detail their horrific narratives.

The accounts were unbearable. Survivor Ruth Elias painfully admitted that Mengele instructed that her breasts be bandaged immediately after she gave birth at Auschwitz in order to observe how long the infant could survive without food. When a week had passed, he instructed Elias to "get ready," which she interpreted to mean that her and her child's executions were imminent. A fellow captive, who happened to be a Jewish doctor, pleaded that she kill her baby to save herself.

"You are young and can live. The baby cannot live," Elias recalled the doctor saying. The physician provided her with a dose of morphine and with a horrified audience looking on, Elias confessed to having killed her child with a lethal injection.

Other testimonials painted pictures of perseverance and humanity. At one point, a man named Zvi Spiegel was asked to stand. One of the older twins (twenty-nine years old) at Auschwitz, Spiegel was charged with assembling younger, male twins for experiments. Nicknamed "Uncle Spiegel," he became a father figure to the young boys, whose parents had more than likely been executed, and taught them math and geography. After liberation, he personally ensured that each of the young boys found a home.

One of the presiding officials scanned the room and asked, "Please stand if you were one of those boys." More than a handful of men stood up. The spectators erupted in a thunderous applause that went on for minutes, and there wasn't a dry eye in the courtroom.

A six-person tribunal, including Simon Wiesenthal and former Israeli Attorney General Gideon Hauser, issued a resolution that read in part, "There exists a body of evidence justifying the committal for trial of the SS physician *Hauptsturmführer* Josef Mengele, for war crimes and crimes against humanity, including crimes against the Jewish people and members of other nations."[111] Calling for a reinvigorated effort to track down Mengele, the tribunal sought to try him for "acts of brutality against the bodies and souls" of his Auschwitz victims.

My mother's years of hard work had paid off. She'd successfully helped illuminate Mengele's war crimes to the world. Following the mock trial, the Israeli, German, and United States governments made a vow to renew their efforts to find Mengele and pooled together more than $3.5 million in reward money. Pleased that the reunion had garnered international attention and cooperation, my mother believed that by returning to Auschwitz she was laying the groundwork for Mengele's capture. In time, it would prove true that her trip to Auschwitz in 1985 was foundational, but for entirely different reasons.

***

By the 2000s, my mother was lecturing more than 150 times per year, and thousands were flocking to the CANDLES Museum on an annual basis. As her popularity soared, so did the demand from others to accompany her to Auschwitz. She was now returning annually, sometimes multiple times per year, and each visit drew media coverage. Her lectures were soul-stirring, but she knew that one could only truly begin to comprehend the horrors of Auschwitz by seeing it firsthand. Viewing Auschwitz as her classroom, she envisioned herself as a teacher who could enlighten her pupils on the topics of discrimination, perseverance, and forgiveness. In 2012, she decided that CANDLES would offer an annual educational expedition to Auschwitz.

As was her custom, my mother took a hands-on role in marketing the trip, advertising it in her speeches and talking it up to everyone who entered her museum. She fired off letters to organizations that might have an interest and plugged it to friends and neighbors. Camera crews from outlets such as ABC, NBC, CBS, and the BBC covered the initial tours, which ramped up publicity in a big way. Participants returned inspired and urged their friends and family members to go as well.

Without fail, the seven-day trip, usually held in June or July, sold out every year. Between 50 and eventually more than 100 guests, hailing from all over the world, annually doled out an average of $3,500 that covered their airfare, hotel, and food costs. The itinerary entailed three days at Auschwitz and a tour of Kraków, including the city's Jewish Quarter. Ages varied and cohorts one summer included both a nine-year old and a ninety-year-old. What began as a small group of people traveling for one week every two years grew larger and larger, evolving into two groups of 100 people each, spanning a two-week period every June.

Motivations differed for each participant. Some were hungry to learn about the Holocaust while others, who were battling their own demons, wanted to understand how my mother had conquered hers. Scores of participants sought to unlock the mystery of how she'd come to forgive the Nazis. A major selling point for all who registered was that this wasn't the average tour. Participants had the chance to gain firsthand knowledge of Auschwitz from a guide who'd personally survived it. Most left with just as many, if not more, questions about this time in history and the inhumanity surrounding it.

The first day of the trip was always met with an air of trepidation. In the inaugural years of the expedition, from 2010 to 2012, we arrived in Kraków on a Sunday and left by coach bus for Auschwitz the following morning. The tension on the bus was palpable throughout the entire hour-and-a-half drive. My mother did her best to quell the group's fears by previewing the day ahead, but words, even those spoken by one familiar with the camp, can't do Auschwitz justice. We later decided that it was best to wait until the second day before going to the camp.

Once at Auschwitz, my mother led us on a day-long journey through the camp, painting vivid pictures of her captivity. The Auschwitz Memorial Museum preferred tours begin at Auschwitz I, but my mother insisted hers begin at Birkenau; it was where her captivity began.

Beginning on the selection platform, she'd open with words that set the stage for the hours to follow: "I firmly believe that there is no other piece of land on this Earth that has been witness to such misery of humanity as the selection platform at Auschwitz-Birkenau."

The barrack that she and Miriam had once been confined to was no more, but she'd point out the precise location where they once slept. On her first night in the barrack, she told of being awakened by a scurrying sound and assumed it to be mice. She'd then reveal to her audiences that rats, as "big as cats," were the actual culprits.

Year after year, tourists were mesmerized as she relived the most harrowing moments of her confinement. She'd point out the kitchen where she was fired upon by Nazi guards and the structure where she'd been restrained while being tattooed. The blood lab was a staple of her tour, and she outlined in graphic detail being stripped naked and subjected to Mengele's inhumane experiments. She would conclude the tour by ushering groups through a section of barbed wire passage, similar to where the iconic liberation photo was snapped.

In 2013, the Auschwitz tour guides escorted us through the Kanada Building, which borders the forest at Birkenau.

"I am not sure that I ever went there," my mother exclaimed. When we entered the building, which resembles a warehouse, she trained her gaze at the ceiling. After staring for a minute, she turned to our group and said, "Oh my! I remember this place. Clothes and shoes were stacked all the way to the top of the ceiling. Miriam and I walked on the heap of clothes and shoes as we were trying to find some that fit us. We finally did." I've often wondered if my mother had a photographic memory or if the images were so nightmarish that she couldn't forget them.

The gas chambers, funereal and intimidating, elicited the strongest reactions. It was difficult for guests to refrain from imagining themselves standing in the chamber, shoulder-to-shoulder with other terrified captives, awaiting death. Knowing this was the most somber stop on the tour, my mother initiated a tradition to mitigate the tension. Upon entering the chamber, guests received a candle and were given the opportunity to light it in memory of a loved one. I attended many of these ceremonies and was privy to some incredibly moving tributes.

A lacrosse coach once accompanied us, and I noticed he wore a bracelet made of net. As he lit his candle, he began wailing profusely and said, "A few years ago, two of my players died in a car accident. I've always blamed myself for their deaths. I wear the strands of their lacrosse sticks around my wrist. After hearing Eva this week, I no longer blame myself and light this candle for these two athletes."

In the evenings, we carved out an hour for nightly reflections where participants could express their emotions. CANDLES staff were present to assist anyone who was having difficulty processing what they'd witnessed.

On one occasion, I witnessed Brielle Hill, a seventeen-year-old, soon-to-be college student, sitting alone and crying. I grabbed my mother and informed her of the situation.

"What is wrong, sweetie? Why are you crying," my mother inquired.

Perplexed, Hill shot back, "How can you smile? How can you be so happy? You keep saying it is on my shoulders as the next generation to prevent this from ever happening again, but I cannot make sense of this place."

Now an expert at comforting distressed participants, my mother consoled the young girl.

"Eva told me to channel my anger and frustration into determination and passion to prevent future Auschwitzes," recalled Hill. "She said I could do my part to change my corner of the world, which will influence others to do the same, causing a ripple effect. When I told her that did not feel like enough, she then asked me, 'Can you write?'

'Yes.'

'Can you speak?'

My mother with members of the IDF (Israeli Defense Forces) at Auschwitz.

COURTESY ALEX KOR

'Yes.'

'Then you will give a speech at our last dinner here in Poland.' It was by speaking to the group that I learned what it means to have the power and responsibility to bear witness." [112] After graduating from college, Hill went on to work for the Anti-Defamation League and is currently on the CANDLES board.

My mother became an expert guide and grew comfortable in talking to total strangers about her past. Periodically, however, a visit to the camp would rekindle her demons. In 1992, she and Miriam were at Auschwitz filming a documentary for ZDF, a German PBS station. The producer wanted a shot of the sisters walking on the train tracks and filmed the scene repeatedly until getting a suitable take. At one point, a German producer interrupted the filming and yelled "Halt!" Instinctively, my mother and Miriam, with their backs to the camera, turned and put their hands up.

She took pride, though, in having been an "alumna" of Auschwitz. The liberation photo of her and Miriam was mounted to a wall at Block 6, and she'd often sit on her walker in the corner and point to herself as groups of people passed by. Many of the guides knew her by name and would introduce her, granting tour groups the opportunity to interact with a survivor.

"I need to go and work the corner!" she'd pronounce when we'd arrive each morning. When I informed her that the phrase had a negative connotation, she just chuckled. A suggestion that a T-shirt with the slogan "Working the Corner of Auschwitz since 1944!" be produced was thankfully not acted upon.

On occasion, her alumni status came in handy. In 1995, security guards attempted to block her and a busload from CANDLES from entering the gates at Auschwitz. My mother stomped off the bus and demanded that the group be allowed in. When instructed that a special pass was required for entry, she rolled up her sleeve and showed off her tattoo. "Do you see this? Fifty years ago, you wouldn't let me out. Now you won't let me in!" The guard immediately opened the gates.

She loved to interact with other tourists at Auschwitz. Once, she was approached by three teenagers, all of whom were students at Jagiellonian University in Kraków. The young men were captivated by her story, leading one of them to drop to his knees.

He took her hand, looked her in the eye, and pleaded, "You have to explain your forgiveness to me so that I can understand." With great empathy, she took several minutes and shared her blueprint for forgiveness.

My mother created quite a presence at Auschwitz, especially as her reputation grew. It wasn't unusual for other visitors to tag along with our tour group. One summer, a group of high school girls lingered uncomfortably around our group until my mother invited them over. The girls were sobbing profusely, prompting my mother to pause her lecture.

"What is wrong? why are you crying?" she asked.

"We are from Germany," one of them responded. "We can't believe that you have chosen forgiveness to heal yourself. Our grandparents could have been responsible for this place."

My mother embraced each girl and reminded them, "It's not your fault. You have nothing to feel guilty about. You are here to learn about the past.

When I see you tomorrow, I want you to smile when you see me. No more crying! You have so much to look forward to."

Another time, we were outside of Block 10, one of the areas where Mengele experimented on the twins. Normally closed to the public, my mother had arranged for a private tour for our group.

Before we entered, I overheard an Australian woman, in an indignant tone, ask a fellow tourist, "Did I hear correctly? She's forgiven the Nazis? I must talk to her!" Having overheard the conversation, my mother approached the woman. Afraid there might be a confrontation, I darted over to intervene but was too late—they were already locked in a conversation.

"Do I deserve to be free from what the Nazis did to me?" my mother asked the woman.

"Yes, of course," came the reply.

My mother then explained, "This is the way that I have found that freedom." The Australian tourist then broke down in tears.

Her talks elicited melancholic reactions, but she underscored that her tale was one of triumph.

"Why are you crying?" she'd ask her audiences. "It's a happy story. I survived! Look at it this way: I beat Hitler, I beat Mengele, I beat the Nazis, I beat the Communists, and I am here to tell my story." [113]

<hr>

As the trip grew in popularity, my mother took immense pride in how many people were genuinely impacted by the visit. Ironically, Auschwitz became a place where she was most alive and comfortable. Her return to Auschwitz was crucial in her healing process and she was determined to help others, even the staunchest of dissenters, find peace.

In 2007, she wrote to Iranian President Mahmoud Ahmadinejad, a prominent denier of the Holocaust. On more than one occasion, Ahmadinejad had asserted that the Holocaust was a "lie and a mythical claim." Infuriated, my mother emailed him an invitation to sign up for the annual trip:

Dear President Mahmoud Ahmadinejad,

My name is Eva Mozes Kor and I have been very troubled since your conference on the Holocaust in December 2006. You stated that the Holocaust never happened, and that it is not true that 6 million Jews and 5 million non-Jews were murdered by Hitler and the Nazis. If your statement is correct, then, I do not exist, but Dr. Ahmadinejad, I DO exist, I am real, and I am alive. So, both things can not be true.

I know that you are a scientist and a politician. As a scientist, you owe it to yourself and to the truth to verify your statements to indeed be true. You asked at your Holocaust Denial conference, "If it happened, where did it happen?" I would like you to come to the Auschwitz Concentration Camp to meet me, the survivor, walk with me on the grounds where it happened, so you could see, touch, hear my story, and VERIFY, VERIFY if it is true or not. [114]

Nearly a year later, she received a brief reply from the Islamic Republic of Iran Presidential email account, wishing her "health and success from the Almighty."

Amid my mother's pilgrimages to Auschwitz, she scheduled a trip in 1997 to return to her hometown of Portz. My sister Rina, a family friend, and I accompanied her. Lodging in Oradea, Romania, we hired a guide to drive us to Portz. Entering the village was like going back in time. There were no cars; only horse and buggies and oxen carts lined the dirt roads.

As we walked down the main street, my mother pointed to an aging building and said, "That was the town bar...a gathering place." A middle-aged man exited the bar, and she engaged him in conversation. Speaking in Hungarian, the two soon became embroiled in an animated dialogue.

"No, no, no!" the man yelled over and over again. He happened to be the county recorder and was charged with oversight of land ownership in Portz.

After my mother had identified herself as a Mozes, the man argued, "No, no—they all died in the war." After a second glance, however, he made a stunning realization: they'd once been classmates. "Oh my gosh," he exclaimed, "I remember you and your twin sister. You were two years ahead of me in grade school. I had no idea that you survived!"

With my mother's bona fides now established, we were given a tour of the village and allowed to see the old Mozes farm. The children of my mother's former neighbors had assumed the property following the war and still lived there. We strolled the entire acreage and viewed the graves of many of my mother's relatives who'd passed away before the war. As we walked, my thoughts turned to pre-1940 and the serene life that the Mozes family had once enjoyed.

My mother and the county recorder stayed in contact, and he attempted to return the Mozes land back to my mother and her three nieces (Miriam's daughters). The resettlement never came to fruition, much to the chagrin of my father, who joked, "Perhaps we could open a bed and breakfast there and call it Count Dracula's Inn."

In October 2018, CANDLES scheduled a fall trip to Portz after previous trips there in 2014 and 2016. The trip back to Romania, marketed as an opportunity to see where my mother's story began, was in addition to the summer expedition to Auschwitz, and there was enough interest that it sold out as well.

Just days before her departure, my mother sustained a complication on an arteriogram, and her hemoglobin was very low. Due to my own work commitments, I was unable to make the trip and begged her not to go. She, of course, waived me off, and her check-up one day prior to her flight yielded a normal blood test. That was good enough for her, and she was off to Romania.

The following evening, I received a call from one of the participants who happened to be a physician.

"Alex, we are in the emergency room in Romania," he began. "We are not sure, but we think your mom has a blood clot in her leg. Should we give her 3,000 units of Heparin?"

It was 3:00 a.m. my time and, half-asleep, I instructed, "Sure, I trust you." I returned to bed, not certain if I'd imagined the entire conversation.

Three hours later, I received a Facebook notification reading, "Watch Eva

Kor give a lecture from her grade school classroom!" I clicked on the link and, in astonishment, listened to my mother, now confined to a wheelchair, lecture from her childhood classroom. Confounded, I began texting the tour group to verify what had just occurred. Had she really just lectured from a Portz school or was I in the midst of a surreal dream?

A text minutes later gave me my answer. "Oh yes, she got the medicine," it read. "She is feeling much better and seems to be doing fine."

In March 1944, my mother had been forced from her childhood home and marched by the police, past her silent neighbors and classmates, on the one road that led out of town. Now, more than seventy-four years later, she was awarded a key to the village of Portz.

By 2000, life was good for my parents. Now retired, my father enjoyed his time watching Purdue, helping at CANDLES, and serving in his role as, in his words, "best supporting actor." Receiving international acclaim for her efforts, my mother finally felt respected in the Holocaust community and was gratified with how much the museum had grown. Inconceivably, she now looked forward to going back every year to Auschwitz and had convinced hundreds of others to share in her enthusiasm. My parents were proud of their children and had grown to love Terre Haute. Entering their Golden Years, they had every reason to believe the future was bright.

Reflections from past CANDLES trip participants

From the moment I met her that first night at dinner, (Monday, July 1) I adored her. She was real with us. She was willing to be an open book. She wanted us to ask her anything, to take as many pictures and videos as we wanted, so that when we go home, we would share with others our experiences with her and our experiences at the camps. We were there to bear witness to what the Nazis did to Eva and the millions of others...

Wednesday, July 3rd was a big day. Nothing really prepares you for seeing the tracks leading up to the guardhouse of Birkenau. It was a powerful moment for me. Knowing that millions of people went down those tracks in cattle cars packed beyond capacity never to come out again, hit me like a ton of bricks. I had tears in my eyes before I even got off the bus. Walking up to the gate from the parking lot was surreal. We toured Birkenau with our guides in the morning and after lunch, Eva would be joining us to talk about her experiences there in Birkenau...

People were drawn to Eva. When other visitors to the camp heard that she was a survivor, they stopped and joined our group to listen to her talk. Eva talked about her experiences at three different locations around the camp. It was an incredibly moving experience that I will never forget. I recorded everything she said to us that day and I am forever grateful that I did that. Little did I know what the next day would bring.

—**Amy Taylor**
Seventh-grade language arts teacher at the Interdistrict School for Arts and Communications in New London, Connecticut

I had the amazing opportunity to travel with Eva to Auschwitz as many others did and I was captivated by her moxie and spirit and kept coming back for more. I traveled again to Auschwitz and to Romania and Hungry with Eva and anyone who has traveled with Eva knows it was always an adventure! However, it was the trip that she was not on that really made me realize how much Eva had taught me. In 2020, I returned to Auschwitz with CANDLES for the 75th Liberation Ceremony and it was the first time I had returned to Auschwitz without Eva. If you had made this journey with Eva, you would know that this was the place where she came alive. Many times, she would be giving us a tour and in-between the very poignant moments there would be smiling and laughing all brought on by our Lady in Blue. She was for me the light in what otherwise would be a very gray and dark place. By embracing forgiveness, Eva Kor led her life by being a light and sharing her shine with all, being the best person she could be. So, that is what Eva Kor taught me, to be a light. I have the power to light up my own life and be the light in a gray place. I miss Eva's light in this world, I miss her funny tweets that would randomly pop up on my phone, and I miss traveling the world adventuring together. She also gave me a network and tribe of friends that are full of some of the best people I know, because I came to learn that the people who are attracted to Eva and her story are special and unique people. So thanks to you Eva I go through life and I try to be a light and shine being the best person I can truly be and it may not be a coincidence that I like to think of my light of having a little tint of blue.

—Stephanie Stabile
Merchant Mariner

Eva was such a bright light and I have so many favorite memories of her:

» *falling asleep in the middle of a crowded room*
» *dancing the Hora on the Auschwitz platform*
» *calling the museum the day after a Poland trip, and hearing her voice on the other end like we didn't just travel across the world and she should be in bed asleep*
» *trying to set people up for marriage wherever she went*
» *spontaneously singing "The Hills Are Alive" at her old apartment in Romania*
» *having her microphone on in the bathroom telling us "I don't care eef you hear me"*
» *doing dangerous things and scaring Alex every trip*
» *catching her by surprise ("Vat are you doing here?!") in New York while she was trying to color in a scarf with a marker because there was "too much yellow"*
» *about to pop off on a television crew until she was given Mountain Dew (thanks to Beth for saving the interview with sugar)*
» *disappearing from the group in Romania because she wanted to take a picture of Dracula's birthplace marker*

I could go on and on. I haven't met a single person that spent any time with Eva and doesn't have a running list of memorable moments. Eva was a beautiful soul. I now work with the HIV/AIDS community in hopes of making the world a better place for other people like you taught me to do. Love you, Duchess.

–Sheri Roach
Friend

My crew and I were privileged to travel internationally with Eva several times—to Auschwitz twice, Romania, Israel, Germany, London—and each trip brought a whole range of experiences and emotions. That was just how it was with Eva. Several of these moments will stay with me always, but one most of all.

We were at Auschwitz for the second time, in 2017, and I really wanted to interview Eva in what she called the "blood lab"—the makeshift barrack where she and the other Mengele Twins suffered through insidious experiments by the Nazis. She wasn't thrilled about the prospect for obvious reasons, but she knew it would be good for the film, and at this point I think she understood we were really onto something.

The location required an extra level of permission straight from the top, which was Wanda Hutny, the longtime curator of the Auschwitz-Birkenau State Museum. She was professional throughout, but working one-on-one with her it became clear that she, the daughter of a Holocaust survivor, was not enamored with Eva's forgiveness. And what made things more awkward was that the interview ended up being moved to a Sunday. Because all interviews have to be supervised by a museum employee, and because most of her staff was off that day, Wanda had to make a special trip to the camp to oversee things herself.

The interview, as I'd hoped, ended up being our best of all. Eva was shaken to be back in this horrible building, but she was tough as nails and determined to show how much she had overcome. You could see and hear the pain and courage and vulnerability in pretty much every answer. We started by talking about what she and the others had gone through here, the logistics of the experiments, how scary and belittling they were and the scars they left, particularly psychologically, and at some point, she mentioned, sort of off-hand, that that's why she didn't feel she was a very good mother sometimes.

That stopped me. Like everyone else who gets interviewed a lot, Eva has a set of talking points she likes to stick to and veer toward, and I'd never heard her mention not being a good mother. And in this room of all places. Now, the interview set-up is I'm looking straight at Eva and everyone else is behind me—the videographers, a couple of people from CANDLES and Wanda—so I couldn't see the effect of what Eva was saying was having on the others. I pushed in on the topic and she went there, quietly but matter-of-factly explaining, with tears often welling, that as a young mother she was still in so much pain and confusion from her Auschwitz horror that she wasn't always able to be there, especially emotionally, for Alex and Rina when they needed her as kids. This was right near the end of the interview, and she kept going deeper and getting rawer, and what I only learned later was that Wanda was silently weeping through all of this.

Immediately after the interview ended, Wanda went over to Eva and leaned down and grasped her, her shoulders shaking, and Eva gave her a motherly pat on the head. We actually have a little of this near the very end of the film. At last Wanda pulled back and through tears told Eva that now she finally understood why her own mother had been so distant when she was growing up. This was happening right in front of me and all I could do was stand there in awe. Eva's forgiveness was now neither here nor there; what mattered was that Eva had opened a door to Wanda's own past and pain and helped her confront and understand it. This was one of those moments—and there were many—when I stopped thinking about the film and simply marveled at the life force that was Eva.

And actually, I later found that moment to be something of a micro-cosm of the whole film experience. A lot of people, Jewish, would come to a screening ready to hate it because this was the "survivor who forgave the Nazis." But once they'd witnessed Eva's full story, her transformation, once they saw that forgiveness was, for her, the only way out and that her example and teachings had eased the pain of so many others, they held her in a new light. This was palpable repeatedly. It was the biggest impact of the film, in my opinion, and it was all due to Eva's courage in facing her past head-on and putting herself out there. One of the last things she told *me in that "blood lab" interview was, "When I come back (to Auschwitz), I don't come back as a victim. I come back as a victorious survivor." Eva was more than that. That extraordinary little woman was the embodiment of inspiration—a celebration of life.*

—Ted Green
Producer of *Eva-A7063*

CHAPTER

11

Burned Again

> "Well, I have had better days.
> I have had worse ones as well."
>
> —Eva

In the early morning of November 18, 2003, I received a phone call from my mother while commuting to work in suburban Washington, DC. Clearly distressed, she cried, "Alex, I got a call from the Terre Haute Police Department. Someone burned down the museum last night after midnight. Everything is gone!" Only two years had passed since 9/11 and I immediately feared there might be a targeted effort to destroy Holocaust museums throughout the country. Concerned about the United States Holocaust Memorial Museum in DC, I phoned to warn them about a potential threat. My fears were unwarranted—the sole target had been the CANDLES Museum.

Devastated, my parents drove to the museum later that morning. With the ashes still smoldering, they strolled the grounds of what had once been my mother's dream. Only its trusses remained. Spray painted in black on the remnants of one side of the building were the words "Remember Timmy McVeigh." The perpetrator of the April 1995 Oklahoma City bombing that had killed 168 people, McVeigh, who'd briefly been a member of the Ku Klux Klan, had been executed on June 11, 2001. The site of the execution just happened to be at the Federal Correctional Complex in Terre Haute, only 4.2 miles away from the museum.

Virtually everything, from my mother's photos and posters of Auschwitz to her collection of personal correspondence, was destroyed. All that remained was a drinking cup from Auschwitz, an angel figurine with a banner that read "Peace," and millions of charred pennies.

"Mrs. Kor," said one of the firefighters. "Why do you have pennies in your museum?"

My mother explained that many of the museum's young visitors had trouble comprehending that 11 million people had perished in the Holocaust. The pennies were collected to visually represent those who'd died.

Filmmaker Bob Hercules, in Terre Haute for work on his upcoming documentary *Forgiving Dr. Mengele*, captured the poignant exchange on camera. He also posed an intriguing question to my mother.

"Eva," he said, "do you have it in your heart to consider forgiveness?"

Still in shock, she admitted, "Right now, I have too much pain and sadness in my heart. But I will work on it."

Three days before the fire, my father had been at the museum, fulfilling his role as docent. Just prior to closing, two short-haired men in their twenties entered. Claiming to be students at nearby Ivy Tech Community College, they told my father that they "just wanted to check things out." The men lingered for several minutes, seemingly indifferent to any of the educational exhibits. After escorting them out of the museum, my father wished them well as they climbed into a pickup truck. Upon second glance, he noticed that the front license plate bore the image of a swastika. An eyewitness later recalled seeing the same truck leave the museum parking lot shortly after midnight on November 18.

The arson investigation revealed that the fire, which generated ten-foot-high flames, had begun just after midnight. Fire marshals estimated that at 12:12 a.m., someone doused a brick with gasoline, hurled it through the window of the museum, and then lit a match. The police investigation and media coverage intensified immediately. Officials interrogated my father about his interaction with the two men and attempted to identify other eyewitnesses. Concerned for his safety, I requested a police patrol for my parents' home. The attack was deemed a hate crime and tagged as a case of domestic terrorism.

Several days after the fire, an undercover policeman overheard a man named Joseph Charles Stockett bragging at a local bar that he'd helped "blow up" the museum. Police arrested Stockett, who'd been convicted of the 1976 bombing of a Planned Parenthood clinic in Oregon, on a firearm possession charge and interrogated him about the fire. Described as a "drifter," Stockett had been in Terre Haute for six months following his release from federal prison. An informant stated that Stockett, nicknamed "antisemitic Joe," harbored anti-Jewish views and was an active recruiter for neo-Nazi organizations. Indicted a month after his arrest in Terre Haute, prosecutors failed to uncover enough evidence linking him to the museum fire.

Mary Wright, the museum's education director, issued a statement on behalf of CANDLES, maintaining that the fire was a hate crime. "We are going on the assumption that it was someone from the Aryan Nation or another such organization," said Wright. "Somebody assumed that if our base of operation was attacked, we would be stopped. This incident has crushed our dreams, but not our determination to help understand hatred and prejudice—that everyone deserves the right to be respected." [115]

The Anti-Defamation League concurred with Wright and announced a $2,500 reward for information leading to the arrest and conviction of those responsible. "Without a doubt, we view this as a hate crime," Richard

Hirschhaut, the league's Midwest director, declared. "We believe this was a deliberate act of hate and those who committed it were hellbent on destroying a place of enlightenment and virtue." [116]

———————

The outpouring of support from the Terre Haute community and beyond in the days following the arson was overwhelming. A day after the fire, more than 150 people, including Indiana gubernatorial candidate Mitch Daniels, convened in the museum parking lot. With camera crews present, supporters hoisted signs declaring the arson to be a hate crime. Hundreds of people later marched in unison from the United Hebrew Congregation to the museum to demonstrate that hatred would not be tolerated in their community. Days later, an interfaith candlelight vigil was held that deeply touched my parents and the Jewish community. More than sixty people attended the vigil.

With each attendee holding a candle, my mother declared, "Through the candle, we are illuminating this dark event. Wherever there is light, darkness cannot exist, symbolically anyway." [117] Having now lived in Terre Haute for more than forty years, my parents had come to love their adopted home. The considerable backing from their neighbors signaled to them that the feeling was mutual.

Despite the mountain of moral support, the task of rebuilding the museum remained daunting. Still working full-time, my mother joined forces with a group of local leaders to formulate a plan of action. Fundraising represented the biggest challenge as nearly $500,000 was required to redevelop the property. The museum had traditionally relied on modest donations, sales from my mother's books, and honorariums from her lectures for its operating budget. My parents needed a miracle to generate the funds needed to re-open the museum's doors. Somehow, they got one.

Inundated with more than 700 calls and emails, my mother and the CANDLES volunteers could barely keep pace with the incoming offers of financial assistance. Correspondence emanated as far away as England, South America, and Israel.

"I have never in my nicest dreams imagined that so many Jewish people would care about a little Holocaust Museum here in Terre Haute," my mother professed to the *Jewish Telegraph Agency*. [118]

Local schools held fundraising drives and friends donated what they could. Students from the Dixie Bee Elementary School hatched a fundraiser where they collected pennies to raise money.

Eighth graders at the Honey Bee Elementary School staged an all-night lock-in to raise money, prompting my mother to joke, "You are prisoners of Mrs. Armstrong. I will not volunteer to be a prisoner again. You think that's fun?" Students at Terre Haute North High School, my alma mater, stood in a Wal-Mart parking lot seeking donations. [119] The Seligman Family, prominent donors to CANDLES, from Michigan, made a substantial donation, which made resurrecting the museum a reality. In total, more than $300,000 was raised in support of the rededication effort, mostly coming from total strangers.

My parents were also uplifted by the amount of emotional reassurance they received. School children flooded my parents' mailbox with letters of encouragement. Several of them, including the following letters, hang in the Indiana Historical Society today:

Dear Mrs. Kor:
I am deeply sorry for the loss of your museum. When I found out that you were coming to talk with us, I was thrilled. I was deeply moved by your speech. You gave me such confidence in my dream, which is to walk on my own someday.
I am deeply sorry for your loss. When I read the article, I was speechless. I have no idea what to say to you except I'm very sorry, and I'll keep you in my thoughts and prayers. [120]

Dear Mrs. Kor:
I am sorry to hear about C.A.N.D.L.E.S. If I could, I would replace all the items you have lost. I wanted to tell you, "If you can forgive the Nazis, you can forgive this horrible man." You are a very brave and strong woman. You have made a big impact on my life. Don't give up. Thank you for sharing your story with us. [121]

The Purdue community also offered significant support, as evidenced by this email from Terry and Mary Jo Johnson, Purdue football season ticket holders who sat near my father:

Dear Michael,

Both Mary Jo and I are devastated to read this morning's Indianapolis Star front page. It tells about a fire that happened to your museum. We just can't believe there remains such cowardly people whose minds are warped with mental backwardness. Such behavior is unacceptable and needs to be dealt with immediately.

You are one of the most wonderful people we know. You are a man of integrity and spiritual strength. Your love for America is visible. We weep for you and your wife. We feel so helpless in your situation. I will be glad to come to Terre Haute to help in any way. Are you going to the Indiana-Purdue game this Saturday? If so, we would like to meet you there at the stadium. Just let me know where your seat is located.

Best regards,
Terry and Mary Jo Johnson [122]

Encouragement came from unlikely places as well. Ailing from chronic shoulder pain, my mother drove to see a specialist in Indianapolis just twenty-four hours after the fire. While filling out paperwork in the doctor's office, a 6-foot-1 man with a beaming smile approached her and asked, "Can I give you a hug?"

The *Indianapolis Star* had just run a story on the fire and a photo of my mother sifting through the rubble made the front page. Startled, she looked up and said, "Wait a second, I should know who you are! My son and my husband would know you."

She stood up and embraced the man who identified himself as Isiah Thomas, a former NBA superstar with the Detroit Pistons and the former head coach of the Indiana Pacers. Thomas was there with his daughter who was having her cast replaced. My mother and Thomas exchanged phone numbers, and he later donated to the museum's rebuilding efforts. In 2007, the *Forgiving Dr. Mengele* documentary premiered in New York City, and I invited Thomas, by then the General Manager of the New York Knicks. He was unable to make it, but later sent my mother a congratulatory box of gourmet popcorn.

From the time she heard about the fire, my mother never wavered about rebuilding. "We'll at least open as good as it was before, but I think it will be even better," she announced. "Even if it takes the last pennies in my account, it will open."[123]

Pressure mounted on her to move the museum to Indianapolis, a more cosmopolitan city with a prominent Jewish population and lush financial resources. Adamant that it would remain in Terre Haute, she defiantly proclaimed, "If we relocate the museum, the terrorists win."

Work on the new museum began in late 2003, and in January 2004, Indiana Governor Joe Kernan invited my parents to the State of the State address in downtown Indianapolis. Prior to the speech, Kernan introduced my parents, who were met with a standing ovation.

"Eva Kor, who survived the Holocaust and the destruction of the CANDLES museum in Terre Haute, has vowed to rebuild," Kernan told the legislative assembly. "Her sacrifice, and that of her husband, Michael, ensures that those who may be exposed to hate, intolerance, and bigotry will also be exposed to love, charity, and mutual respect. Our communities are places that we are proud of because of the people that call them home."[124]

My father had last been in the state house fifty years prior when he took his pharmacy boards. When Kernan shook his hand, my father bore a grin a mile-wide, and later remarked, "Only in America can a prisoner shake hands with the governor!" Three days later, my mother was presented with the "Spirit of Justice" award from the Indiana Civil Rights Commission.

Despite the recognition, my parents remained saddened by yet another act of antisemitism. True to form, my mother chose not to dwell on the negative. Driven to rebuild the museum, she focused solely on erecting a better facility that would continue to educate about the epidemics of hate and discrimination.

"You can only do in your life what you can do," she told the *Terre Haute Tribune Star*. "Distressing over it will not change anything."[125]

In a paper in the *Indiana Magazine of History* entitled, "The Firebombing of the Terre Haute Holocaust Museum," author William B. Pickett aptly depicted my mother's optimism in the face of tragedy. "No doubt the most important reason for the public response, however, was Eva herself: her dedication as

Groundbreaking for the new CANDLES Holocaust Museum and Education Center, 2004.

COURTESY CANDLES HOLOCAUST MUSEUM

a witness, a storyteller, and an educator," Pickett wrote. "The fire brought out in her an admirable grace, true to her message of peace and forgiveness. When the television reporters at the scene asked for her reaction, she replied, 'Well, I have had better days.' After a slight pause, she added, 'I have had worse ones.' In the days and weeks that followed, she reached a national audience. 'I am,' she said, 'an eternal optimist. I do this because what I do in my little corner of the world might make a difference.'" [126]

Despite an exhaustive effort by the police and the FBI, the arsonists were never apprehended. Given her decades-long obsession with hunting down Mengele, I worried that my mother would be consumed with finding the firebombers as well. This time it was easier for her to let go. Her focus was on moving on from this terrible chapter, and she rarely spoke about finding the perpetrators.

"I thought I have only two choices when I see anything tragic: be destroyed by it or rise above it," she said at the time. [127]

On April 3, 2005, the museum, rebuilt on the same site, was rededicated. Once again, I emceed the event and like before, a handful of survivors, elected officials, and religious leaders attended. This time, they were joined by several of the students who'd raised money for the reconstruction.

"I'm asking you a special favor," my mother implored the crowd, "to remember today as a shining example of triumph over evil." [128]

The CANDLES Museum after the rebuild. COURTESY TROY FEARS

The new space, expanded to 3,700 square feet, boasted a more elaborate entryway with a vaulted ceiling, elongated windows, a library room, offices, and a display room. Artwork created by local school children and updated visual depictions of Auschwitz lined the freshly painted walls. Newly created memorials recognized additional peoples who'd been persecuted and murdered by the Nazis, including Jehovah's Witnesses, gypsies, the physically and mentally handicapped, and homosexuals. Resolute that the arson would not be forgotten, my mother kept burned drywall from the old museum and some burned books for display.

Years back, a group of students had gifted my father a six-pack of Coke that had been decorated to commemorate his freedom and love for America. The memento had been destroyed in the fire and this same group of students—now in their mid-twenties—returned and presented him with a new six-pack of Coke. Upon accepting the replacement gift, my father beamed with pride, his smile every bit as radiant as it had been the first time around.

The original museum was built with my parents' money and my mother's grit. This time it was a true collective effort. The arsonists destroyed the museum, but in the process, unified an entire community and put CANDLES in an international spotlight.

"As strange as it might sound, the world has learned about our little museum," my mother explained. "If he was trying to destroy the message we were trying to teach, he has accomplished exactly the opposite."[129]

My parents left the rededication ceremony with a newfound optimism. Buoyed by two years of compassion, empathy, and love, they were reminded once more that hate never wins. In the wake of another heinous act of discrimination meant to break their spirit, they'd risen from the ashes yet again.

CHAPTER

A Different Platform

> "When you have a small megaphone, very few people hear you. Through all this what I hope is happening is people are Googling me and finding out what my message is."
> —Eva

hough unwanted, the media coverage of the fire further propelled my mother and her mission into the limelight. As her profile grew, her CANDLES office was besieged with requests for her to speak and annual visitor tallies to the museum skyrocketed. In the past, invitations for her to lecture typically came from Indiana and from around the Midwest. Staffers now fielded calls from both coasts and occasionally overseas. Saying "no" was never her strength and she felt compelled to accommodate every request. Educating her audiences remained her priority, but she also felt an obligation to fundraise for CANDLES, and the newfound demand offered an opportunity to do so. For every stipend she received, she donated a significant percentage back to the museum. Her elevated status enabled CANDLES to grow, but her ambition to uplift others extended well beyond the Terre Haute border. Standing on a new and vastly different platform, she was more poised than ever to do so.

Beginning with the Russian propaganda film of the liberation in the winter of 1945, my mother always seemed to be a magnet for the camera. Her photograph at the 50th anniversary celebration at Auschwitz had made the *The New York Times* and even her ignominious moments, like the Capitol incident, were caught on film. Following her public declaration of forgiveness, more and more television personalities came calling to request she come on their program. Appearances on *Good Morning America, 20/20, Geraldo,* and *Larry King Live* all brought the Mengele twin story to light and helped make her a household name. Now media-savvy, she was very much at ease in divulging details of her Holocaust past to millions. She had come a long way.

Back in the late 1980s, she had been invited to appear on *The Oprah Winfrey Show.* Tied up at my morning podiatry clinic, I briefed a fellow resident that I needed to step out and find the nearest television. Miffed, he reminded me that we had patients to see.

"Yes, but my mother is on *Oprah* right now!" I exclaimed. Unaware of my mother's history, my colleague thought I was joking. He followed me to a doctor's lounge, and we plopped ourselves in front of a TV just in time to watch my mother conduct one of her first major television interviews.

At the show's conclusion Oprah asked, "Eva, if people want to help you, how can they reach you?"

Without hesitation, my mother blurted out her telephone number and said, "Just call me!"

Incredulous, I screamed, "She just gave out our home phone number on national TV!"

As the media appearances and newspaper articles mounted in the wake of the CANDLES museum's rebirth, she became somewhat of a luminary in the survivor community. Her story was captivating, and her deadpan humor added to her likeability. Audiences were staggered when this diminutive woman smiled and laughed when discussing the most horrific of childhoods.

While many fellow survivors remained upset with her decision to forgive, scores of new admirers lined up after learning about her approach. In the early 2000s, my mother had agreed to participate in a documentary chronicling her forgiveness of Mengele to be directed by Bob Hercules and Cheri Pugh. The two followed her for four years, even accompanying her on a pilgrimage to Israel. *Forgiving Dr. Mengele* premiered at the Gene Siskel Film Center in Chicago on February 24, 2006. Living in Washington, DC, at the time, I had high hopes for a premiere in the nation's capital. The city's Jewish Community Center expressed interest and plans were set for a spring debut. The Center's theater held 280 people, but despite the executive director's interest, he was skeptical that we'd sell many seats. A half-empty theater would not sit well with my mother, so I quickly got to work.

Six weeks from the premiere, it appeared the executive director was right— only twenty tickets had been purchased. Given her newfound celebrity, I convinced my mother to hold a "meet and greet" the day of the premiere for those who'd purchased a ticket. An email blast to my network promoting the event hit the mark and we'd soon sold half the ticket allotment. I next reached out to every Senator and Congressman on Capitol Hill and within two weeks, we were at 80% capacity. Before I knew it, calls from a "who's who" of DC politicians were hitting my voicemail. Senator Joe Lieberman's office phoned with a request that the Senator's wife Haddashah, whose parents were Holocaust survivors, speak with my mother. A staffer from Dick Cheney's office called to offer regrets that the Vice President would be unable to attend. Several weeks after the premiere, Barbara Bush's secretary rang. Just twenty years prior, George H. W. Bush had witnessed my mother's eviction from the Capitol. Now, Mrs. Bush's secretary was calling to express regret that the former first lady couldn't make the showing.

On the evening of the premiere, the Jewish Community Center's executive director was stunned to see scalpers hawking tickets outside the theater. Inside, a capacity crowd, including family, friends, and Washington's political bourgeoisie, watched in awe as the film portrayed my mother's exoneration of Mengele.

The wave of publicity was a long time coming. For decades my mother had tried in vain to convince the media to cover the Mengele twin story and help her locate Mengele. Now, the press couldn't get enough of her.

As my mother's star rose, however, so did the level of vitriol that was directed at her. Detractors continued their refrain that she was an attention monger and shameless self-promoter. The fact that she donated most of her honorariums back to CANDLES and never became rich (she lived in her small, modest home up until her death) didn't matter. Their contempt was never more evident than during the 2015 trial of Oskar Gröning.

A former Nazi stationed at Auschwitz, Gröning was on trial for at least 300,000 counts of accessory to murder. Nicknamed "The Accountant at Auschwitz," Gröning was tasked with counting and sorting money taken from prisoners, and responsible for their personal belongings. Upon witnessing a Nazi guard smash an infant's skull against a truck, Gröning purportedly told his superiors that he could no longer work at the camp. His request denied, Gröning claimed that he manipulated his schedule to avoid bearing witness to executions over the next few years. His application to transfer to the front-line was finally granted, and in 1944 he fought in the Battle of the Bulge, where he was wounded.

Following the war, Gröning was imprisoned in a former Nazi concentration camp before being deported to a farm in England and used as a slave laborer. After his release, he returned to Germany and remained there for the next seventy years.

In 2005, Gröning, who'd grown disgusted with a growing population of Holocaust deniers, went public and acknowledged his role at Auschwitz. Though refuting that he'd directly participated in executions, he professed to having observed Nazi executions and admitted to having stolen money and jewelry from captives.

"I would like you to believe me," he pleaded. "I saw the gas chambers. I saw the crematoria. I saw the open fires. I would like you to believe that these atrocities happened because I was there." [130]

Despite his admission, Gröning didn't feel personally culpable for the actions of the Nazis, maintaining he'd only witnessed their crimes.

"Not of my acts, because I never killed anyone," insisted Gröning. "But I offered my aid. I was a cog in the killing machine that eliminated millions of innocent people." [131] Revealing that he'd been tormented with decades of grief, he begged for forgiveness from the Jewish people and from God.

Indicted in September 2014, Gröning's trial began the following spring in Lüneburg, Germany. Though he was now ninety-three, the courts ruled that Gröning was still fit to stand trial as an accessory to murder at Auschwitz.

In his opening statement, he declared, "For me there's no question that I share moral guilt. I ask for forgiveness. I share morally in the guilt, but whether I am guilty under criminal law, you will have to decide." [132]

More than sixty third-party plaintiffs, including my mother, were called in to testify. As the court proceedings began, protestors gathered outside the courtroom with signs reading, "Don't forget Auschwitz."

Prosecutors painted Gröning as an avowed Nazi who'd chosen to enlist in the war effort at the age of nineteen. "Through his activities," they asserted, "he provided the Nazi regime with economic advantage and supported systematic killings." [133] Gröning's attorneys held steadfastly that the former bookkeeper had only been a witness, not an active participant in the killings at Auschwitz.

Prior to the trial, my mother wrote to Gröning requesting he answer a series of questions during the trial and stating the following:

It is true, but sad, that we cannot change what happened in Auschwitz. I am hoping that you and I, as former adversaries, can meet as people who respect one another as human beings and can relate to one another to understand, to heal, and to express thoughts that would not be possible any other way. Any time adversaries meet to repair a relationship, they learn a great deal about themselves and how people function. It cannot be done on television, by telephone, or by Skype; it can only be done face to face. [134]

While other witnesses vehemently pushed for Gröning's conviction, my mother reminded the public of his humanity.

"On the first day of the trial," she recalled, "I introduced myself and reached out to shake his hand. The strangest thing happened. He was trying to say something as he was sitting sideways in his chair. He turned white and fell backwards, not saying a word. He was holding onto my arm, so he did not hit the floor. At that moment he was not a Nazi but an old man who fainted and I was trying to save him from falling. I screamed, 'He is falling, and I can't hold onto him—he is a big old guy!' This was not the interaction I was hoping for. I knocked out an old Nazi." [135] Gröning was driven to the hospital, but not admitted.

The following day, she approached Gröning in an office adjacent to the courtroom and thanked him for accepting some responsibility for his actions. As he rose to greet her, my mother, fearing that Gröning might fall again, hugged him. In return, the former Nazi planted a kiss on her cheek.

"I was a little bit astonished," she admitted. "It was not planned. This is what you see when you see two human beings interact. He likes me, how about that? I am going back to the US with a kiss on my cheek from a former Nazi.... This shows that former enemies can get along as human beings. What on earth do we want to tell the world? Killing each other has never created anything good. I want to teach young people that even former Nazis and survivors can get along." [136]

Unbeknownst to my mother, someone had snapped a photo of the embrace. To the surprise of many and disgust of some, she shared the photo on Twitter later that day. An accompanying caption read, "I know many people will criticize me for this photo, but so be it. It was two human beings seventy years after it happened. For the life of me I will never understand why anger is preferable to a goodwill gesture." [137]

In July 2015, Gröning was convicted of facilitating mass murder and sentenced to four years in prison.

Crestfallen, my mother commented, "I would like the court to prove to me, a survivor, how four years in jail will benefit anybody.... He's still rationalizing it. He's trying to minimize his role as much as possible by saying he only stood and watched. But it could be that bearing witness to what he did in this court case is the best thing he's ever done in his life. Isn't that sad?"[138]

My mother's compassion was met with a plethora of criticism from other survivors who accused her of "repeatedly staging her forgiveness." A joint statement from other witnesses read, "We cannot forgive Mr. Gröning for his participation in the murder of our relatives and another 299,000 people—especially since he feels free from any legal guilt. We want justice and we welcome the resolution that this trial brings."[139] In a condemnation of my mother's call that Nazi prosecutions cease, fellow witnesses asserted that she shouldn't have agreed to testify if she didn't believe in such prosecutions.

Gröning's attorneys unsuccessfully appealed his conviction, and he died in March 2018 at the age of ninety-six while hospitalized prior to the start of his sentence. Gröning's conviction represented one of Germany's final attempts to close the book on Nazi war criminals, but for my mother it was just the latest in her ongoing exercise in forgiveness. It was also proof that, no matter how loud the voices of her critics grew or how much attention she received in the media, she would remain true to her personal mission of not only espousing, but continuing to practice the life-changing commitment to forgiveness. Yet, as the world increasingly tuned into her message of forgiveness, a significant part of her story remained in the dark.

In 2015, filmmaker Ted Green attended my mother's lecture at Clowes Memorial Hall on the Butler University campus. The 2,200-seat auditorium was filled to the rafters while others, hoping for a ticket, waited outside. Having produced films on UCLA coach John Wooden, a Martinsville, Indiana native, and Indianapolis's all-Black Crispus Attucks High School, Green was well-versed in Hoosier lore, but knew very little about my mother. He was there that night only at the convincing of a friend.

Mesmerized by my mother's narrative, Green was also struck by what she hadn't said. Her lectures seemed to include a part one—her early childhood up through Auschwitz and liberation—and part three—her forgiveness of

My mother with Ted Green, producer of *Eva A-7063*. COURTESY WFYI

the Nazis in 1995 and all that followed. But part two—the fifty-year gap in between—was missing. Curious, Green fancied the idea of making my mother the subject of his next film.

She wasn't an easy sell. It hadn't yet been a decade since the Mengele documentary premiered and she was laser-focused on her lecturing. An initial conversation exposed another major obstacle. It became immediately apparent to Green that she was reticent to speak about "part two," the years of anger, bitterness, and the hunt for Mengele. It was still too painful for her. Initially reluctant to consent to the project, she finally relented, and filming began in 2016.

Determined to unearth what she hadn't disclosed, Green sought to better illuminate her and explain her controversial forgiveness of the Nazis. Quickly taking a liking to him, my mother and Green became joined at the hip:

"I spent so much time with her during the two years of production," Green reflected. "We really came to get a kick out of each other and loved to joke and tease. But it was the sad times that stick with me most because they made me understand and appreciate her and her courage. In fact, one afternoon specifically unlocked it all." [140]

"It took time, but then it exploded," Green recollected. "One afternoon about a year in, co-producer Mika Brown and I visited Eva at her house in Terre Haute just to shoot some B-roll of the voluminous, old-school metal filing cabinets in her attic that housed her materials from her time hunting for Josef Mengele. It figured to be kind of a blah day, but at this point Eva had come to trust me and our discussions had grown deeper, and as Mika was setting up her camera Eva started talking off-handedly about the Mengele hunt. I pushed her a little, and she started in about how quickly she went from international hero to outcast—even among her fellow survivors—culminating in her arrest in the Capitol Rotunda.

"At some point I dropped my head and said—mostly to myself—'I can't imagine how alone you must have felt.' And then it came. 'So alone! I've always felt alone!' she bawled. And the tears fell hard.

"Mika showed great instincts and swung the camera to Eva and went in tight, and Eva noticed but was beyond caring. And over the next thirty minutes she opened it all, how lonely she felt at first in the United States, her anger and hurt over the Mengele investigation, the years of rejection, all of it. When Mika and I finally left and stepped out into the bright sunshine, I remember thinking, 'Now we have a story.'"

Over the course of two years, Green came to understand the isolation that her perspective on forgiveness necessitated. Near the conclusion of filming, his crew traveled to Israel to interview the Csengeri twins, Lea and Yehudit, the last people alive from my mother's barrack in Birkenau. The Csengeris, my mother, and Miriam had been the closest of friends for years, but my mother's announcement of forgiveness had precipitated a major falling out. Assuming things had thawed a bit, she looked forward to the visit.

Her hopes were quickly dashed when Green shared that the Csengeris' consent to be interviewed was contingent upon her not being there.

Upon hearing the news, she broke down and said, "Ted, I don't want you to do that interview."

Following several minutes of silence, Green informed her that he had to, and she replied, "I know."

"Eva's forgiveness helped her and others and brought her great fame which she loved," Green pointed out, "but she paid a price for it too."

After the lengthy filming process, *Eva A-7063* finally debuted at Clowes Hall on April 5, 2018, before premiering at locations nationwide. Green was struck by how filmgoers' perceptions changed after viewing the documentary.

"It amazed me when it first happened, but then it became the norm: We'd screen it to a mostly Jewish audience that had come red-faced and ready to hate it—this was the survivor who did the unthinkable: forgive the Nazis. But they'd walk out feeling a lot differently than when they walked in," said Green.

"It really hit home during a screening at the Miami Jewish Film Festival, a screening that was initially canceled because of member objections before Dr. Michael Berenbaum urged them to give it a chance. As the crowd filed in, the anger was palpable, and no small amount of the glares were directed at me. But the reaction was stupendous, and during the Q&A afterward an elderly gentleman stood up—I learned later he was also a survivor—and said through tears, "I still can't go all the way Eva did. But now I understand why she did it."

In June 2019 a Mengele twin from New York who'd previously been furious about my mother's forgiveness of the Nazis called to make amends to her. After seeing the documentary, he came to realize that her forgiveness hadn't been easy, and that'd she struggled with the same pain that he'd experienced for decades. The call meant the world to her.

Back home, buoyed by an educational toolkit that accompanied Green's documentary, Indiana Governor Eric Holcomb established an "Education Day" on January 27, 2020, the anniversary of the liberation of Auschwitz. A generous donation enabled the toolkit and documentary to be sent to every middle school and high school in the state, and the education program later was distributed nationally as part of the PBS Learning Media.

The documentary included a marquee cast—Michael Berenbaum, Stephen D. Smith, Wolf Blitzer, Lucette Lagnado, and Elliott Gould among others, with my mother's friend Ed Asner as narrator—and was the first film or book to thoroughly portray my mother's life, including the fifty years she'd previously been reticent to talk about. The footage of the arrest at the Capitol Rotunda was particularly searing, but Eva insisted it be included.

"Truly, Eva led me, the whole crew and WFYI [Indianapolis's public radio, TV, and news station] on the journey of a lifetime," Green remarked. "If the film helped in any way to reveal this irrepressible, massively accomplished yet scarred and vulnerable woman a little further, I'm happy. It was her courage that made it possible."

<hr>

Along with Mary Wright, my mother had co-authored *Echoes From Auschwitz*, a self-published memoir, in 2000. Given the monumental events that followed—namely the fire, the Mengele documentary, and additional trips to Auschwitz—she felt it necessary to go back to the drawing board. Encouraged by her good friend Peggy Tierney, she co-authored a second book in 2009 with Lisa Buccieri entitled *Surviving the Angel of Death*, published by Tanglewood Press. In the book, my mother recapped her upbringing in Portz and captivity at Auschwitz and dovetailed into her philosophy on forgiveness. Featuring the liberation photo of her and Miriam on the cover, the interior included many photos of the Mozes Family and of Auschwitz. Book tours followed, and she always kept copies handy to give to tour attendees, museum visitors, or in some cases random strangers.

Not long before the book was published, Twitter launched. From day one, my mother was intrigued by "Tweeterland" and immediately recognized the online platform as another way to further her message through the written word. Ultimately amassing more than 33,000 followers, her Twitter adventures became the stuff of legend.

Well-versed in using her cell phone for texting and phone calls, she was far from an expert in social media. The CANDLES staff created an account for her, and they tried in vain to educate her on how to use it. Periodically, they would tweet out information pertinent to the museum or an upcoming lecture.

Out of the blue one day, I received a call from a staffer who was concerned that a controversial tweet had been shared from my mother's account. Sure enough, my mother had secretly mastered the platform and tweeted out an opinion on a political matter. Until this point, I didn't have a Twitter account, but I signed up for one right away in order to monitor her tweets. My standard phone call greeting to her quickly evolved from "Hi, Mom" to "Mom, you cannot post that!"

Twitter provided a new medium for her to spread her mantra of forgiveness, shed light on the stories of other survivors, and call attention to ongoing antisemitic attacks. Her followers could often find 140-character messages of hope and inspiration along with photos of her flashing a peace sign. For those interested in history, she'd post pictures of Auschwitz and tweet out anecdotes on the Holocaust. Periodically, she'd even retweet my posts on proper foot care.

The social media platform also exposed tens of thousands to her sense of humor. Just one day prior to her passing, she tweeted, "Can you believe that today I can get chicken McNuggets near Auschwitz? That would have been wonderful 75 years ago." It wasn't uncommon to find her interacting with celebrities like Ed Asner on Twitter, and on one occasion she invoked song lyrics to catch the attention of one of her favorite performers. Tweeting at Mick Jagger, she wrote:

You had heart surgery yesterday like mine. Like U, "My Beast of Burden" was a bad heart valve. Although it took me a while to get "Satisfaction", I was told "You can't always get what you want". I am sure you will be back on your stage, like me.

Never one to be shy, she wasn't hesitant to voice her opinions on societal issues as well. In December 2018, she posted:

While I am safe in my home I have not forgotten about Syria, Sudan, China,

Cuba, Venezuela, North Korea, Congo, Yemen, Iran & sadly many more who yearn 2 be free-74 yrs. ago I was dying in Auschwitz & the world was silent-let's not be silent tweet 4 freedom 4 all the oppressed people!"

As I kept a watchful eye on her account, I came to realize that there were some unexpected benefits to her being online. In February 2018, my mother called to tell me that she'd gotten stuck inside a local car wash. The car wash's exit door had failed to open automatically, and she remained lodged in her vehicle on the car wash's conveyor belt. In Terre Haute for a family visit, I left my father and sped over to the car wash. An attendant greeted me and reassured me she was fine.

On the drive home, the Vigo County Sheriff called and asked my mother if she was okay. "Why do you ask?" she replied.

The Sheriff informed her that his office had received more than 100 calls expressing concern for her safety. Area 911 operators had also been deluged with calls from her distressed Twitter followers.

While stuck in the car, she'd tweeted out a photo with the caption: "2-10-18: I was trying to wash my dirty car. I must have made a mistake. I am stuck inside the car. I paid for it, and I want my car washed. It couldn't be that difficult, I have done it many times in the past. I am in Terre Haute, IN at 2500 and Hulman." Her legion of followers had grown concerned and had bombarded the Sheriff's office with pleas for help.

After the car wash adventure, I came to realize that Twitter not only allowed her to speak her mind but occasionally offered a safeguard as well. Given her experiences in Mengele's lab, she was averse to having strangers touch her. Flying often for her lectures, she abhorred body searches at security check-points. During one trip, she felt that the agent had been particularly rough and tweeted, "As I lecture about surviving Auschwitz, I barely survive the TSA body search. I detest it." A few hours later, TSA responded on "Tweeterland," and her future trips were without incident.

Though now an octogenarian, my mother still loved connecting with younger audiences. Twitter offered that opportunity, as did other mediums that she came upon by accident. In the summer of 2017, she apprised me of an upcoming trip to Los Angeles. She'd agreed to appear on a podcast, and had consented to an interview with another media outlet with which she was unfamiliar. Having grown more concerned about her health and frenetic schedule, I tried to dissuade her from going. Once again, she got her way. After her interview for the "Sixx Sense" podcast, she made her way over to the BuzzFeed offices, which were located just off the Ventura Freeway. During her interview, the traffic got so loud that the recording engineer had to repeatedly interrupt her and rerecord. The finished interview made noise of its own, and generated close to 200 million views. Several months later, she was floating in the Dead Sea when a crowd of people approached her, having recognized her from the BuzzFeed video.

Awards and honors poured in as my mother grew in notoriety and stature. In 2015, she was invited to be the commencement speaker and awarded an honorary degree at my alma mater, Butler University. Before a capacity crowd of

My mother receiving an honorary degree from Butler University, 2015.
COURTESY BUTLER UNIVERSITY

My mother and I on the red carpet at the 2017 Indianapolis 500.

more than 8,000 people who gave her multiple standing ovations, she detailed her life's story to an enthralled assemblage of 1,000 graduates. Disclosing that she couldn't hug her parents upon being liberated from Auschwitz, she urged the graduates to hug their parents at the graduation's conclusion. Motioning for me to come up on stage, she locked me in a deep embrace as we both wept. No Butler Bulldog basketball win could ever eclipse that moment. In the weeks that followed, inspired donors contributed more than $50,000 to endow a scholarship for Butler's Peace and Conflict Studies program in her honor.

In 2017, Governor Holcomb presented her with the Sachem Award, Indiana's highest civilian honor, and a year later DePauw University also bestowed upon her an honorary degree. She was honored at the Kennedy Center in Washington, DC, by the Anti-Defamation League, received the United Way's "Heroes Award," and was recognized as a "Living Legend" by the Indiana Historical Society. Having received so many accolades in 2017, the *Indianapolis Star* ran a year-end column titled "For Hoosier Holocaust survivor Eva Mozes Kor, 2017 was the year she went viral."[141]

The star turn took her to another place where she felt instantly at home:

the Indianapolis 500. Long characterized as a "Mario Andretti-like" driver by my father, my mother was officially recognized for her lead foot in 2017. In April of that year Bob Bryant, president and CEO of the Indy 500 Festival, announced that she'd serve as the grand marshal for the 101st running of the Indianapolis 500.

"Eva Mozes Kor is a hero and the ultimate renegade," pronounced Bryant. "Despite a childhood that was consumed by utter devastation, she decided to live her life based on hope, forgiveness, courage, and selflessness. Eva's compassion, resilience, and spirit is an inspiration to us all. We are proud to have her serve as the Grand Marshal of the 2017 IPL 500 Festival Parade, and we can't wait to celebrate her!" [142]

"It's surreal because I know I am a survivor of Auschwitz, and that picture of liberation is always clear in my mind," she said in the press release. "From there, marching out of Auschwitz, to being a grand marshal, it's two different worlds that you cannot comprehend it really."

Referencing my father's digs about her driving, she added, "When I was in real estate I was always running to appointments and was driving a little bit faster than the speed limit. So, I said I wanted to meet [Andretti], finally, and I asked him what was his speed and he said 'A lot more than the 30, 35, 40 or 45 you've been driving.'" [143]

It turned out that my mother and Andretti shared more than just a love for fast cars. An identical twin as well, Andretti was eight years old when his parents fled their hometown of Montona, Italy, at the end of World War II. Fearful of living under communist rule, Andretti's parents shuffled their twin boys and daughter to a displacement camp in Udine, Italy, before being sent to a refugee camp in Tuscany, where they lived for seven years.

During a prerace exchange, my mother told the Indy 500 champion that my father had often compared their similar driving styles. In response, Andretti told her that my father should be proud of her. [144]

In recognition of those who'd overcome great obstacles, the 2017 Indy 500 parade's theme fittingly read, "Accelerating the American Spirit." My mother and her family had once been scorned as they were driven out of Portz en route to Auschwitz. Seven decades later, she was waving an American flag to thousands of onlookers who bellowed out her name and showered her with cheers.

My mother was to be on the red carpet of the Indianapolis Motor Speedway two hours before the start of the race. Arriving late due to a traffic jam, I flagged down the driver of a golf cart who graciously agreed to give us a ride. Confused as to where to enter the VIP staging area, the driver ended up going the wrong way until a 6-foot-4 long-haired man draped in tattoos intercepted us. The good Samaritan was Nikki Sixx, cofounder of

My mother with Nikki Sixx.

the rock band Mötley Crüe. *IndyStar* photojournalist Michelle Pemberton had the brilliant idea to introduce Sixx and my mother. Just as Pemberton suspected, the two of them hit it off immediately. My mother later tagged Sixx in a tweet and announced that she wished to be "a rock star like him." The heavy metal star subsequently tweeted back: "Eva my sweetheart you've been a rockstar your whole life. Thank you for inspiring so many." After she appeared on the "Sixx Sense" podcast months later, the two developed a close friendship up until her passing.

The prerace party also allowed her to rub elbows with some of auto racing's luminaries, including Andretti and J. R. Hillenbrand, along with several new and unlikely acquaintances. During the festivities, I found her talking to two men who looked vaguely familiar.

"Who were those two guys that you were talking to?" I asked.

"Oh, I'm not sure," she responded. "One guy invented something and the other guy, I think he is a music professor."

Returning minutes later, the two men greeted us, and my mother introduced me. I shook their hands and asked for their names. "Oh, I'm Rob Angel, and my friend is Mike Mills." Angel invented Pictionary, and Mike Mills was a founding member of the music group REM. Later, I found my mom holding court with actor Jake Gyllenhaal.

Never failing to promote my bachelorhood, she later tweeted, "I have never been to a bigger nor better party than the Indianapolis 500 and with my son Alex, who is single and looking."

Cognizant that this latest honor provided an even bigger medium for her message of forgiveness, she acknowledged, "When you have a small megaphone, very few people hear you. Through all this what I hope is happening is people are Googling me and finding out what my message is." She added, "The bigger the megaphone the more people will hear you. And the idea that we can heal this world, I mean look around, there is so much suffering, so much meanness, and a little bit of common sense coming from an eighty-three-year-old survivor of horrors might get some people to take a look. And that's good enough for me…. What I would like to tell young people is if you do the right thing in life and work hard and make a contribution to society, anyone can be a grand marshal." [145]

Like my father, my mother was a music aficionado and was touched when not one, but four songs were composed with her in mind. In 2017 a German metal group, Saltatio Mortis, introduced a song entitled "*Todesengel*" (translated as "Angel of Death") in tribute to her and Miriam. Fittingly, the band's self-proclaimed motto reads, "He Who Dances Does Not Die"—most apropos for her and Miriam.

Todesengel

by Saltatio Mortis

We were children of Todesengel
Girls of the same shape
The same bodies, the same clothing
We were only ten years old

A-70-6-3
A-70-6-4**
Two tatoos on children's skin
We were numbers, we are alone
A nightmare built of only hate
Sleep in my arms, Achot.***

Fly with me to distant stars
into the Heavens...
I protect us from the black wings****
to show you a better world...

But never sleep as a corpse
Never Sleep with the dead, Achot
Have no fear and no doubt
We will be liberated from this affliction

Take my blood and my body
My pride and my face
But you will never break my will
because I am not your victim!

Sleep in my arms, Achot.

Fly with me to distant stars
into the Heavens...
I protect us from the black wings
to show you a better world...

And I forgave the Todesengel
What he did has hurt me
Anger and Hatred are black seeds
which can only grow into war

Never give up, start dreaming!
Make your dreams come true!
Actions speak louder than words
Forgiveness is so wonderful

Fly with me to distant stars
into the Heavens...
I protect us from the black wings
to show you a better world...

Fly with me to distant stars
into the Heavens...
I protect us from the black wings
to show you a better world...

That same year, Scottish songwriter Raymond Meade produced *The Railway People*, a BBC documentary on the Holocaust. For the soundtrack, he recorded a song which included a poem entitled "How Could It Be" recited by mother. The documentary went on to win an Emmy. As the songs and documentaries accumulated, I recognized that they would be instrumental in keeping my mother's voice alive whenever she passed. However, nothing would honor her voice so vividly as a project that emerged from the Shoah Foundation around this time.

As mentioned previously, in 2016 the Shoah Foundation at the University of Southern California launched the Dimensions in Technology (DIT) venture to capture the narratives of thirteen Holocaust survivors, including my mother.

With Stephen Smith, Director of the Shoah Foundation, and my mother's hologram.
COURTESY ALEX KOR

Her participation in the project wasn't accidental. Having previously heard about Shoah's plan, she phoned Stephen Smith, Executive Director of the Shoah Foundation, and requested to take part. "So, we made a little announcement about the fact we were starting this project," Smith recalled. "I get a call the next day from a lady called Eva Kor. I didn't know her at that point in time. And she says, 'I want to be one of those 3D interviews.'" [146]

During the call, Smith attempted to discourage my mother from participating, citing the project cost and experimental nature of the technology. "Whatever it is, I need to be one of the survivors!" she urged. Still reluctant and not familiar with her narrative, Smith agreed to meet her in Washington, DC. After thirty minutes, my mother's persuasiveness wore Smith down and he consented to her inclusion.

In 2016, she traveled to Los Angeles for a week's worth of interviews, each one lasting approximately five hours. With 116 cameras hovering around her, she shared about her time at Auschwitz, the conception of CANDLES, and her work to promote peace and forgiveness. During the filming, she was peppered with more than 2,000 questions related to her experiences at Auschwitz and wore her traditional blue outfit for each session.

Participating survivors were granted one day off during the week of filming, and many of them headed over to Rodeo Drive for shopping. My mother had other ideas. Somehow, she'd arranged to lecture to a class of ninth graders at a school in Watts. Arriving to find the school, situated in an impoverished and crime-ridden area of Los Angeles, surrounded by barbed wire, she proclaimed, "It's the 'barracks of Watts!'" The level of security wasn't the only surprise. She soon found herself dismayed by the way some of the students had chosen to dress that day. Indeed, as she traversed the country and talked to so many different young people at so many different schools, it was common for her to grouse privately about their wardrobe choices and then, later, to admit that she had to work on not judging people by how they dressed. My mother was far from perfect, but she was self-aware, and she tried to work on this particular disposition even in her twilight years.

Debuting at the CANDLES museum in early 2018, the exhibit enabled visitors to interact with and ask questions of my mother in a virtual interview. In 2020, CBS's Leslie Stahl featured Shoah's DIT project on *60 Minutes*. Interviewing my mother's digital likeness, Stahl engaged in a spirited question-and-answer session:

"Hi, Eva. How are you today?"

"I'm fine, and how are you?"

"I'm good. So how old were you when you went to Auschwitz?"

"When I arrived in Auschwitz, I was ten years old, and I stayed in Auschwitz until liberation, which was about nine months later when we were liberated."

The DIT program remains permanently available at the USC Shoah Foundation in Los Angeles; the Illinois Holocaust Museum and Education Center in Skokie, Illinois; the CANDLES museum in Terre Haute; and handful of other museums around the country. Temporary exhibits have popped up at Holocaust museums around the world, preserving the testimonies of an ever-shrinking population of survivors.

Thrilled that her account would be permanently preserved, my mother commented, "I think it's a great privilege for an eighty-two-year-old person to realize that I might be able to talk to young people fifty years from now and they can hear my voice."

CHAPTER

13

Crossing the Goal Line

"I am ready to go home."

—Mickey

A s my mother evolved into a media darling, my father continued to keep a low profile. Content with attending Purdue football and basketball games, he spent much of his time writing letters to newspaper editors and working at CANDLES. Despite growing more comfortable in his lectures, in sharp contrast to my mother he rarely ventured outside of the museum and never spoke outside of Terre Haute. In 2018, the Vigo County Historical Society honored him with a six-foot Coke bottle that featured several icons significant to his life's story. (Coincidentally, the original Coke bottle contour had been designed by the Root Glass Company based in Terre Haute.) Included was a 1946 photo of him drinking a Coke float from a soda fountain in Vienna,

My father serving as a translator for the 250th Engineer Combat Battalion. COURTESY ALEX KOR

Austria. The bottle still stands at the entrance of the museum.

As he grew older, we had many deep discussions about world affairs, his views on the future, and how he hoped to be remembered. Even on his worst days, he stayed glued to the news and was gravely concerned about the global rise of antisemitism. He fretted over the instability of Israel and remained a staunch believer that the Israeli people had a right to live in peace in the Middle East. While my mother preferred the spoken word to express herself, my father was most at ease with a pen and paper. He continued to write to the *Terre Haute Tribune-Star* in support of Israel and on an array of other topics. Always thoughtful in his approach, he, like my mother on *Oprah*, listed his personal phone number at the conclusion of each letter.

Printed in 2011 the following editorial addressed Israel and ended with his typical dry wit:

As a Survivor of the Holocaust, the fate of Israel, unfolding in the current storm in the Middle-East, is very close to my heart and mind. The Chief "Engineer" of the American Response Operation, is Secretary of State Hillary Clinton. I am concerned; because in her long public career, Mrs. Clinton did NOT exhibit a great "friendship" for the State of Israel.

If I had the opportunity to invite a few friends and foes (of Israel) for a cup

of coffee at my favorite fast-food restaurant, the following would be the thesis of my remarks: "It is an established fact that the "neighbor" states surrounding Israel, have only one mission: To shove the people (of that country) into the Mediterranean Sea. Since the Jews (of Israel) CANNOT swim that well, this project is NOT a viable option" —Michael Kor [147]

Other editorials proved to be prescient, like this one that he sent to *Time* magazine:

I am an American Jew and a Veteran of the US Army; I was serving in the latter stage of the Korean War (stationed in Osaka, Japan). I, also, happen to be a survivor of the Holocaust.

The month-long Israel-Hezbollah War is now history. The cease-fire, imposed by the "international community," left Hezbollah armed and claiming Victory! The Resolution #1701, ironed out by the U.N., has a key provision: Hezbollah must be disarmed. But now, the World Body, the Secretary General and key States, who were involved in crafting the Document, are engaged in Diplomatic Mumbo Jumbo, and the disarming of Hezbollah is NOT even "on the table" (as journalists like to say). It has been reported that one hundred Israeli soldiers have fallen in one month of combat. I am NOT an expert in statistics (I worked in drug stores all my life). But in my opinion, considering the population of Israel, it is analogous to five thousand GIs losing their lives—in the same time frame—vis-a'-vis the population of the United States! It truly saddened me, when I saw in the World Media (and a substantial segment of the American Press) actually rooting for Hezbollah over Israel!! Our society (and journalism itself) has changed considerably in the last few decades. When (or where) did we take the wrong turn as to what constitutes right from wrong? —Michael Kor [148]

His missives were not all political. When his former college PE teacher passed, he penned the following tribute, which appeared in the *Terre Haute Tribune Star:*

The death of Coach John Wooden has opened up my album of memories with very enjoyable "snapshots." Mr. Wooden was my gym teacher at Indiana State, which at the time was known as Indiana State Teachers College (ISTC). The year was 1948—while I was on a long waiting list for my acceptance at the Purdue University School of Pharmacy. When Coach Wooden won his first NCAA

Championship at UCLA, I sent him a congratulatory note. I began my letter as follows: "Mr. Wooden, you may not remember me. My name is Mickey, and I was the shortest guy in your PE class." I received a gracious Letter, dated April 13, 1964. He thanked me for taking the time to write. And proceeded to discuss the "strategic" aspects of the Conference Championship and ultimately the NCAA Tournament Title. I have this letter framed and hanging on the wall over a small desk where my PC is now located. Coach Wooden made a major impression in my life. I tried to emulate his philosophy and his great vocabulary as I have gone through life. Yes, Mr. Wooden was the finest human being I have ever met.... And on a few occasions, he demonstrated to me how to shoot a jump shot which has a chance to culminate in two points. —Michael Kor [149]

By my conservative count, he sent more than 300 such letters to various news outlets over the course of his lifetime. I learned that my uncle Shlomo employed the same tactic, sending scores of letters to Israeli newspapers to express his own concerns. I can only surmise that their parents underscored the importance of making sure their voices were heard. While not a 3D hologram, the letters are a vivid memento of my father that echo his quiet, unassuming presence and keep his voice alive for me today.

While my mother adopted forgiveness in the mid-1990s, my father was slow to come around. He wrestled to forgive, and my parents occasionally debated forgiveness at the dinner table. In 2013, my mother, father, and I were invited to participate in a dialogue between Holocaust survivors and second and third generation Nazis. Dubbed "Weimar, Repair the Future," the conversation would be held in a small village near Weimar, Germany, a short distance from the former Buchenwald concentration camp. Following my acceptance of the invitation, my father agreed to join me. However, as he thought more about it, and specifically the event's proximity to Buchenwald, he changed his mind. Even after seventy years, he couldn't bring himself to go back to Europe.

Still hoping he'd participate, the event organizer paid for a film crew to travel to Terre Haute and interview him.

When the producer asked, "If you were to come to Germany, what do you think that you would see?"

My father broke down and responded, "I have so many bad memories of Germany. If I were in Germany and walking down the street of cobblestones, when I would look down at the street, I would still see blood running through the cobblestones. I am sorry but that is how I feel."

My father with Coach Wooden in Terre Haute in 1997. COURTESY ALEX KOR

In the *Forgiving Mengele* documentary, he choked up as he articulated his struggle to forgive: "My war story, my prison, it was so sad that a human being couldn't sit through it. A person would just vomit and leave the theater. That's the reason I never talk about it. I have forgiven the Germans, but not the stockade, not the wires. The shouting, the yelling—I don't want to see them again!" [150]

Even as he felt he could not return to Europe, his perspective still evolved as he remained stateside. In a symbolic gesture in 2010, he called a press conference to announce that he was forgiving the family of a famous NBA player of German descent. Not entirely certain if the player's family was affiliated with the SS, my father hoped to demonstrate that his stance on forgiveness was changing. Later that fall, he spoke at the museum and formally made amends to Germany.

"I would like to declare my forgiveness to the German people for their World

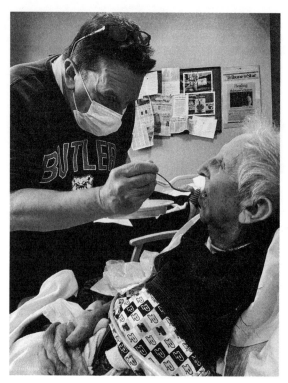

With my father in his final year. COURTESY ALEX KOR

War II atrocities," he declared. "And hopefully I will have the opportunity before I leave this planet to visit Frankfurt and Berlin and shake hands with their citizens."[151]

A thirteen-year-old boy in attendance later shared, "I think it's good he's forgiven the Nazis. I don't know if I could do that." My father composed a formal letter of forgiveness and sent it to the German government. He never received a response.

In 2019 Bruno Dey, a former Nazi guard at the Stutthof concentration camp, was tried for complicity in the murder of 5,000 prisoners. My father didn't remember Dey, but their time at Stutthof overlapped and my father was asked to provide a statement. I really didn't know what he was going to say but anticipated it would include a call for punishment. Instead, his comments surprised me.

"The war killed a lot of people," he said. "In war, you do not think about consequences, you just keep fighting and firing guns. Every day in Stutthof, we were afraid for our lives, but it is all forgotten now. You can no longer keep track and you do not choose your feelings. My feelings are that in war, people are caught in events that they cannot control. The war is over and he [Dey] should be forgiven. The war is over."[152]

By this point my mother had passed, and I believe his forgiveness was in tribute to her legacy. Following his statement that day, I remember him looking at me and saying, "Mom would have liked that."

Markus Goldbach, my father's lawyer in Germany, later wrote to me: "The story of your dad is so important to mention and to show the world. This should include his marriage to Eva and his decision to support her now that she has passed away. This is a form of true love." [153]

Goldbach was right. My parents' marriage was never perfect, but each understood the others' perspective on forgiveness and appreciated it. Knowing my mother would never be content

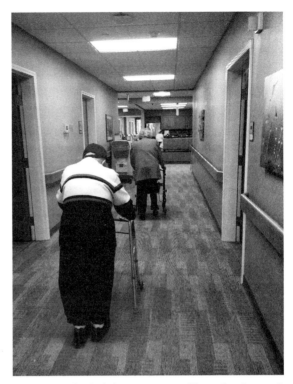

My parents in their latter years—still moving forward.
COURTESY ALEX KOR

staying at home, my father gave her the latitude to lecture around the world. Conversely, she knew that he preferred to keep a low profile and recognized his reticence in talking about his past. For fifty-nine years they shared a life together in Terre Haute. They didn't always see eye to eye, but loved and respected each other until the very end.

My father's final days lasted for years. In July 2016, he was hospitalized with a urinary tract infection and then discharged to a nursing home in Terre Haute. My mother notified me that he wasn't doing well and I flew in from Baltimore to see him, arriving to find his nursing home room vacant.

"He's being fed," said the attending nurse, who then directed me to the dining hall. Scanning the room, I noticed a withered, decrepit man being spoon fed. On second glance, I realized that man was my father! I couldn't believe it. I'd been with him just two months prior and he was now unrecognizable. Barely able to open his eyes, he tried in vain to identify the stranger standing in front of him. We didn't know it at the time, but the episodes of forgetfulness he'd experienced earlier that year were morphing into full onset dementia.

I'd never seen my father in this condition and couldn't fathom how he'd declined this rapidly. Convincing myself that this was just an aberration, I returned to see him the next morning in an upbeat mood. As I approached his room, I heard a desperate cry for assistance: "Someone help me! Someone help me!" My father had become entangled in his IV line and there was no one around to help. Within a few hours, he was readmitted to the hospital while I tried to locate a better nursing home. I found a facility on Terre Haute's north side that was willing to admit him and was relieved when Rina, who'd been living in San Francisco, informed us she was moving home to help care for him.

I'd just gotten back to Baltimore when my mother called to tell me that his condition had deteriorated. He was barely eating and wasn't responsive.

"Prepare for the worst," she advised. Fortunately, Rina arrived in Terre Haute shortly thereafter, and her return lifted his spirits. Though he didn't initially know who she was (he called her "Missy"), he started to eat more and regained his strength. The trouble was that he slept through the day and wasn't ambulatory.

Rina wasn't a big sports fan, but came up with an ingenious idea that proved to be a Hail Mary. My father had attended Purdue football games since the 1980s and loved predicting the outcomes of their contests. I'd post his forecasts on my Twitter feed and several of my friends based their wagers on his prognostications. Rina hoped that the Boilermakers' 2016 televised home opener might revitalize him and somehow, it did. He woke up shortly after she switched on the game and rooted on his alma mater as they pounded Eastern Kentucky by a 45-24 score. He was able to recall players' names and analyzed game situations as if he were John Madden. Rina had the TV ready to go every Saturday, and my father's condition subsequently improved. Unfortunately, Purdue's did not, as they went 2-9 following their opening victory, but that didn't seem to matter. My father's appetite returned, he got stronger, and the effects of his dementia were less apparent. Rina's reintroduction of Purdue football helped extend his life by a few years, and words can't express how grateful I am to her.

In 2019, I moved back to Indiana for work, allowing me to spend more time with my father. Normally reticent to speak about his legacy, he shared with me that he hoped to be remembered as a Holocaust survivor who'd beaten impossible odds. Inches away from being gunned down at the age of nineteen, he'd extended his life by seventy-six years through sheer willpower, unyielding optimism, and, as even he would admit, luck.

A lover of sports analogies, he once said, "If my life is like a basketball game, I am in my second overtime. I had hoped for a six or seven overtime game." He also wanted to be known for his integrity, character, and patriotism. Dating back to his 1945 written account of his liberation, my father's greatest desire was to repay his debt of gratitude to his adopted country, the United States of America.

In his final days, I reminded him that he had recompensed more than his fair share given his numerous contributions as a husband, father, community servant, and veteran. He was proud of what he'd overcome, but, even in the end, remained haunted by survivor's guilt. In February 2020, he gave one of his last lectures and tearfully alluded to the painful, permanent separation from his mother in 1941.

"My mother saved my life," he told the audience. "It doesn't get any more painful." [154]

———————————

The timing of my homecoming was fortuitous given that my mother would pass just a few months later. On that fateful July 4 morning, I struggled on how to break the tragic news to my father. By 1:00 p.m. Poland time (6:00 a.m. EST) we'd yet to publicly announce her death, and I feared he'd hear before I could reach him. Around 5:00 a.m. EST, I phoned Rina with the somber news and we mulled over how to inform him, ultimately deciding that she would time her lunchtime visit with my call. My fingers trembled as I dialed his number and I fortunately caught him on my first attempt. He detected right away that something was wrong and asked if I was okay.

"Dad, I need to tell you something," I said, trying to contain my emotions. "Mom just passed away in our hotel room."

He asked if she'd been in pain and said, "Alex, this is very important to me. Were you with her when she passed away?"

With tears in my eyes, I confirmed that I had been.

"That is all you can ask for," he replied. "I am very proud of you."

In the weeks that followed, he fell into a worrisome depression, and my daily pep talks made little impact.

Finally, I told him, "Mom wouldn't want you to be sad. She'd want you to smile and be thankful. Be grateful that you had her for fifty-nine years." He promised to address his grief over the coming days, and he kept to his word: his mood lifted, his crying ceased, and his piano playing resumed. While he shared his deep affection for my mother to me, he rarely disclosed his feelings to the public. An interview he gave to a British filmmaker in 2015 was a rare exception and illustrated his deep passion for her. My father spoke about how her beauty and "very admirable" army uniform first attracted him to her.

"What does Eva mean to you?" he was asked.

"I wouldn't be alive without her," he replied. "She takes care of me."

What most moved me, though, was his response to the filmmaker's final question. When invited to encapsulate his feelings for his wife of fifty-nine years, he stated simply, "I would run into a burning building for her."

My father was a staunch defender of my mother, even after her passing. Several days after her passing, Deborah Lipstadt, a professor at Emory University and author of the book *Denying the Holocaust*, wrote an op-ed in the *Washington Post*. The hit piece, choked with false assumptions and outright lies, threw dirt on my mother's grave and infuriated both me and my father. I contacted the *Post*, and they printed a retraction and correction several days later. My father requested a framed copy of the retraction and proudly hung it in his room.

In the summer of 2020, my father experienced another UTI and neither oral nor IV antibiotics were effective in fighting the infection. He'd stopped eating, had difficulty swallowing, and our only option was to put him on a feeding tube. The night before the tube was to be administered, he fell and was sent to the emergency room. Fearing the worst and knowing that he'd not eaten in two days, I (in my best Mario Andretti imitation) sped the entire seventy miles from Indianapolis to Terre Haute.

A throwback to our football days. COURTESY ALEX KOR

As I walked into the ER, my father proudly proclaimed, "There is my son! He is a podiatrist in Indianapolis! How are you tonight, Alex?" I was astonished at his vigor. The medical staff had found a way to feed him, and he was now feeling fine, even without a Purdue game. The ER doctor reminded me that Witham Health Services, my new employer, had an extended care unit and recommended I get my father there. Three days later, he was transported to the unit in Lebanon, Indiana, where we got to see each other nearly every day for the next two years.

My office was a stone's throw from my father's room at Witham, and the close proximity allowed for much father-son bonding and belly-aching laughter. One morning, I walked in to check on a patient whose room was adjacent to my father's.

I asked if she'd slept well the previous night, to which she responded, "Dr. Kor, I sleep well every night because your father serenades me to sleep every night at 8:00 p.m.!"

Early on during his time at Witham, I received a phone call urging me to get to his unit immediately. I assumed he'd fallen, or perhaps worse, and sprinted to the dining room. Refusing to eat, he began wildly gesturing at the cream and crimson colored bib the staff had applied to his neck. I immediately removed the bib.

"Finally, someone understands," he mumbled. "I am a Purdue fan; I will not wear an Indiana University bib!" The other staff and residents roared with laughter, and my father resumed his lunch. From that point on, he only wore Purdue bibs that were made especially for him.

From July 2020 to August 2021, he received great care and cherished my daily visits—even during COVID, when I communicated with him from outside his window.

One day while riding his stationary bike, he said, "Alex, can you come over here?"

"Sure," I replied. "How can I help you?"

"Alex, I am *so* happy to be alive," he gushed. "I can see you. I see Rina a lot. I watch the news on TV. I eat good. I am so happy. I think I can live forever."

In October 2020, he celebrated his ninety-fifth birthday by eating cake and, of course, watching a Purdue football game. He continued to play the piano at every opportunity, his repertoire including "Besame Mucho" by Tino Rossi and a variety of Dean Martin, Bing Crosby, and Frank Sinatra numbers. When he wasn't feeling well and didn't want to play the piano, *I'd* play Dean Martin's greatest hits in his room, and *he'd* sing along for hours. I think I've heard "That's Amore" at least 100 times!

In August 2021, he had a bad week and wasn't eating, nor playing the piano—a real sign that he wasn't himself. One evening, after I'd helped him eat and take his medicine, his stomach spasmed and he threw everything up. His face was ashen, and he'd stopped breathing. Panicked, I immediately called for help. This was the same manner in which my mother had died, and my mind raced back to that humid night in Kraków.

"Dad, come on! You can do it, hang in there!" I urged.

Two nurses administered oxygen and his blood pressure slowly improved. As his grip got stronger, so did my hope. I left him with the nurses and rushed over to the hospital where I luckily found a pulmonologist. After explaining that my father had aspirated, the doctor raced with me to his room and began suctioning him. He was transferred to intensive care where I remained at his side until midnight, but his vitals weren't stable, and I wasn't confident that he'd make it through the night.

A dour mood greeted me the following morning at the hospital. My father's nurse, with a look of grave apprehension, shared that his vitals and lab results weren't good. He was sleeping and unresponsive as I sat next to him. Not surprisingly, ESPN's College Gameday was on television and, as if he were awake, I began previewing the upcoming games to him.

About an hour later, his nurse walked in and exclaimed, "What is going on in here?"

She then revealed that since I'd started conversing with him, his vitals had significantly improved. "He hears you!" she emphasized.

Still skeptical, I continued my football analysis until a voice interrupted me again.

"Hi Alex," said my father. "How are you?"

A day later, my father showed significant improvement and was returned to his regular room.

I paid him a visit and as I walked in, he said, "Alex, there you are. I have a question: where are my socks?"

"Dad, your socks are on your feet," I replied.

His expression turned grim, and he whispered, "You know, I think I am ready to go home."

"What do you mean?" I probed.

"I want to see your mom again and all of my brothers," he replied.

Thinking he might be delusional, I asked when he thought this might occur. He didn't hesitate: "Oh this will happen in two months."

Almost exactly two months later, I paid him my daily visit, knowing he was nearing the end. He was weak and his breathing was labored.

Looking me squarely in the eyes, he murmured, "Alex, I am not doing good."

On October 18, we watched our final football game together. Around 10:00 p.m., his nurse Bill came into the room and encouraged me to go home and get some sleep, but I refused: I knew my father would pass soon, and I wanted to be on hand to say the Kaddish if he did.

"Alex," Bill replied, "you know there are three Jews in this room!"

I went home and slept poorly, my cellphone pressed against my head. No calls came, and I held onto hope that maybe my father had improved. I hopped in the shower around 5:50 a.m. and as I toweled off, noticed a voicemail on my phone. I didn't listen to it and immediately called Bill, who delivered the news that my father had passed at 6:01 a.m. on October 19. Just as Bill promised, he'd said Kaddish.

I went to Witham Hospital to say goodbye one last time and, as I did with my mother, kissed him. On October 24, 2021, as "Taps" played per his wishes, he was buried next to my mother at the Highland Lawn Cemetery in Terre Haute. Approximately fifty mourners huddled under a tent as a monsoon descended on the burial site. As the Rabbi said Kaddish, the sky erupted, accompanied by a booming peal of thunder. The ground shook, and the Rabbi paused to look at me in disbelief. Addressing the mourners, he declared what we all knew to be true: my mother had picked an opportune time to make her entrance at the memorial.

In a twenty-seven-month span, I'd lost both my parents. One of my great regrets is that I'd failed to ask my mother what role I should play in extending her mission. I never got that chance because she passed so suddenly. Conversely, my father and I had many conversations about his hopes for me. He was proud of me and desired that I continue to remember and honor my mother. In the months that followed, I spent much time contemplating how I could carry on both of their legacies.

CHAPTER

Fortunate Son

> "I hope that you are both proud of me."
>
> —Alex

Despite having not grown up in a wealthy family, I've always felt blessed beyond measure. Though we'd lost most of our extended family in the Holocaust, my parents ensured that Rina and I were raised in a home filled with love and compassion. The values they instilled in me, coupled with the exceptional education they provided, paved the way for a successful career as a podiatrist. In 1990, at the age of twenty-nine, I began my practice at the Welborn Clinic in Evansville, Indiana. Fulfilling a lifelong dream to serve on the medical staff for a NCAA Division I school, I also assumed the role of team podiatrist for the athletic department at the University of Evansville.

My experience in Evansville was wonderful, and I remain close with many of the friends I met during my five years there. Though satisfied with my career, Evansville lacked a significant Jewish population, and I set my sights on a more diverse city. After announcing that I'd accepted a position in Atlanta, a colleague's wife sensed my hesitancy in relocating.

"Look Alex, just think of this as an adventure!" she encouraged.

I've heeded her words, and the last twenty-nine years have been quite the journey. My podiatry career has taken me to Colorado, Illinois, Ohio, Georgia, Washington, DC, Maryland, and Wisconsin. I'm now "back home again in Indiana" and work as a podiatrist in suburban Indianapolis.

My "nationwide podiatry tour" has brought much reward, though I've had my struggles as well. In my early years in Evansville, a patient called me a "Jew boy," and I was once asked if Jewish people had horns. In a separate encounter, a patient inquired if I was going to "Jew" him on his medical bill. After taking a deep breath, I offered that his next three visits would be free. While living in Galesburg, Illinois, I began receiving anonymous, threatening letters. My first correspondence arrived in 1998, and on occasion, I still receive hate mail from this individual. Having lived all over the country, I've sadly learned that no geographic region is devoid of hate.

While my career has far exceeded my expectations, I can't say the same for my dating life. Despite my mother's endless advertising of her "single, Jewish son," I remain a bachelor. I've logged many hours on a variety of dating platforms and attended the "Matzoball," a Jewish singles party held every Christmas Eve, on many occasions, but have yet to find the right female companion. I remain optimistic, though unlike my parents, will not be offering up my personal phone number in these pages.

Since 1987, when I was first diagnosed and successfully treated for testicular cancer, I've been lucky to remain cancer-free. Unfortunately, I've lost many other family members over this time period. My uncle Leib lived most of his life in Connecticut and prospered as a lumber yard executive. In 1980, after having relocated to Florida, his car broke down on the side of the highway. While walking to find a payphone, he was struck by a car and died instantly. My uncle Shlomo enjoyed a lengthy career as a newspaper executive in Tel Aviv, Israel. With a poor grasp of the English language, he rarely spoke to my father, who knew little Hebrew. One day, Shlomo informed his children that he wished to speak to his brother back in the States. Though surprised, his children assured him they'd arrange a call. On the day the brothers were to talk, Shlomo died of natural causes.

My "adopted grandparents," Lt. Colonel Andrew J. Nehf and his wife Carolyn, have both passed away. I'm still in contact with their children and grandchildren and remain eternally grateful for what Lt. Colonel Nehf did for my father. On occasion, the sight of a can of Coke triggers the memory of their fortuitous encounter and lifelong friendship.

Though I still have cousins overseas, Rina, me, and my cousin Robert (Leib's son) are the only living descendants of the Kor Family in the United States. Rina has also never married and has worked primarily in the nonprofit sector. Taking after my father, she prefers to keep a low profile. Having settled on the West Coast, we rarely get to see each other, but I hope she knows how much I appreciate her and all that she's done for our family.

Though I'm getting older, having children remains a dream of mine. Having long yearned to be a father, I still aspire to someday play backyard sports with my kids and take them on family drives through the countryside. More than anything, I'd love to tell them about their grandparents' remarkable tale.

<hr>

After finalizing arrangements to send my mother's body back to the United States, I departed Kraków and flew back to Indiana. The flight home was always arduous, but this one was especially grueling. Alone, I stared out the window and wondered what the future held. How would my father and Rina cope with her passing? What would become of the museum? Who would carry my mother's torch forward? Unable to sleep, I grabbed a pen and paper and transcribed my thoughts:

As I fly back to the United States after losing my mother on July 4, I am flooded with a million emotions. Although I should probably be sleeping and getting rest, the pain in my heart will not allow such leisure. There is no remedy that will suffice. I would think that there would be a finite supply of tears, but the dam is broken. I should be (and am) grateful for having both of my parents for fifty-eight plus years, but the pain is constant. In the last few years, I have been amazed how well a majority of my friends have handled their losses. But, after the events of July 4, 2019, I must now battle this demon. Therefore, with a pen in hand and a day of travel ahead, I feel obligated to allow my emotions to paint this page.

It is my belief that whether you are eight-years-old, eighteen-years-old or fifty-eight-years-old, having a loving mother is important. And, I had a loving mother. If I knew that on the morning of July 4th, my mother would be gone, I would have told her many things. If I had one more chance to talk to my mom, I would tell her that she was a great mother. If I could see my mom one more time, I would tell her that I love her with all of my heart. If I could spend one more day with her, I would tell her I am still trying to have a family (but luck has been an issue). If I had one more meal with my mom, she would know that I (and all involved parties) did everything we could to save her on 7/4/2019. If I had one more minute with my mom, I would give her one more kiss and a long hug.

But I realize that these wishes are nothing more than an impossible dream. How do I channel my pain that this loss has produced? Is it possible to utilize the energy from these unfulfilled desires into positive action? Well, I hope so. That is, at some point, I will indeed try to continue my mother's life work. There is unfinished business. Like my mother, I want my life to count for something. Moreover, from her perch in heaven, as she eats a few more McNuggets while chatting with my aunt, Miriam, she will say: "… Hi Sweetie. You are doing great. I love you, too…"

My mother's passing made headlines in *The New York Times, The Washington Post,* and multiple news outlets around the world. On August 4, 2019, a celebration of her life was held at Indiana State University's Tilson Auditorium. United States Senator Todd Young, Indiana State President Debra Curtis, and former Terre Haute mayors Jim Jenkins and Duke Bennett were among those who paid tribute to her.

On August 18, 2019, a second celebration of her life was held at Clowes Memorial Hall on the Butler University campus. Among the event's speakers, I was joined Davidson Men's Basketball Coach Bob McKillop, whose team had visited Auschwitz with my mother the previous year; Holocaust scholar Michael Berenbaum; and Indiana Governor Eric Holcomb. Together, we paid tribute to her life and legacy. The previous spring, my mother and Peyton Manning had both been named as "Indiana Living Legends," and I referenced the NFL great as I concluded my eulogy:

If we consider a sports analogy, think of my mother as the best player on a football team, perhaps like Peyton Manning when he played for the Indianapolis Colts. Unfortunately, when he hurt his neck in 2011, the Colts won only two games. To achieve the same success, Manning's teammates needed to play harder, more as a team. They did not. With my mother no longer here as the quarterback, we cannot afford the same outcome.… We all need everyone to rally around my mother's legacy to keep her memory alive forever, always being mindful of her passion for CANDLES and Holocaust education. This must be a cohesive effort that utilizes all resources and avenues for the advancement of her message.… I urge each and every one of you to get involved…

Over the years, I have frequently heard my mother say, "If one person throws a pebble in a lake, a small ripple will be produced. If two people throw pebbles in a lake, two ripples will occur, and you have a ripple touching a ripple. If fifty people throw pebbles in a lake, a small wave will result, and all of those ripples are touching one another. This is the effort that we need to extend my mother's legacy.

I had a dream shortly after my mother's passing. I heard something like, "Omaha! Omaha!" It was my mother from the "pressbox from heaven." She was calling an audible. To score a touchdown, my mother is calling a trick play that involves me throwing a pass to everyone in this room. In other words, please throw thousands of pebbles in that lake so that all of us can create ripples of hope, healing, and humanity, to complete my mother's unfinished business.

In a symbolic gesture, I then tossed a football from the stage to Dr. John Abrams, a dear family friend, reiterating that we all had a responsibility to pass her message forward.

Tributes from around the country flowed in. My email inbox was flooded with condolences from dignitaries, past trip participants, and other survivors. Raymond Meade, who'd previously composed a song in my mother's honor, wrote another tune entitled "Indiana Blue" in her memory.

Indiana Blue

by Raymond Meade

I felt like I'd just found you
And I wanted you to be there
For when life throws up its problems
And we have to seek our shelter
But though now my heart weighs heavy
I wasn't there or ready
For the time that none of us know
I didn't want to have to let go

If the price of love is pain
It's a price that was worth paying
When I had you in my life
Time stood still at times
If I have to let you go
Then I have to let you know
I'll always love you my Indiana Blue

I saw the way you carried
Eastern European barbarians
And how you turned them into dust
And then flew away a bluebird
I'm glad no rules residing
If there's hearts set on colliding
We shared joys and common worries
But I'm just sad our time was hurried

If the price of love is pain
It's a price that was worth paying

When I had you in my life
Time stood still at times
If I have to let you go
Then I have to let you know
I'll always love you my Indiana Blue

When I saw you for the last time
And we hugged and said our goodbyes
I never thought it was the last time
Or I'd have told you more than goodbye
And I hope you'll travel safely
And you found your way to family
You will always travel with me
In my heart and in my memories

If the price of love is pain
It's a price that was worth paying
When I had you in my life
Time stood still at times
If I have to let you go
Then I have to let you know
I'll always love you my Indiana Blue
I'll always love you my Indiana Blue
I'll always love you my Indiana Blue

My initial efforts to prolong my mother's legacy entailed defending her honor and began immediately following her death. On July 16, 2019, just twelve days after her passing, Emory University professor Deborah Lipstadt took aim at my mother's stance on forgiveness in a *Washington Post* editorial entitled "She survived Auschwitz — and eventually forgave her persecutors. Should others?" In her dubiously timed essay, Lipstadt examined the Jewish philosophy of forgiveness and called into question my mother's public declaration:

"Kor always insisted she was forgiving these perpetrators in her name only. Nonetheless, many survivors were troubled by her actions. I watched them grimace as audiences gave her standing ovations and the media described her as someone 'who found it in her heart' to forgive, the implication being that survivors who did not follow her lead were unable to rise above their resentment. Survivors told me they felt they were being depicted as hardhearted, while Kor was being celebrated as the hero, someone bigger than they." [155]

Mischaracterizing my mother's approach, Lipstadt went on to claim that she had granted forgiveness on behalf of others as well:

"What rankled many survivors, and their children, was not her forgiving but her public and rather dramatic bestowal of amnesty on all Nazi murderers, including those who had done little—if anything—to demonstrate that they grasped how terribly wrong was their attempted annihilation of an entire people. She appeared to be giving them not just her personal forgiveness but theirs, too." [156]

My grief instantly morphed to outrage. Infuriated that she'd chosen the occasion of my mother's death to opine about forgiveness, I engaged in a heated email exchange with Lipstadt. On July 19, *The Washington Post* printed a minor retraction and included my response to Lipstadt's hit piece:

Regarding Deborah E. Lipstadt's July 17 op-ed, "Should we forgive the Nazis?":

My mother, Eva Mozes Kor, announced in 1995 her forgiveness of Nazis. More importantly, my mother forgave the Nazis on her behalf only; she was explicit about that. Anyone interested in my mother's complicated life and legacy should watch the recent documentary "Eva: A-7063," which includes insight from esteemed Holocaust scholars Michael Berenbaum and Stephen D. Smith, as well as the recently deceased Wall Street Journal reporter and author Lucette Lagnado. My mother was far from perfect, but she inspired a lot of people, and I am very proud of her. [157]

Lipstadt was entitled to her opinion, but her op-ed was littered with inaccuracies, and I took issue with her gutless approach. Why hadn't she made her opinions known before? Had she even bothered to fact-check her work? Why hadn't she ever attempted to interview my mother? Even a cursory search of the internet would have unearthed my mother's definition of forgiveness which reads in part, "Each person can forgive only in his or her name. One cannot forgive in the name of all Holocaust survivors. Forgiveness is a very personal thing, but if we feel troubled and hurt by learning about the victimization of others, then we have the right to take action."

Sadly, she wasn't alone in seizing the opportunity to condemn my mother's message.

Just days after Lipstadt's editorial, Efraim Zuroff, a writer for *The Jerusalem Post*, inexplicably compared my mother's forgiveness to the Apollo 11 moon landing. In his bizarre correlation, Zuroff asserted that while the moon landing and my mother's forgiveness had garnered worldwide publicity, moral sacrifices were required for both to occur. In Zuroff's view, the triumph of the moon landing was forever tainted given that several of the scientists responsible for building the V-2 rockets had been Nazis. In my mother's case, Zuroff devalued her declaration of forgiveness and questioned why she hadn't pushed for atonement from the perpetrators.

"What ties these two issues together is the question of how to relate to those who committed the crimes of the Holocaust," wrote Zuroff. "One could suggest that in both cases the motivation of Kor, on the one hand, and the Americans behind Operation Paperclip on the other, was to produce some good out of evil. Kor was ostensibly offering survivors and others a means of 'liberating' themselves from hatred and hostility, while the US officials were helping to defend the Free World from potential Soviet aggression. But at what price and under what conditions? Did Kor or the Americans ever ask for an apology or detailed testimony about the crimes they had committed and witnessed?" [158]

Throughout the editorial, Zuroff threw cheap shots at my mother, and again, I felt compelled to respond by email. A year later, the pattern repeated itself: another column, with more unfounded criticisms, another email from me, and no response. The news outlet was no better. Despite multiple requests that they do so, *The Jerusalem Post* never issued a retraction in either instance.

As much as this continued criticism rankled me, I had to shift my focus as my mother's passing had resulted in new avenues for me to help extend and

In front of my mother's mural in downtown Indianapolis, her bobblehead in hand.

COURTESY ALEX KOR

elucidate her message. Some efforts were more monumental than others. Literally. In 2020, with the support of local philanthropists, artist Pamela Bliss immortalized her with a 53-foot mural on the side of the 500 Festival Building in downtown Indianapolis. Other Hoosier legends who'd been previously honored with a mural included author Kurt Vonnegut, Indiana Pacer great Reggie Miller, and poet Mari Evans. Portraying my mother flashing her signature peace sign in her signature blue attire, the likeness was accompanied by her credo: hope, healing, and forgiveness.

At the unveiling, Ted Green declared, "She stood 4-foot-9 in real life, but she was a giant." [159]

In a press release, Indiana Governor Eric Holcomb added, "Eva has left an everlasting impact on Hoosiers, our country, and our world. This mural will be an enduring reminder of her spirit of forgiveness and love." [160] The mural will remain for the foreseeable future.

On a more diminutive level, I worked with the National Bobblehead Museum in Milwaukee to produce a bobblehead of my mother's likeness. The figurine depicted her flashing the peace sign and listed her Auschwitz tattoo number at the base. The initial allotment of 300 bobbleheads evaporated in no time. Bob McKillop, who retired as Davidson's basketball coach in 2022, placed one of the statues on his desk as a permanent reminder of his team's 2018 trip to Auschwitz.

"I keep her bobblehead prominently displayed on my desk," McKillop shared. "When I meet with coaches, donors, others, etc., they come into the office with various agendas on their mind. The first thing they ask me about is, 'What is that? Who is she?'" [161]

In the winter of 2022, I collaborated with the Indiana Historical Society to establish a new exhibit in my mother's honor. "Eva Kor from Auschwitz to Indiana" includes never-before-seen artifacts (including replica dresses that she and Miriam wore in their youth), original film footage from the *Eva A-7063* documentary, and my mother's Dimensions in Technology hologram. Privileged to be the keynote speaker at the opening, I announced, "In her memory, I challenge all of you to learn my mom's story, her life lessons, and the impact that she made on the world. Moving forward, it is my hope that her legacy will live on in the hearts and minds of children for generations to come." The exhibit will remain in place until the fall of 2024.

Though I could never replicate her dynamic presence, I've lectured on forgiveness many times since her death. On the morning of October 7, 2023, I was scheduled to fly from Chicago to Belgrade, Serbia, to speak on forgiveness as part of a "Women in the Holocaust" symposium. That morning, I heard reports of a significant Hamas attack on Israel. After gathering more information, I grew concerned about traveling abroad. "What would my mother do in this situation?" I asked myself at O'Hare International Airport. The answer was an easy one, and I boarded the plane bound for Europe with little reservation.

The flight to Belgrade took nine hours, including a layover in Munich, Germany. At the conference, I lectured for fifteen minutes and then flew home the next morning. Several friends who'd gotten wind of my travels, especially coming on the heels of the Hamas attack, questioned me as to why I'd make such a long journey for such a brief address. After my initial reluctance, however, I thought nothing of the trip: I'd go to the end of the earth to spread my mother's message.

Given that my mother spent the last twenty years of her life lecturing to health care providers, doctors, nurses, and researchers about medical ethics, I've taken a keen interest in continuing her work in this area. Since 2020, I've lectured to podiatry and medical students on medical ethics and usually lead off with a hypothetical question: "In your medical training, what would you do if you were forced to join a club or organization that conflicted with your ideals?" My question alludes to Dr. Hans Münch, and his path from medical student to Nazi. Often startled by my query, my audiences come to understand the correlation after hearing about my mother's history.

My father's death also inspired numerous tributes from friends, civic leaders, and patrons of the museum. Shortly before he passed, I established a scholarship in his honor at Purdue that will be annually awarded to a pharmacy student. In April 2023, more than 130 people attended a fundraising dinner to support his scholarship and a similar scholarship established in my mother's honor at Butler. Purdue basketball coach Matt Painter and newly hired Army Coach Kevin Kuwik, who'd been an assistant coach on the Davidson team that toured Auschwitz, both spoke, and the event generated more than $20,000 for the two scholarships.

In June 2024, I will help lead the CANDLES annual summer trip. Instead of our traditional expedition to Auschwitz, we will journey to Riga, Latvia. It will be my first visit to my father's boyhood home, and the itinerary will also include the Riga ghetto, Kaiserwald Concentration Camp, and Rumbula Forest, where my grandmother was murdered. I can only imagine the emotions the trip will evoke.

An initiative launched in the fall of 2023 pays homage to both my parents. The story of the Davidson basketball team's 2018 journey to Auschwitz generated much publicity-receiving mentions in *The Washington Post* and the 2021 book, *Unbracketed: Big Time College Basketball Done the Right Way*. That trip was especially meaningful to me, and the memory of it remains so, because of the way that it fused my parents' passions. My father, the former pupil of John Wooden, loved college athletics. He believed in the power of sport to change lives, and not just the lives of those who played the games, but the lives of those who watched from the sidelines as well. My mother dedicated her life to educating anyone who would listen, but especially young people, on the Holocaust. She would try to meet students wherever they were, but there was no greater, more vivid classroom than when they could walk with her through Auschwitz. For these reasons, the trip to Poland with the Davidson men's basketball team remains deeply symbolic to me of the power of their combined legacies.

As many people have said following that trip, it was a singular experience, in no small part because of Davidson's head coach Bob McKillop and the type of program he built at Davidson over his 33-year career there. The team did not bring a basketball. They came to learn. And they came to listen to my mother. I treasure the images of those young men walking hand in hand with my mother through the gravel, making certain she did not stumble as they retraced the path of her liberation together. Likewise, I cherish the more somber moments, when my mother led them to the selection platform to share the story of how she lost her parents, or when the players would wander off on their own, head in hands, to wrestle with the weight of what they were learning. I remember Coach McKillop hanging back, staying quiet and introspective, deferring to my mother. I remember the players asking profound questions, crying, processing, and chatting with my mother. I remember how much they all cared. And I remember the after-effects, how the team rallied around one another during the following season, and how they continued to stay in touch with me and communicate how much my mother's story had moved them. I could tell there was a lasting effect to our journey together. As Coach McKillop said, that trip changed not just their team, but their college as a whole.

Hoping to touch a broader population of student-athletes, Stacy Gallin, a co-leader of the 2018 trip and founder of the Benjamin Ferencz Institute for Ethics, Human Rights, and the Holocaust, initiated conversations with me and several others about building on Davidson's life-altering experience. Our talks resulted in the establishment of the Athletes Against Antisemitism and Discrimination consortium. Announced in the fall of 2023 and in partnership with CANDLES, the consortium aims to embolden student-athletes to stand up and speak out when faced with intolerance, and will offer a comprehensive curriculum including books, videos, and interactive online discussions. We ultimately aspire to annually fund a trip to Auschwitz for other college athletics teams. Though he never visited Auschwitz, my father, who was such a devout fan of college athletics, would be proud that my mother's work will live on through this initiative.

Beyond this initiative, my parent's everlasting legacy lies in the sustained mission of the CANDLES Holocaust Museum and Education Center. As a board member, I'm engaged in spreading the museum's mission and finding others to join our cause. As the only Holocaust Museum in the state of Indiana, my parents would both want CANDLES to play a vital role in curbing antisemitism in our state and around the world. I'm committed to ensuring that happens.

Over the course of their lives, my parents were an inspiration not just to me, but to tens of thousands of people. I'm often asked what lessons they taught me, and though too numerous to list them all, I'd like to close this book with several of the most impactful things I learned from them:

Think of one thing that you can do every day that can make the world a better place: That sounds simple, and it is. If you see garbage, pick it up. Hold the door for someone. Call a friend you haven't spoken with in a long time. Simple acts of kindness add up and make the world a better place. They also improve health. According to the Mayo Clinic, kindness has been shown to increase self-esteem, empathy, and compassion, and improve mood. My father was no Elton John, but his brief, daily piano performance put a smile on so many faces, whether at the museum or in his nursing home.

Several years ago, a friend of mine shared that her father had been diagnosed with terminal cancer. My mother, still alive at the time, consoled her and then gifted her with a mini flashlight.

"She said if I felt sad and alone, to use the flashlight to remember there is always light in the darkness and that everything would be okay," my friend recalled. We all have someone in our lives who needs a flashlight. We can all do something to make the world a better place.

Have a sense of humor: Given what they'd endured, it's astonishing that my parents both retained such an incredible sense of humor. Laughter is great medicine, and humor was one of their coping mechanisms in their post-Holocaust years. My sweatshirt reading, "My Mother Survived Auschwitz and All I Got Was this Lousy Sweatshirt," still sits in a box in my apartment. It's a testament to my mother's ability to poke fun at the most dire of circumstances. Likewise, my father loved telling jokes. While employed as a pharmacist in Japan during the Korean War, he loved telling the joke of the GI who skipped down the hall:

"Sir, why are you skipping?" asks his commanding officer.

The GI answers, 'Sir, my doctor told me to take one a day and then skip a day!'"

If two survivors, who'd lost hundreds of family members in the Holocaust, could find humor on a daily basis, then we all can.

Make your time on this earth count for something: Don't just exist. Leave an impact on others. My mother circled the globe preaching forgiveness because she wanted to uplift those who were battling their own personal demons. Albeit sad, it's fitting that she passed away while educating others at Auschwitz. She yearned to make a difference right up until the end. In her last year on earth, she advocated that forgiveness workshops be taught in prisons and implemented in treating those afflicted by post-traumatic stress disorder. My father followed suit, only in a different manner. Though he rarely left the confines of Terre Haute, except to watch his Boilermakers on the hardwood or gridiron, he made his voice heard in the hundreds of editorials he composed and in the lectures he delivered later in his life. We all have a contribution to make to society.

Memories are the source of our strength and the motivation for our actions: "Forgiving is not the same as forgetting," my mother often reminded her critics. Tormented by years of agonizing memories, my parents leveraged their painful recollections for the betterment of others. Most mornings, they walked into the CANDLES museum, only to be greeted by concentration camp photos, pictures of their deceased loved ones, and other excruciating reminders of their Holocaust history. Rather than hide from it, they confronted their past head on, and in the process helped remind countless others why the Holocaust can never be forgotten. All of us have painful memories; it's what we do with them that counts.

Forgiveness is really nothing more than an act of self-healing and self-empowerment: My mother coined forgiveness as "the miracle of medicine," adding, "It's free, it works, has no side effects, and if you don't like how it makes you feel, you can always take it back and be angry again." For decades, she was burdened by her anger, and it affected every aspect of her life. Her forgiveness, sparked by her encounter with Münch, gave her a new outlook and, I have no doubt, saved her life. The infamous sign at the entrance at Auschwitz reads, "Work Sets

With my parents—my heroes. COURTESY BUTLER UNIVERSITY

You Free." If she'd had her way, my mother would have erected a new marker reading, "Forgiveness Sets You Free." We all have the power to forgive those who have wronged us, not for their benefit of them, but for ours.

Prejudice is the cancer of the human soul: From the time I first observed separate bathrooms in Louisville, Kentucky, my parents preached respect. Teaching me to see past the color of someone's skin and focus on their actions, character, and heart, my parents practiced what they preached. They welcomed our German neighbors when it would have been easy to shun them and encouraged me to build friendships with Mark Hord and other kids who didn't look like me. It saddens me that racism remains such a scourge in our society and that antisemitism continues to rise. Senator Robert F. Kennedy once proclaimed, "What we need in the United States is not division; what we need in the United States is not hatred; what we need in the United States is not violence or lawlessness; but love and wisdom, and compassion toward one another, and a feeling of justice toward those who still suffer within our country, whether they be white or they be black."[162] Kennedy made that declaration in Indianapolis, Indiana, on April 4, 1968, on the tragic occasion of Martin Luther King's assassination. More than fifty years later, his words are more relevant than ever.

Never give up: It's staggering to reflect on all that my parents endured at Auschwitz, Buchenwald, and beyond. Hunger, thirst, the bitter cold, and the suffocating heat all paled in comparison to the loss of their parents and siblings and the psychological torture inflicted upon them. "Everything can be taken from a man but one thing: the last of the human freedoms—to choose one's attitude in any given set of circumstances, to choose one's own way," wrote Victor Frankel. [163] Though very young, my parents, who were also blessed with luck, were determined to outlast the Nazis. From my mother's will to survive Mengele's experiments to my father's never-say-die attitude during the death march at Magdeburg, they chose, in the face of all odds, to live. Theirs is a lesson for us all.

My work to preserve my parents' legacies has only begun. They bestowed on me their boundless and unconditional love. At the very least, I owe it to them to carry on their messages of resilience, optimism, and forgiveness. At the close of *Eva: A -7063*, the camera zooms out as my mother looks to the heavens and says to her own departed mother, "Mom, I will tell your story. I hope that you are proud of me."

Since my parents have passed, I often conclude my lectures by looking skyward and uttering, "Mom and Dad: I will tell your stories. I hope that you are both proud of me." My desire, as I write these final words, is that they'd be gratified with this effort as well.

And on that final note, let me offer you, the reader, my congratulations: you've survived my book.

Epilogue

T he Hamas attacks in October 2023 began shortly after Graham and I started writing this book. My thoughts went to Israel, a country whose people remain dear to my heart. It's where my parents met, and I have many fond memories of visiting relatives there as a child. The majority of my remaining family members still live there, and I still journey there every few years to compete in the Maccabiah Games (the Jewish Olympics). Yet while this recent terror and violence are the worst against Jews since 1945, antisemitic behavior remains a global issue. In late October 2023, FBI Director Christopher Wray testified before Congress that antisemitism had reached historic levels. Closer to home, the Anti-Defamation League's Midwest Office, which covers nine states, has received four times as many reports about antisemitic incidents since October 7 than it normally does each month.

This is not new. In the early 1970s my family was often targeted for being Jewish in our hometown of Terre Haute, Indiana. As a kid I dismissed these incidents, which included having swastikas scrawled on our windows, as typical teenage hijinks, and thought they'd dissipate as I got older. Instead, they have only increased in frequency and intensity.

Not a day goes by that I don't think about my parents. I miss them dearly, but I'm grateful that they aren't physically present to witness the horror unfolding in our world. The tragic events that have transpired in Israel coupled with the rise of antisemitism would have devastated them both. I've no doubt that they would have vocalized their opinions—my mother via Twitter and my father with a heartfelt letter to the *Terre Haute Tribune Star*—but the heartbreaking violence and continued discrimination would have adversely affected their already-fragile health. I could not stand to see them suffer any more than they already had.

When Graham and I set out to write this book, my initial motivations were to tell my father's story and elaborate on my mother's often told, but not always accurate, journey to forgiveness. As amazing as her narrative is, my father's tale is equally extraordinary. Portraying their lives remained paramount throughout the writing process, but I soon realized that this project could serve an even greater purpose.

Over the years, I've met many children and grandchildren of Holocaust survivors in Israel, Germany, and Poland. In my experience, second and third generation survivors respond in different ways with respect to telling their parents' or grandparents' stories: One group is very active, drawing strength from their heritage and their continued involvement in burnishing the memories of their forebears. A second group lacks initiative, mainly stemming from an uncertainty about how to proceed. A third group is apathetic and opposed to being engaged.

I commend those who remain committed in doing their part to continue the legacy of their loved ones. I hope this book encourages them to stay the course and, where possible, to double down in their efforts. I also hope that this book moves those in the latter two groups to take a more active role in keeping alive the stories of their parents and grandparents. The world needs you. With each passing season we lose more Holocaust survivors whose stories deserve and need to be told. The obligation we bear in carrying on their legacies may seem daunting. It may feel like the weight of the world is on our shoulders. I can certainly relate. Given the tragic state of affairs in the world around us, I've had many moments of self-doubt since my parents' deaths. However, we have a collective responsibility to pass our survivors' accounts on to future generations and to do our part to ensure a Holocaust never happens again. This book represents my effort at preserving my parents' story for future generations, and hopefully it will inspire more children and grandchildren of survivors to do the same. We all need to look at our responsibility not as a burden, but as a blessing.

That said, my wish is that all readers, regardless of their backgrounds or stations in life, will be motivated by our words. My mom often said, "If I can make a difference in the life of one person, I will feel that I accomplished something on this earth!" By the time of her passing, she had made a difference in so many lives that it added up to much more than "something," and the impact continues to ripple outward today as those whom she influenced carry forward her stories and life lessons. Yet, in playing the long game, we must also not lose our sense of urgency. The time to act is now, and we can start with the work that is right at our fingertips.

I want to spur other descendants of Holocaust survivors to make a difference, so that their parents' and grandparents' stories do not fade from memory. I want to help the staff and Board of Directors of CANDLES Holocaust Museum make their efforts even more fruitful and sustainable. I want to help young medical students and residents understand the importance of learning about the Holocaust in making them better doctors and researchers. I want to be involved in taking more college athletic teams to Auschwitz to learn about the Holocaust in an effort to make them better people.

In light of current events, one might suggest that our efforts, along with the work of millions and millions of others who've fought against antisemitism over time, have failed. On the contrary, I maintain that compassion and education will always vanquish hate. Each new generation holds our future in their hands. We must continue, tirelessly, to educate them about the Holocaust and to share the narratives of survivors of the Holocaust and all genocides, for as my mother declared shortly before her passing, "our work is far from done."

—Dr. Alex Kor, February 2024

Acknowledgements

O ne of the life lessons that my father instilled in me was to always to look my fellow man or woman in the eye, shake their hand, say thank you, and acknowledge the efforts of others. He was so humble and appreciative of his friends, colleagues, co-workers, and acquaintances. With my dad looking down on me, I have so many people to thank and acknowledge.

Over the years, I have been very fortunate to have had many people positively influence my life and mentor me. Bob Fisher, my first tennis coach at Woodrow Wilson Junior High in Terre Haute, was just that person. He provided me with the necessary skills to be successful on and off the court. David Craig, ATC, the former long term Certified Athletic Trainer for the NBA's Indiana Pacers and a NATA Hall of Famer, entered my life as a teenager, ultimately guiding my professional career in medicine. My Butler University tennis coaches, Bill Burgman and Nick Davis, provided me with guidance during my time dealing with the challenges of being a student-athlete. And, last but not least, Dr. John Grady, my residency director at the Jesse Brown VA Medical Center in Chicago, IL, trained me to be a capable and knowledgeable podiatrist but also a better person. To all of my mentors' credit, to this day, all have continued to be involved in my life.

In addition, I have been blessed with many friends that have played a major role in my life. Mark Hord, a childhood friend since the age of 10, has shared with me and my parents the great times (e.g., Purdue football games, the US Open Tennis Championships, playing tennis tournaments) and the sad times. I have valued his friendship and have always admired his style, grace, and perspective. Joe Gentry, my doubles partner at Butler and thereafter, has always been very supportive of my efforts. My Evansville, Indiana, friends, including Coach Jim Crews, Julie Vittori, Dr. Andy Saltzman, Pat Wempe, PT, and Mike McCall have all helped me in so many ways over the years. Coach Todd Schayes, from Denver, Colorado, and also a Maccabiah participant, was a frequent visitor to the Kor household and remains a close friend. Others that deserve mention include Dr. Steve Chatlin, my former service chief and a colleague in the Washington, DC, area; Dr. Kevin Bolinger, a Professor at Indiana State University; Dr. Tom Reifsnyder, a Terre Haute native who is a vascular surgeon at Johns Hopkins; Dr. Selim Benbadis from Tampa, FL; Sam Levin from Terre Haute; Dr. Barry Feig from Houston, TX; Brian J. Campbell from Washington, DC; Tom Bowers from Baltimore; Paul Cole from Cincinnati; Troy Fears, Amy Grove, and Trent Andrews from CANDLES Holocaust Museum; Jody Blankenship from the Indiana Historical Society; Cathy Baker from Terre Haute; Mark Tamar from Los Angeles; Dave Berkey, Joe Bastian, Scott Walker, John Tooke, Rob Stanton, Rocky Erickson, Dr. Mike Bush; Dave Peach; Mitch Henck; Dr. John Hester, podiatrist with the Boston Celtics, and Dr. Howie Osterman, podiatrist with the Washington Wizards; and, Coach Bob McKillop from Davidson College. In the good times and the bad times, your collective friendship has been everlasting.

Because sports played a major role in my life, I would like to thank all of my coaches along the way in making me into the person I am today. Those include Charlie Gurman, Bill Upman, Jack Webster, Bob Fischer, Duane Klueh, Dan Hopkins, Charlie Seitz, Bill Burgman, and Nick Davis. Without the structure that sports and in particular tennis provided me, I do not think that I would be where I am today.

Along the way, I was very fortunate to have had incredible educational opportunities while in Terre Haute at Thornton Elementary (Mrs. Biggins), Woodrow Wilson Junior High School (Tom Keller), and Terre Haute North High School. Once I matriculated to Butler University, in the freshman English class of Dr. Howard Baetzhold, I first learned the art of telling a story and gained a greater appreciation for the written word. After graduation from Butler, I also learned the intricacies of writing a scientific paper at Purdue University under the tutelage of Dr. David R. Lamb.

These acknowledgements and quite frankly this book would not have been possible without the input, support, and selflessness of Peggy Tierney, founder and President of Tanglewood Books; Dr. John Abrams, a local ophthalmologist whose heart and generosity are second to none; Ted Green, filmmaker and producer/director of *Eva: A-7063*; Stacy Gallin, D.M.H., the Founder and Director of the Benjamin Ferencz Institute for Ethics, Human Rights and the Holocaust; and, of course, teacher Beth Nairn. Ted's and Beth's input and incredible ability to not only donate their efforts but provide invaluable facts and anecdotal stories was critical in making this book a must read.

Lastly, I would remiss if I did not thank Chris Fenison, President of Pediment Publishing, for believing that these stories should never be forgotten; Jerry Logan, who has served as our editor and whose creative and literary talents have been an incredible asset; and, of course, my co-author Graham Honaker. Graham, from the bottom of my heart, I would like to thank you for spearheading this effort and pushing me ever since we started on this quest in the late summer of 2023.

On one of the last days of my dad's life, with a tear streaming down his face, he looked at me and said, "Alex, nothing lasts forever." My father loved to play the piano and one of his favorite songs was "Autumn Leaves." Popularized by many, including Nat King Cole and Frank Sinatra, I can still hear my father playing and singing:

Since you went away the days grow long
And soon I'll hear old winter's song
But I miss you most of all my darling
When autumn leaves start to fall

Knowing that the true meaning of "Autumn Leaves" speaks to the inevitable changes of life and loss, and that we all need to gain a greater appreciation of "the beauty of each passing moment before it too fades away," in my dad's memory, I thank you all.

—*Alex Kor*

"To dream, the impossible dream." The lyric is derived from Eva Kor's favorite song, "The Impossible Dream," but aptly summarized my feelings upon tackling this project. My high aspirations were coupled with a daunting uncertainty. In addition to Alex's personal account, a mountain of historical research coupled with photos and archival materials would be required. To ensure our accuracy, we also needed an all-star team of editors. With the help of many hands, our dream became a reality.

Jerry Logan, my co-author on two previous books, served an invaluable role as our chief editor. His wordsmithing skills are one-of-a-kind, and he was a tremendous source of emotional support along the way. Jerry: One day, I'll learn where commas are to be placed!

As always, Chris Fenison and Pediment Publishing were phenomenal to work with. I'm most grateful that Chris took my call three years ago, and proud that this is the third book project we've collaborated on.

This book would not have been possible without the contributions of Beth Nairn, trusted friend of the Kor Family and elementary school teacher in Patricksburg, Indiana, and Ted Green, producer of the award-winning documentary *Eva A-7063*. Both Beth and Ted provided research, historical context, and personal insights that were instrumental in accurately chronicling Eva's and Mickey's lives.

Stacy Gallin championed this book from the get-go and served as an additional set of eyes on the manuscript as well. Her foresight and leadership on Davidson's 2018 journey to Auschwitz was instrumental in the trip's success, and I dream of the day when we can provide another team with the same experience.

It's impossible to list all the support from friends and family but I do want to recognize the following: Alison Guiney, Ed and Beth Valdettaro, Trena Roudebush, Zach Everson, Bill "Seadog" Logan, Joyce Logan, Matt Beldner, George and Judy Andrus, Susan and Bill Kleinman, Bob McKillop, Teresa Schofield, Bill and Kay Shover, Nancy and Denny Lawton, Art Kodroff, Greg and Renny Silver, Charlie Moyer, Tom and Deborah Slaton, Julie and Cook Griffin, Jason Lantzer, Gordon Kaplan, John and Diane Abrams, Harriet Schor, Margo Lemberger, Ronnie Katz, Rabbi Erez Sherman, Phyllis and Ilana Sambuco, Alex and Georgeann Brown, Julia Whitworth, Chris and Sally Wirthwein, Michael Lofton, Tom Deuschle, Jaime Smith, Allie Kenney, Patti Lamb, Jennifer Stringer, Kim Goad, Todd and Linda Maurer, Sandy Lynch, Mark and Deb McFatridge, Bill Dugan, JoJo Gentry, Maythi Calvert, Ena

Shelley, Rock and Mary Sue Gurka, Curtis Stennett, Ken LaRose, Duane and Linnea Leatherman, Betsy Weatherly, Kelly Oles, Lauren Houldsworth, Mike and Krista Deese, Greg Rakestraw, Catherine Pangan, Mitch Henck, Trent Cowles, Mitch Daniels, Barb and Thad Matta, Brent and Jan Sandman, Mike and Mary Chapman, Jeff Blade, Andrea Freund, the Emmons Family, Dennis and Sandy Sasso, Rachael Burt, Brent and Jan Sandman, Lauren Houldsworth, and my Butler University Advancement colleagues.

I've had three professors who played a major role in developing my writing skills: Christy Buchanan, Mark Leary, and Pat McDunn. Bob Hammel remains the best mentor in the world, and thankfully he didn't have to spare as much red ink on this project!

I'm so thankful to my family for providing love and unconditional support: my wife Sarah and daughters Bella and Kate offered overwhelming encouragement throughout the writing process. I love you very much. I remain so appreciative to family members Nancye Claypool, Tom Honaker, Eliot and Sarah Honaker, Greta and Brian Koning, Mark and Daryl Snyder, Liz and Ian Ware, Mary and Joey Parks, Bob and Nancy Traer, and Paul and Kathy Morsbach.

Finally, I'm eternally grateful to Eva and Mickey Kor—my personal heroes who daily provide me with inspiration and a sense of purpose. They embodied the best of the human spirit, and their friendship was an incredible gift. As I put the finishing touches on this book, I'm dining over chicken nuggets and raising a cold glass of Coca-Cola in their honor. May their memories live on forever.

—*Graham Honaker*

Chapter 2: The Taste of Freedom

1   As quoted in Mickey Kor's *"Mickey's Story"* essay

2   Ibid.

3   Ibid.

4   Ibid.

5   Ibid.

6   Ibid.

7   Ibid.

8   Ibid.

9   Ibid.

10   Ibid.

11   As quoted in Mickey Kor's *"The Great Massacre"* essay

12   Ibid.

13   Ibid.

14   Ibid.

15   Ibid.

16   Ibid.

17   As quoted in Mickey Kor's *"Sailing Where to??"* essay

18   Ibid.

19   Ibid.

20   "A love of America, and a love of basketball," Readers' Forum *Terre Haute Tribune Star*, February 26, 2017

21   As quoted from Mickey Kor's *"My Way to Freedom"* essay

22   Ibid.

23   Ibid.

24   Ibid.

25   Ibid.

Chapter 3: Hope Was in Short Supply

26   Eva Mozes Kor and Lisa Rojany Buccieri, *Surviving the Angel of Death*, *(Tanglewood Publishing Inc., Terre Haute, Indiana)*, 2009, *3*

27   Ibid., *8*

28   Ibid., *10-11*

29   Ibid.,*12*

30   Ibid., *12*

31   Ibid., *13*

32   Ibid., *6*

33   Ibid., *13*

34   Ibid., *9*

35   Ibid., *14-16*

36   Ibid., *18*

37   Ibid., *20*

38   Ibid., *22*

39   Ibid., *22-23*

40   Ibid., *23*

41   Ibid., *24*

42   Ibid., *25-28*

43   Ibid., *29*

44   Ibid., *32-33*

45   Ibid., *33*

46   Kor and Buccieri, *Surviving the Angel of Death*, 33

47   Ibid., *35*

48   As quoted in Bob Hercules and Cheri Pugh's, "Dr. Forgiving Mengele — The Angel of Death" documentary

49   Kor and Buccieri, *Surviving the Angel of Death*, 38-39

50   Kor and Buccieri, *Surviving the Angel of Death*, 40-41

51   Ibid., *45*

52   From 2001 speech on "Healing and Forgiveness"

53   Kor and Buccieri, *Surviving the Angel of Death*, 47–49

54   Ibid., *64*

55   Ibid., *65*

56 https://www.npr.org/2015/05/24/409286734/
    its-for-you-to-know-that-you-forgive-says-holocaust-survivor

57 From "Dr. Forgiving Mengele — The Angel of Death" documentary, Bob
    Hercules and Cheri Pugh

58 "Eva Kor and the Work of Forgiveness," *Wabash Magazine*, Eva Kor and
    the Work of Forgiveness–*Wabash Magazine*, November 16, 2016

59 Kor and Buccieri, *Surviving the Angel of Death*, 89

60 Ibid., *86*

61 Ibid., *92*

62 Ibid., *94*

63 Ibid., *95*

Chapter 4: Love Language

64 As quoted in Beth Bailey, "The Holocaust Survivor and Jewish Refugee
    who Became an American Soldier" by Beth Bailey, June 8, 2021, The
    Holocaust Survivor and Jewish Refugee Who Became an American
    Soldier (coffeeordie.com)

65 As quoted in Andrew Silverstein, "How one newspaper column saved
    lives, reunited families and changed the course of Jewish history," *The
    Forward*, September 10, 2023, How the Seeking Relatives column saved
    lives and changed history–The Forward Footnote: For years, my dad
    listed his birthdate as 10/25/1929. It's my understanding that the US
    GIs (or someone at liberation) told him to add four years to his date of
    birth. The rationale was that he lost four years of his life in the camps,
    hence he should get those years back. It wasn't until Beth Nairn found
    his birth certificate in the early 2000s that we got confirmation of his
    correct date of birth.

66 As told to Alex Kor

67 As quoted from Mickey Kor's "My Voyage From Europe to the US" essay

68 "A love of America, and a love of basketball," Readers' Forum *Terre Haute
    Tribune Star*, February 26, 2017

69 Ibid.

70 Kor and Buccieri, *Surviving the Angel of Death*, *112-113*

71 Ibid., *114*

72 Ibid., *118*

73 Ibid. *121*

74 Ibid., *122-123*

75 Ibid., *123*

76 Ibid., *126*

Chapter 5: The Unlikeliest of Destinations

77 As quoted by Mark Bennett, "Lessons From a Dark Chapter in Hoosier History," *Terre Haute Tribune Star*, October 2, 2020

Chapter 7: For Herself

78 Kor and Buccieri, *Surviving the Angel of Death*, 129

79 As quoted in "Superfan" in the *Purdue Alumnus magazine, September 2017*

80 As quoted in Robert E. Dollos and Robert L. Soble, *The Los Angeles Times*, February, 1985

81 As quoted in John Conroy, "On the Trail of Josef Mengele," *The Reader*, November 25, 1993 On the Trail of Josef Mengele—Chicago Reader

82 As quoted in Tom Murphy, "The son of Nazi 'Angel of Death' Josef Mengele…," *UPI*, June 11, 1985

83 As quoted in "Son Says Mengele's Dead, Tells Why He Kept Silent," *Los Angeles Times*, June 11, 1985

84 As quoted in John Conroy, "On the Trail of Josef Mengele," *The Reader*, November 25, 1993 On the Trail of Josef Mengele—Chicago Reader

85 As quoted in Ronald Soble in "US Secrecy Keeps Cloud of Doubt Over Mengele Death," *Los Angeles Times* by Ronald Soble, March 3, 1989

86 As quoted in John Conroy, "On the Trail of Josef Mengele", *The Reader*, November 25, 1993 On the Trail of Josef Mengele—Chicago Reader

87 Ibid.

88 Ibid.

89 Hans Münch—Wikipedia

90 As quoted in Alexander Smoltczck, "The Doctor and His Victim," *Der Spiegel* 1999

91 As quoted in Debra Nussbaum Cohen, "The Nazi Victim Who Forgave Her Perpetrators," The Nazi Victim Who Forgave Her Perpetrators, My Jewish Learning

92 Ibid.

Chapter 8: It's Not the Critic Who Counts

93 Eva Kor — The Forgiveness Project

94 Ibid.

95 Ibid.

96 As quoted by Susan Olp in the Billings Gazette, March 25, 2015

97 Personal email to Alex Kor

98 Ibid.

99 As quoted in Bob Hercules and Cheri Pugh, "Dr. Forgiving Mengele — The Angel of Death" documentary

100 Ibid.

101 Ibid.

102 From Eva Kor speech

103 As quoted in Debra Nussbaum Cohen, "The Nazi Victim Who Forgave Her Perpetrators," The Nazi Victim Who Forgave Her Perpetrators, My Jewish Learning

104 Ibid.

105 As quoted in Marjorie Ingall and Susan McCarthy, Reasons to Forgive—or Not Forgive, The Tablet, October 4, 2022

106 Ibid.

107 As quoted by Julian Borger and Hans Kundani, "Drugs Firm Sued by Auschwitz 'Guinea Pig," The Guardian, February 18, 1999

108 As quoted in cbsnews.com staff, "Bayer Accused of Aiding the Nazis," CBS News online, February 18, 1999

Chapter 10: You Can Go Home Again

109 As quoted in, "Mother Here I Am: Tearful Eva Kor," Terre Haute Tribune Star, January 28, 1985

110 Nancy Segal, The Twin Children of the Holocaust: Stolen Childhood and the

Will to Survive, Monoray Publishing, 2021

111 As quoted in "Jerusalem Listens to the Victims of Mengele," *New York Times*, February 7, 1985

112 Personal communication to Alex Kor

113 As quoted in Amy Taylor, "From Final Tour of Auschwitz with Survivor Eva Kor," July 17, 2019

114 Personal communication to Alex Kor

Chapter 11: Burned Again

115 As quoted in Joanne Laurier, "Arson Destroys Indiana Holocaust Museum," World Socialist Website, November 20, 2003,

116 As quoted in Jo Napolitano, "Vow to Rebuild Burned Holocaust Museum," *New York Time*, November 25, 2003

117 As quoted by Dianne Francis D. Powell, Remembering the CANDLES museum fire, *Terre Haute Tribune Star*, November 16, 2013

118 As quoted in "Anti-abortionist Suspected in Arson at Holocaust Museum," *Jewish Telegraphic Agency*, December 31, 2003

119 "Students stage lock-in to raise money for CANDLES Holocaust Museum," *Terre Haute Tribune Star*, by Sue Loughlin, March 18, 2005

120 Letter from Indiana Historical Society

121 Ibid.

122 Personal communication to Mickey Kor

123 As quoted in Jo Napolitano, "Vow to Rebuild Burned Holocaust Museum," *New York Time*, November 25, 2003

124 As quoted in Joseph Garza, "A Place of Honor," *Terre Haute Tribune Star*, January 14, 2005

125 As quoted in Peter Ciancone, "CANDLES Holocaust Museum celebrates reopening," *Terre Haute Tribune Star*, July 4, 2005

126 As quoted by William B. Pickett, "The Firebombing of the Terre Haute Holocaust Museum," *Indiana Magazine of History*, September 2004

127 As quoted in Jo Napolitano, "Vow to Rebuild Burned Holocaust Museum," *New York Time*, November 25, 2003

128 "Holocaust Museum celebrates reopening after arson fire," WTHR

website, April 3, 2005, Holocaust Museum celebrates reopening after arson fire (wthr.com)

129   As quoted in Jo Napolitano, "Vow to Rebuild Burned Holocaust Museum," *New York Time*, November 25, 2003

Chapter 12: A Different Platform

130   As quoted by Lawrence Rees, "The Life of an Auschwitz Guard," *Politico Magazine*, July 13, 2015

131   As quoted in "Auschwitz 'bookkeeper' charged with 300,000 counts of accessory to murder," *The Times of Israel*, February 2, 2015

132   As quoted in Abby Phillip, "The moral guilt of Oskar Groening, the 'Accountant of Auschwitz," August 21, 2015

133   As quoted in Kacper Pempel, "Decades After Auschwitz, Former Guard Charged With Accessory to Murder," September 16, 2014

134   8f144e28-f848-44a3-9bfb-e483eec3ce0d (candlesholocaustmuseum.org)

135   As quoted in Sarah Kaplan, "An Auschwitz survivor's radical forgiveness as she hugs Nazi," *Washington Post*, April 27, 2015

136   Holocaust Survivor Eva Kor Embraces Former Nazi Guard Oskar Groning—ABC News (go.com)

137   As quoted in Stephanie McNeal, "A Holocaust Survivor Has Written About Why She Shook A Former Nazi's Hand," Buzzfeed.news, April 26, 2015

138   Why this photo of a Holocaust survivor and a former Nazi guard is going viral—HelloGigglesHelloGiggles

139   As quoted in Kashmira Gander, "Oskar Groening trial: Auschwitz survivor Eva Mozes Kor criticised by co-accusers for saying ex-SS officer should not face trial," *The Independent*, April 28, 2015

140   Personal account by Ted Green

141   "For Hoosier Holocaust survivor Eva Mozes Kor, 2017 was the year she went viral," by Robert King, *Indianapolis Star*, December 29, 2017

142   Eva Kor, Inspirational Champion of Human Rights, Named Grand Marshal of the 2017 IPL 500 Festival Parade—500 Festival

143   As quoted in Alex Modesitt, "Terre Haute's Eva Kor serves as grand marshal of 500 Festival Parade," *Terre Haute Tribune Star*, May 27, 2017

144 Only in Indiana: Eva Kor and Mario Andretti share a spot in the Winner's Circle, wthr.com

145 As quoted in Alex Modesitt, "Terre Haute's Eva Kor serves as grand marshal of 500 Festival Parade," *Terre Haute Tribune Star,* May 27, 2017

146 As quoted in Leslie Stahl, "Artificial intelligence preserving our ability to converse with Holocaust survivors even after they die," CBS News, March 27, 2022

Chapter 13: Crossing the Goal Line

147 Reader's Forum, *Terre Haute Tribune Star,* February 7, 2011

148 Personal correspondence from Mickey Kor

149 Reader's Forum, *Terre Haute Tribune Star,* June 11, 2010

150 As quoted in Bob Hercules and Cheri Pugh, *Dr. Forgiving Mengele—The Angel of Death* documentary

151 As quoted in Brian Boyce, "Holocaust survivor Michael Kor issues letter of forgiveness," *Terre Haute Tribune Star,* September 18, 2010

152 As quoted in *Terre Haute Tribune Star,* July 26, 2020, Mickey Kor Offers Nazi Guard Forgiveness

153 Personal communication to Alex Kor

154 As quoted in Sue Loughlin, "Holocaust survivor celebrates 85th birthday," Terre Haute Tribune Star, October 25, 2013

Chapter 14: Fortunate Son

155 As quoted in Deborah E. Lipstadt, "She Survived Auschwitz—And Eventually Forgave Her Persecutors. Should Others?" *Washington Post,* July 16, 2019

156 Ibid.

157 *The Washington Post,* Editorial Section, July 19, 2019

158 As quoted in Efraim Zuroff, "Reconciliation, Never Forgiveness," *The Jerusalem Post,* July 25, 2019

159 As quoted in Jordan Erb, "'Larger than life': Mural of Holocaust survivor Eva Kor coming to downtown Indianapolis," *Indianapolis Star,* October 12, 2020

160 Ibid.

161 Personal communication with Bob McKillop

162 JFK Library Website Statement on Assassination of Martin Luther King, Jr., Indianapolis, Indiana, April 4, 1968, JFK Library

163 Victor Frankel, *Man's Search for Meaning*, Beacon Press, 1946